PROFILES FROM PRISON

Adjusting to Life Behind Bars

Michael Santos

Criminal Justice, Delinquency, and Corrections
Marilyn D. McShane and Frank Williams, Series Editors

Westport, Connecticut
London

Library of Congress Cataloging-in-Publication Data

Santos, Michael, 1964–
    Profiles from prison : adjusting to life behind bars / Michael Santos.
        p. cm.—(Criminal justice, delinquency, and corrections, ISSN 1535–0371)
        Includes bibliographical references and index.
    ISBN 0–275–97889–3 (alk. paper)
    1. Prisoners—United States—Biography. 2. Prisoners—United States—
Psychology. 3. Imprisonment—United States. 4. Prison administration—United
States. 5. Prisoners' writings, American. I. Title. II. Series.
HV9468.S246 2003
365′.6′092—dc21   2002193045

British Library Cataloguing in Publication Data is available.

Library of Congress Catalog Card Number: 2002193045
ISBN: 0–275–97889–3 (alk. paper)
ISSN: 1535–0371

First published in 2003

Praeger Publishers, 88 Post Road West, Westport, CT 06881
An imprint of Greenwood Publishing Group, Inc.
www.praeger.com

Printed in the United States of America

The paper used in this book complies with the
Permanent Paper Standard issued by the National
Information Standards Organization (Z39.48–1984).

10   9   8   7   6   5   4   3   2   1

Copyright Acknowledgment
All photos courtesy of Michael Santos.

Profiles from Prison

CONTENTS

ACKNOWLEDGMENTS

Over the sixteen years that I have been confined, I have had the good fortune to receive encouraging support from several of America's leading criminal justice scholars. By giving me their time, they have helped bring meaning to my life. Through their support, I have become convinced that I can do more than prepare for release, as I did during the first half of my imprisonment. Indeed, their friendship has convinced me that I can lead a productive life as I move through this second half of my imprisonment by making actual contributions to society despite the fences and obstacles surrounding me.

I am grateful to Dr. Marilyn McShane. Marilyn has been like a sponsor to me since the early 1990s. She has helped me with my education, and given me opportunities to contribute to her edited projects. With this work, Marilyn guided me from the beginning. She not only helped with every aspect of this book's development, including its editing, but also opened a new relationship for me with Greenwood/Praeger Publishing. As a federal prisoner, I do not have access to a word processor or the tools of modern technology. Marilyn, therefore, generously performed the laborious task of converting my typewritten work into a digital format as we prepared for publication. Without her, this book would not exist. I am grateful to Marilyn for her continuing support.

The first reader for each of the chapters presented here was my long-time friend and mentor Dr. P. Bruce McPherson. Although I met Bruce while I was in the incipient stages of my term, he has treated me more like a son than a student. Bruce is an invaluable friend, and I am indebted to him. His guidance in all areas of my life has made me a better person.

I am grateful to Carol Zachary, her husband Jon Axelrod, and their children, Zachary and Tristan. They are my liaisons to society and constantly work to help me feel like I am more than a prisoner. I extend this same gratitude to Bill Ayers, Mary Bosworth, Skeydrit Bahr, Todd Clear, George Cole, Francis T. Cullen, John J. DiIulio Jr., Sabra Horne, Tara Gray, Carole Goodwin, Joel Lomberg, and Norval Morris. Special thanks also go to Suzanne Staszak-Silva, my editor at Greenwood for her faith in this manuscript.

None of my work would be possible without the generous and consistent support of my beloved sister Julie Santos and her husband, Tim Ufkes. They have remained by my side, full of encouragement, from that day in 1987 when an arrest changed my life. Because of them, I have been able to lift myself from melancholia and do more than time while I serve this lengthy prison term. My younger sister, Christina, and my mother, Frances Sierra, have been equally supportive throughout my term. In time, I pray that my work will help assuage the humiliation I caused my family members through my indiscriminate actions during the recklessness of my youth.

SERIES EDITORS' PREFACE

One of the great ironies of criminal justice policy is that we regularly hypothesize about the causes of crime, legislate punishment, propose treatment and prevention programs, and design elaborate laws, programs, or penitentiaries all without ever asking offenders why they commit crimes. Although there is a rich literature of prison writing and research, little of it seems to directly translate into new policies or procedures. This is unfortunate, as meaningful insights can be gleaned from both the explicit and the subtle messages of those who inhabit the world behind bars. The reader should come to realize that, as different as this world may seem from ours, it is a real world. What you read is not just the inmates' view of life, it is, ultimately, a reflection of our condemnation of that view.

Over the years famous writers such as Solzhenitsyn, Timerman, and Dostoyevsky have been able to bring readers deep into their prison experiences. However, some of the most exciting works have come from those who have educated themselves behind bars and become master storytellers in their own right: Rideau and Wikberg, Washington, Hassine, McCall, Martin, and now Santos.

The men profiled in this collection are intriguing and contradictory spirits, confused and savvy, contrite and defensive, funny and sad, and, oh, so very human. Within these pages are unique lessons on the poverty of the human condition—not one created by dustbowls, floods, or famines, but one we have engineered in America. It is not the creation of some executive from HBO; it is what the American public, through our actions or inactions, have made it.

We are pleased to introduce the reader to our friend Michael Santos. He is a consummate student and social observer. We are grateful to him and to his subjects for their willingness to share their thoughts and ideas. We believe that they hope, as do we, that this work leads us all to some discussion, some reconceptualizing, and, perhaps, some change.

Marilyn McShane and Frank P. Williams III

INTRODUCTION

THE CONVICT AND THE PENITENTIARY

Historians tell us that in the early days of the penitentiary system in America, prisoners usually served fewer than two years, and they served those sentences under a system that is strikingly different from ours today. Indeed, in those days, when a convicted criminal was assigned to a prison, the individual was blindfolded and led to a single cell. He never left that cell. He was prohibited from having any contact with the outside world. And, he was punished severely for any attempt to communicate verbally, or in any other way, with other prisoners. It was a system of total control and total isolation. A prisoner had nothing more than a Bible and his thoughts to help him pass and serve the time.

THE MODERN PRISON

Some two-hundred years later, American prisons have changed. Instead of subjecting felons to relatively brief periods of incarceration under austere conditions, most prisoners today serve long sentences in electronically wired or walled communities that are complex and relatively open. Administrators now offer their versions of human development programs, some of which are optional, others in which prisoners are required to participate.

In 2002 prisoners may send and receive mail. They may have limited access to telephones, televisions, and radios. They also may be allowed to visit regularly with approved family members and friends. In some prisons, inmates may participate in courses that could lead not only to high school equivalency certificates, but college degrees as well.

Those who take a superficial look at the prison system frequently walk away with an impression that the rather simple concept of isolating a man in a cell as punishment has evolved to one that not only punishes past behavior but actually helps shape future behavior. I frequently watch as administrators guide judges, politicians, and other community leaders on tours through the prisons to display the many attributes of their enlightened correctional institutions. Lieutenants and correctional officers walk in front and behind these tours to make sure that prisoners do not disrupt the staff member's spiel about the wonderful opportunities provided to inmates.

Even the names associated with incarceration have changed. Instead of guards watching over convicts in prison, administrators like to think of their staff members as "correctional officers" who have the responsibility of supervising "inmates" in "correctional institutions." My experience of being confined in the federal Bureau of Prisons system since 1987 suggests that although the system has changed and continues to change, it is in no way correctional. This is not to imply that people in prison do not have opportunities to improve themselves. They do. My point is that the system is closed to accurate inspection from outside sources. Also, it takes few steps to encourage personal growth. Except in cases of prison riots or other sensational disturbances, those in the broader American community have little information about what goes on inside the communities of the confined. Even those who tour the prisons hear only staff-member reports. When they can, administrators often take steps to suppress the voices of those they confine.

Despite having lived virtually my entire adult life as a prisoner, I have yet to meet a prison employee who corrects the behavior of an inmate. Instead, staff members slavishly follow policies, rules that were established by other administrators with more authority. Correctional officers are petty bureaucrats. They operate the prison, they do not interact. In particular, staff members manage large numbers of prisoners; humanness associated with the individual prisoners rarely is part of the supervisory equation. This is not an indictment of any particular prison employee, but rather a considered statement based upon my observations after having been confined for a significantly long period of time in four separate federal prisons at varying security levels.

MY OWN JOURNEY THROUGH PRISON

My sentence results from a course of illegal actions I undertook as a younger man. In my early twenties, I wrongfully initiated and led a scheme to distribute cocaine. After I turned twenty-three, I was arrested, tried, and convicted of operating a continuing criminal enterprise. Although neither weapons nor violence was alleged in the cases against me, and I had never been incarcerated before, I was sentenced to serve a forty-five-year term. If nothing changes, and if I continue to receive expected time off for good behavior, my release will occur in 2013, when I am forty-nine. By then, I will have served nearly twenty-seven years in prison, well over half my life for the bad decisions I made during the recklessness of youth.

I have never been bitter about the time, never blamed the system or anyone else for the predicament I put myself in. My problem, I realized, had its roots in my own thoughts, attitudes, and behavior. When I began serving the term, it was my intention to make some changes in my persona and my life, to do everything possible while I served my sentence to prepare myself to lead a crime-free, law-abiding life upon my release. I began by searching for a meaningful postsecondary education.

Although a native of Seattle, after sentencing I was sent to begin my term behind the forty-foot concrete walls that surround the United States Penitentiary in Atlanta. While there, I began studying at the university level through correspondence, and later in courses that professors from Mercer University taught inside the penitentiary's walls. Mercer University awarded me the bachelor of arts degree in 1992.

Studying had become my escape from the frustrations of confinement. By working to obtain educational credentials, I hoped to distinguish myself in some way and to prepare myself for the obstacles I expected to face after my release. Also, I hoped that by educating myself I could find some way to contribute to the world during my confinement. It was all part of a design that, I hoped, would lead to my redeeming myself for the crimes that led me to prison. In summary, I wanted to earn freedom—from the prison, but also for myself.

To that end, after earning my undergraduate degree, I approached several universities around the country with the hope of continuing my studies. I wanted to find a graduate program or professional school in which I could enroll. It was a problem because my incarceration would prevent me from attending any classes, listening to any lectures, or using the type of library necessary for research. I wrote to people from the academic arena in search of mentors. With persistence, and after sending out scores

Michael Santos

of unsolicited letters that went unanswered, I found several people who were willing to guide me. They not only opened doors for me, but through a vigorous correspondence helped me on my educational journey.

Hofstra University waived its residency requirement and allowed me to study toward a master of arts degree independently. Debbie Willet, a librarian at Hofstra's Axinn Library, agreed to help me by packaging and sending me books on loan that I needed to complete my studies. And the professors under whom I studied were willing to work around the obstacles my predicament presented. In 1995, eight years into my sentence, Hofstra awarded me a master of arts degree.

ADJUSTMENT IS IN THE ATTITUDE

With the possible exception of an insane asylum, the culture in which prisoners live is different from any other culture in America. For the most part, the principles that govern Western civilization shape the behavior of most Americans. Prisons, on the other hand, are governed much more along the lines of communism—where individuality is discouraged and a single authoritarian party has no accountability to the people whom it controls or the people whom it is supposed to represent.

Academic studies helped me move through the first decade of my confinement. By working toward credentials that I expected would make a difference in my life upon release, I had a reason to navigate my way through the minefield-like environment of every prison where I have been held.

Others, I found, were not so concerned with preparing themselves for release. Many focused only on passing their time as easily as possible. Indeed, many of the men with whom I have served time over the past fifteen years live as fatalists, believing they are powerless to change their lives. Because of such perceptions, many of the men with whom I have been confined since 1987 see no reason to put forth a sustained effort to develop skills that will help them reverse their criminal behavior upon release. Nor do these men feel any need to atone for their criminal convictions. Rather, the vast majority, consider themselves victims in need of assistance and attention rather than perpetrators of crime who should express remorse. Although many acknowledge having committed wrongful acts, they claim that their convictions were unconstitutionally obtained, or, more frequently, they claim that they have received excessive sentences.

Such perceptions influence the way prisoners adjust to their confinement. Those who fail to see any connection between their current behavior and their future, act accordingly. Instead of looking for opportunities to grow, they look for opportunities to ease their time in prison. By conditioning themselves to live in prison, however, many simultaneously condition themselves to fail in society.

USING ETHNOGRAPHY

Ethnography provides a writer like me the best opportunity (within the broad domain of the social sciences) to explore the prison culture and to obtain data related to that culture and the varying ways in which men adjust to the reality of incarceration. Ethnography might be thought of as descriptive anthropology, where anthropology is the study of humans— how they behave, how they react to certain contexts and circumstances, how they reveal the human condition. The operative word is descriptive. Thus, I seek to tell the reader about life in prison through the stories of certain prisoners. I am not a practicing social scientist, I am a prisoner. Nonetheless, my experiences in graduate studies taught me how to collect, analyze, and present ethnographic data. The stories that follow were not obtained casually, nor are they prepared for the reader, in a strictly anecdotal manner. Each chapter (or vignette of prison life) includes selected experiences related to adjustment to life in prison; explication of the prison structures, policies, and informal organization without which the vignettes would not be grounded; and, finally, my analysis of the case and observations for the reader to consider. Through this ethnographic inquiry— the stories of men living out prison sentences and adjusting in various ways to the institution—I hope to help readers come to better understand the culture of the contemporary prison in the United States.

THE SUBJECTS

In an effort to introduce readers to the world in which I live, I have asked nineteen men of various backgrounds and with a variety of sentence lengths and time served to describe their own perceptions of the prison experiences, including their adjustments, both positive and negative. I did not use scientific methods to select the prisoners profiled. Selecting prisoners randomly, for example, might not have provided the reader a reasonable sense of the prison experience as I and others live it. Instead of judging the men, I strove to respect their own perspectives of their experiences and expectations as I described their different patterns of adjustment.

I conducted the interviews informally, by telling each man about my efforts to help others understand the prison system and the people that it holds. If an individual agreed to participate in the project, we sat down and talked for a few hours. We spoke on the prison yard, in our assigned rooms, in the library, in bathrooms, or anywhere we could find some privacy. They told me about their experiences while I kept handwritten notes. From the notes I composed a story, which I then typed and shared with each participant to check its accuracy. Each participant assured me that I have reflected his experiences and views accurately.

As Virgil guided Dante through the circles of hell, I am asking the reader to allow me to serve as a guide through this ever-growing subculture of the American prison system. I offer my sixteen-year experience of living in prison as verification of my competence to lead this journey.

THE MATTER OF GENERALIZATION

Over two million people are locked in American places of confinement—a figure that has far more than doubled since my term began a "short" sixteen years ago. This fact of life troubles me, as I am sure it does many citizens. Through this work, I hope to leave readers who have little or no knowledge of these communities of the confined with a general understanding of the workings of the prison. By providing profiles of people from different backgrounds, together with commentary that compares other adjustment patterns with my own experiences, the work in its entirety should help readers understand how prison experiences shape perceptions, how those perceptions shape one's adjustment, and how that adjustment influences one's behavior in preparing for release after confinement.

Readers should not expect this book to describe every aspect of prison any more than a book on French wine can describe every delightful aspect of the French culture. No single work can accomplish such a goal. There is much that I could not cover, either because of space limitations or because the information is beyond my access. I could not describe, for example, the perceptions and beliefs of staff members. Staff members would not talk formally with me about their beliefs or the reasons behind policies that present problems for so many prisoners.

I tried to speak with John Harrington, for example, who is a department head at Fort Dix. I had hoped to provide more balance to the work by having him comment on what the prisoners said. He told me that as a senior staff member, it would not be appropriate for him to engage in a discussion of prison policy with me. I received the same response from lieutenants who are responsible for enforcing the rules.

It would have been helpful to have had a staff member's insight into why some policies seem to exacerbate inmate problems with the system and also why there does not appear to be any way for a prisoner to distinguish himself formally in a positive manner within the classification system. Why would a so-called correctional system offer no vehicle for an inmate to demonstrate merit, remorse, or rehabilitation? While some staff members deplored such policies in private conversations with me, they made it clear that it would not be appropriate for them to speak formally on the matter.

THE SETTING

All of the prisoners in this work are confined with me here at Fort Dix, a low-security federal prison in New Jersey. Located about halfway between New York City and Philadelphia, and housing over four thousand men, Fort Dix is the largest single federal prison in the United States. It is so large that it is divided into two separate compounds, each holding approximately two thousand men. One warden serves as chief executive officer of the entire facility, and inmates regularly transfer from one side of the prison to the other for program participation.

Although the men featured here all are currently inmates at Fort Dix, many describe experiences in other federal and state prisons. Some of the men have histories of and proclivities for violence, others are nonviolent. Some of the men are serving long terms, others shorter terms. Some of the men have served only a few months on their current commitment, some will soon be released after serving nearly twenty years. Some of the men were well educated before they came to prison, others are illiterate.

Taken in its entirety, I am confident that these narratives will leave readers with an understanding of living in any men's prison in the United States. Unfortunately, I cannot comment on women in prison, as I have no information regarding their status or predicament. The reader should be aware, however, that women represent the fastest growing segment of American prisoners.

ORGANIZATION OF THE TEXT

My goal has been to present an accurate picture of the prison subculture from the perspective of the men who live inside these fences. (Please note that the names of administrators and other prison personnel have been changed in the interest of privacy.) I have divided the work into four separate sections according to the length of sentence each inmate is serving.

First, the lilliputian-time prisoners are serving terms up to five years. These are considered short-term offenders. The second section, on bantam-time prisoners, profiles men serving between five and ten year sentences. The elephant-time prisoners make up the third section. Their sentences are between ten and twenty years. Finally, the last section presents profiles of men who are serving more than twenty years. These men are serving towering time.

In an effort to provide some continuity to the work, I have preceded each section with commentary. This opening section suggests some themes for consideration—some common elements in the lives of each prisoner featured or complexities and unusual circumstances in their lives.

As the reader moves through this work, noting how each man's life has been shaped not only by choices he made, but by conditions under which he now lives, I ask the reader to consider John Dewey's notion that there is no absolute good. Rather, for Dewey, the aim of living was the ever-enduring process of perfecting, maturing, and refining man's nature. As Dewey suggested, the bad man is the man who, no matter how good he has been, is beginning to deteriorate, to grow less good. The good man is the man who, no matter how morally unworthy he has been, is moving to become better. Such a concept makes one severe in judging oneself and humane in judging others.

LILLIPUTIAN-TIME PRISONERS

GULLIVER'S SUBCULTURE

Some readers may remember Jonathan Swift, the eighteenth-century satirist who introduced readers to the island of Lilliput in his classic book, *Gulliver's Travels*. Lilliputians were characterized by their diminutive stature. If we think of today's prison system as a group of scattered islands isolated off the coast of the American mainland, then let us imagine and consider those prisoners serving fewer than five years as the lilliputians of an isolated subculture, or of America's Devil's Islands.

With two million people inhabiting American places of confinement, administrators make use of classification systems designed to hold offenders together according to their relative threat to security. With so many people incarcerated, however, it is inevitable that in any given confined population, some short-term—or lilliputian prisoners—will share a cell with prisoners who may be serving life terms or have not lived outside of prison fences for more than twenty years. Lilliputian offenders are people who come from backgrounds as disparate as the children of a federal judge and the children of an organized crime boss. Do the perceptions of those serving very different amounts of time have an impact on their adjustment to prison, on their ability to prepare for life outside prison walls after release?

The men whom I profile in this section tell us about their own adjust-ments to confinement. All four describe terms that are less than five years, but two of them, the first and last, have served longer terms. The Watergate offenders, Charles Colson, G. Gordon Liddy, John Ehrlichman, H. R. Hal-deman, and John Dean all served less than five years, as did activists Angela Davis and Fathers Daniel and Phillip Berrigan.

One of our subjects, Pup, says that at one stage of his initial confine-ment, when he was held in a single cell and was contemplating his future, he thought about using his time to develop his mind and work toward acquiring skills to make a new life upon his release. When he was removed from the isolated cell, however, and cast into the open community of thousands of other hardened felons, he reconsidered his strategy.

Many prisoners find no stigma in coming to prison. In some large cities, such as Baltimore and Washington, fifty percent of all black males be-tween the ages of eighteen and forty have some intimate experience with the criminal justice system. With most children growing up in families with relatives or friends in prison, many (while still young) believe it inevitable, that it is only a matter of time before they themselves are living inside of cages. To them, terms such as *shank, lockdown,* and *the hole* need no explanation. Whereas other children respect and fear the power of the law, children who grow up in prison visiting rooms see guards as an odious but normal part of life; as one of Aesop's fables suggests, familiarity breeds contempt.

Pup was familiar with the criminal way of life. For him, prison was like an immense social club, an opportunity to connect with established criminals who could help him launch a new and more lucrative career as a drug dealer. He had no fears about returning to prison after his release.

Al Pezlo, the second prisoner in this section, comes from a different background. Whereas Pup's background and experience as an armed crim-inal gave him instant credibility in any penal environment, Al, a college-educated and extraordinarily successful entrepreneur, describes some of the frustrations that accompanied his comeuppance. Through Al's profile, I provide readers with a basic introduction to the differences between *new law* and *old law* offenses, and how the sentencing system today removes discretion from sentencing judges. Whereas the old law left judges with the power to take personal circumstances into consideration when impos-ing sentences, under the new law, judges who sentence federal prisoners must impose sentences according to a strict set of guidelines that remove individual circumstances from the equation.

Ellis Rogers is another white-collar offender. Upon his arrival in the federal prison system with no prior criminal history, Ellis was surprised to find himself sharing silverware with people whom he says would have been considered favorably for inclusion in a book such as *Who's Who in the Criminal World.*

All people who come to prison must learn to live in the immediate company of others who embrace values that vary dramatically. The four thousand men incarcerated at Fort Dix come from more than ninety different counties. Some cling to perspectives that patriotic Americans find offensive. Yet the most extreme views, as Ellis found out after September 11, 2001, come from Americans who are convinced that they live as victims in their own country.

Finally, I present the story of Billy Williams. Unlike many inmates, Billy adjusted as a model prisoner. He did not look for a hustle. Instead, he worked a full-time prison job and avoided problems throughout his term. Men who accept jobs, as Billy did, perform long hours of manual labor, carrying pipes, digging ditches, and installing fences. However, you will learn, as Billy does, that felons never seem to work their way clear of the scarlet letter of a criminal conviction.

Prison old timers often advise the new residents not to live halfway, with the body inside but the mind outside. According to them, prisoners should forget about family and friends outside of prison because everyone was bound to abandon them anyway. When one is waiting for letters from home, or visits, the time drags on. When the mail stops coming, many fall into deep states of depression, wondering why they have been abandoned. The old-time convicts suggested that it was best not to depend on anyone. To find some independence within the prison walls, one must create a hustle to support oneself, take a job in the prison factory, or find a routine to move through the years. By abandoning all hope for the outside world, they suggest, prisoners remove the possibility of further disappointments.

Old-time convicts also claim that anyone can obtain respect in prison if he is willing to pay the price. That means "to go all the way, to take any perceived offense to the wall." They argue that respect comes to those who succeeded in instilling fear in others. Ironically, it is not only prisoners who give the most violent people in prison leeway, but staff members too. Prisoners who were notoriously violent in Atlanta's penitentiary received single-man cells, were allowed to pass through the chow line twice, and were placated by staff in order to avoid having to deal with the tirades and bloody messes the men otherwise would leave behind.

Readers should be aware that the attributes of one who has respect in prison are not quite the same as one who has respect in society. In society, people like Al Pezlo and Ellis Rogers have respect. They graduated from college. They are faithful to their wives. They paid taxes, contributed to their communities, and their current predicaments notwithstanding, respect and abide by the law. In prison, however, their accomplishments do not entitle them to respect. Instead, such characteristics make them easy marks for abuse. A so-called respected prisoner would not have been frustrated in the same ways as Ellis and Al were, as the reader shall learn.

Ellis encountered difficulties in his adjustment because other prisoners did not respect him. They were not impressed by anything but violence, which Ellis's background did not prepare him for. Similarly, Al encountered problems with prison staff members because they did not respect him. Had he been one of the men who causes problems for administrators, he would have received the medical attention he needed without the aggravation and belittling he encountered. The respect they had in the community did not translate into respect behind fences.

Jack Henry Abbot, a former long-time convict, wrote about the prisoner mentality in his book *In the Belly of the Beast.* Abbot observes that the only response to disrespect that he knew was violence. After serving well over a decade inside maximum-security prisons, he was released. Soon thereafter he was eating in a restaurant. The waiter "disrespected" him by not serving him fast enough. Abbot responded by plunging his knife into the waiter's abdomen. The act resulted in his return to prison, the only society in which Abbot was prepared to live.

The men whom I feature in this section, of course, would conclude their terms before five years expired. But how would the choices they made impact their lives after confinement? Men such as Al Pezlo and Ellis Rogers were only months into their relatively short terms. Both were well educated and had lives that were well established, waiting for them upon release. After some initial frustrations, both recognized that the best way to pass through their time was to keep their opinions to themselves about the absurdity of confinement. It made no sense to offer suggestions that might change anything, as both staff and inmates resented any suggestions that challenged the norm. Prison was a temporary phase in the lives of Al and Ellis, an aberration that they would move beyond once the gates closed behind them. For them, the only objective was to make it out. They quickly learned that the best way to reach that objective was to go with the flow.

Pup, on the other hand, had nowhere to go after his term expired. He quickly lost sight of any reason to use his time in a positive way. Instead, he grooved with the swing of things in prison, making contacts that would lead to greater criminal ventures upon his release. Pup would tell you that he adjusted to the environment created by the prison system.

I present the stories as they were told me; as a prisoner, I had no way of verifying the background of the men. My now extensive experience of living in prison, however, has given me a keen eye and a reasoned judgment, and I am confident that the profiles presented herein will help readers develop an accurate feel for incarceration and how these lilliputian prisoners have adjusted.

THE SCHOOL OF CRIME: BENJAMIN "PUP" COLLIER

One prisoner describes how he graduated to the world of drug dealing from armed robbery.

As a young child, Benjamin Collier had aspirations of becoming a gangster. He was raised in Harlem, an urban, predominantly African American community on the northern tip of Manhattan Island. His parents were law-abiding, church-going citizens. Their upright behavior, however, did not carry much influence with the young Benjamin. "There was no fun in it," he says. His father had urged Benjamin to read the Bible and other books of a spiritual nature as a kind of intellectual nourishment, but Benjamin explains that when he was young he would have preferred to swallow cement blocks rather than "listen to whatever Pops had to say 'bout the Good Book." Benjamin was drawn to the life of a thug, to the streets, eager to be accorded the homage he saw everyone paying the loud and slick-talking gangsters who brazenly controlled Harlem.

By the time he was ten, Benjamin regularly was lingering until the late hours of the night on the street corners with his role models—some of the neighborhood hoodlums. Someone christened Benjamin with the nickname Pup, and even now, at forty-two, he introduces himself and is known by this childhood moniker.

After having served the past ten years in prison for convictions related to the distribution of narcotics, Pup now waits patiently for the next two years to pass for his release. When he gets out this time, he will be forty-

Benjamin "Pup" Collier

four, and he professes that he "will do something constructive" with his life. He has no definitive plan but insists that he will make decisions quite different from those he made the last time he was released. Despite having begun his criminal life before he was a teenager, Pup says his first period of incarceration did not come until he was twenty-eight, when he received a lilliputian sentence of two years for robbery. Pup describes that first encounter with the criminal justice system as a New York State prisoner.

THE "HARLEM HOODS"

At thirteen he regularly was burglarizing neighborhood stores. He started out shoplifting with friends. Later, as he and his friends grew more resolute, they began breaking into the stores at night through windows or doors they pried open, walking away with anything their hands could carry. After the burglary, Pup and his friends had the problem of converting their stolen merchandise into cash—and money, ultimately, was what they were after. They needed it to buy drugs, to gamble, and to polish and embellish their image as Harlem hoods.

By the time he was sixteen, Pup had discovered the magical powers of firearms. "People punk out when they feel a gun pressing into the back of their neck," he said. With a gun he could commit robberies instead of burglaries, steal money itself rather than merchandise that he would then have to transport, store, and sell.

After one of those neighborhood old heads blessed him with a pistol, Pup committed his first robbery. He put the loaded gun to the head of a numbers runner who was working for a Harlem bookie. "This is a robbery!" Pup wrapped his arm around the victim's neck while pressing the gun's barrel into his head. "Give me all your money, and we won't make it a homicide." It gave him a feeling of power, invincibility. After that first taste of robbery, Pup was hooked.

"The only other crime I considered," Pup says, "was selling drugs." Yet he was enticed with the action of robbery. With a gun in his hand, everything was fast, and he snatched his reward right away. "Selling drugs in Harlem is an honorable score too," he says, "but you have to find customers first. There's too much competition. Selling drugs is like work, and work was for suckers." At that time in his life, Pup thought, robbery was faster and easier.

Until he was twenty-eight, Pup described himself as a hood, robbing whenever he found himself in need of money. He never had to kill anyone, but without elaborating he now says that did not mean his guns went without use. Pup held up grocery stores and other hoodlums, but his specialty became robbing taxicab drivers. Pup robbed so frequently, he says, that he cannot even estimate how many times he stretched his arm around a cab driver's neck and pulled from the back seat, pressed a gun against his skull, and ordered him not to move while his accomplice, a female, rummaged through the driver's pocket to steal his money. Robbing cabs became easy, almost second nature to him and his partner. They could do it whenever they needed money. Sometimes they did it for fun.

FIRST STOP: RIKER'S ISLAND

Finally, Pup was arrested. He had led a life of crime since he was a child. At twenty-eight he was getting his first taste of the criminal justice system by being processed through the Riker's Island Jail in New York.

After his arrest, Pup was taken to court and ordered to stand for a lineup. As expected, one of his victims identified him, and within hours Pup was transported in the back of a windowless van—the paddy wagon—to the notorious Riker's Island Jail. During the processing rituals, guards took his fingerprints and photographs. Scores of prisoners were being booked into the jail, and the guards were pushing them through an assembly-line procedure, moving them from one station to the next with the indifference of warehouse workers handling packages. At the end of the line, Pup was ordered to stand naked for inspection, then escorted into a crowded and noisy bullpen holding about fifty other prisoners. At Riker's Island, he was not required to exchange his clothing for a jail uniform. Rather, like everyone else on "The Island," he wore his own clothing.

Pup's description of it makes the bullpen sound like a packed dungeon. There were no windows, but with the constant buzzing of the overhead fluorescent lights, it was never dark. The room was a rectangle of three cement walls covered with a flaking coat of a drab, lifeless, gray paint; a series of floor-to-ceiling, evenly-spaced vertical steel bars sealed off the fourth wall. One long bench stretched along a wall, but there were no seats or furniture in the cell. A filthy, stainless-steel toilet stood like a monument in the corner of the tank.

The ventilation system in the room was awful. Everyone was breathing the same, stale, uncirculating air. It was dirty, clouded with cigarette smoke as well as the noxious fumes that emanate from so many unwashed mouths and bodies, reeking of sweat mixed with stress and fear. A disgusting rancid odor lingered in the air, and each breath felt like an assault on one's nostrils and lungs.

Pup had heard rumors of the Riker's Island Jail all his life. The name of the game among his Harlem crowd was to stay out of jail, but there was no shame in going. Those who spent time on "The Island" or "Up-state" in one of the many New York prisons frequently were treated with a measure of deference and respect on the streets. In Harlem, Pup explained, confinement does not have the stigma attached to it that lawmakers and law enforcers would prefer. On the contrary, confinement is a proving ground. Those who pass through it can come home to honor, he says, the type that in other communities might be extended to a man who returned from military service.

For well over a decade Pup had been making his living as an armed robber. Using the threat of lethal violence, Pup stripped others of their dignity and possessions. He used a gun and exploited the shock that comes with such a surprise to embolden him. And yet, those experiences did not prepare him for what he encountered in those first hours of confinement. Indeed, when Pup walked into that bullpen, sans firearm, he felt vulnerable, disoriented, and out of place. Pup was afraid, but he knew from the hostile looks around him that he had better not allow his face to reveal his fear.

He was one of some fifty rough looking prisoners. Some were standing in groups, others were sprawled out on the sticky, dirty cement floor. He did not witness any violence in the room, but while sitting in the corner, talking to no one, he could feel others scoping out potential victims. Rapes, extortions, and stabbings, he knew, were only a holler away. Perhaps as close as the next cell. Pup passed three days in that tank before he finally was bailed out.

During those seventy-two hours, Pup says he does not think he slept at all. He was trying to take it all in. He expected that his family was going to bail him out, but he did not know how long that would take. Even so, Pup knew that he was guilty of robbing scores of cabs, and now that he was caught, he was going to have to get used to imprisonment.

Sleep would not have been easy anyway because of the noise. It came from the other prisoners, the other holding tanks, the institutional announcements over the loud speakers, and the slamming of steel doors. Every thirty minutes or so the guards would come by to bring in a new group of prisoners and take others out. He sat in his corner observing the people around him, hoping that his name would be announced, that he had been bailed out.

A lot of guys, Pup noticed, moved around freely inside that bullpen. It was obvious they had spent a lot of time in confinement. Living in cages seemed to be a normal experience for them. Most of them were physically imposing, pumped up from years of weight lifting and scarred from knife fights. Many had no teeth, an open mouth revealed a black hole. Pup wondered how they lost their teeth. Was it a home run swing to the grill? Would he have his teeth after leaving prison?

Despite the fifty other guys around them, these prisoners would drop their pants to the floor and lower their cheeks onto that nasty, steel toilet without the slightest sign of embarrassment. Another prisoner might have been eating or sleeping inches away. It did not matter. In fact, while sitting on the toilet for a bowel movement, between gaseous pops, one of these superconvicts might order someone who looked frightened to fetch him some "shit paper," bring him a smoke, or find him something to read.

Pup estimated that ninety percent of the people held in the tank were inner-city blacks or Hispanics who knew something about ghetto living. There were always four or five Wall Street types in the cage for something or other, and they personified fear. Pup watched their movements, watched the jailhouse regulars descend upon them.

"Yo, playa. Can a nigga get some smokes up off you?"

"A-yo, my man, you gonna eat that lunch?"

"Let me git that dinner bag, ya heard?"

Pup's years in the streets, if nothing else, conditioned him to adopt that look of hardness that let others in the bullpen know there were easier targets to try.

Pup's bail finally came through on his third day and he was released. He returned to the neighborhood and was welcomed by his friends of the street. "A-yo, Pup been up on The Island," he would hear people say. And despite the fear that had been gnawing inside his stomach while he was in there, the streets brought him back to life. He was proud that others knew he did not crack under the pressure of confinement. His peace did not last long, though, as less than a month later Pup was ordered to return to the courthouse for another lineup. Now that he had been identified for the one taxicab robbery, prosecutors were able to match Pup's method of operation with scores of other robberies.

Pup stood for the second lineup, and another of his victims quickly identified him. Detectives arrested him for this offense, too, but this time he was not taken back to Riker's Island. Instead, he went to The Tombs, another jail-type facility, but with seemingly better management and conditions. Instead of being dumped into a crowded holding tank, Pup was processed into The Tombs and led to a single-man cell. While alone, he was able to think more clearly, to focus on what was best for his life rather than dealing with minute-to-minute survival.

Pup's lawyer met with him while he was held in The Tombs. The lawyer explained the overcrowding in the state's correctional system and said that the authorities only wanted a conviction. If Pup would agree to plead guilty, the lawyer said, he could structure a plea agreement for Pup to serve about eighteen months that would cover all the taxicab robberies to date. Otherwise, the prosecutors would charge him with every taxicab robbery that matched Pup's method of operation. They both knew that could be a lot. Pup agreed to accept the plea agreement that would end his exposure to even more jail time.

During the three or four days Pup was at The Tombs, in the solitude his single cell provided, Pup thought about going away for the next year and a half. While he was gone, he reasoned, he could free his system of drugs, get in better physical shape, maybe even complete some schooling. But his planning was interrupted when he was ordered to chain up. Pup was being transferred back to The Island.

He stayed in the crowded and noisy tanks on Riker's for two weeks that second time before he was bailed out again. The second time, he says, was easier than the first because he knew what to expect. He did not feel afraid anymore, felt the jail was similar in many ways to the streets of Harlem. Pup was finding that he was almost in his own element there. In the midst of the crowd, those plans he had been making—while locked in a single cell at The Tombs—began to vanish, like wisps of early-morning fog.

When Pup was released on bail he knew that he was supposed to return to court forty-five days later to be sentenced and to commence his term. Instead, Pup chose to ignore his responsibility. While out on bail he reverted to robbing and using drugs. For ten months Pup ran around the streets of Harlem like a nomad, trying to stay one step ahead of the bounty hunters who were trying to bring him in. They finally caught up to him, and as a result of his extended flight, the judge sentenced Pup to a term of two years instead of the eighteen months he had been expecting.

RETURN TO RIKER'S

Pup returned to Riker's Island. This time, however, Pup had been convicted, and so he was not sent to one of the crowded holding tanks. Instead, he was assigned to a housing unit where prisoners were either serving time or waiting for transfer from the jail to prison. On his way into the unit, thoughts again began to consume Pup's mind about what he was going to do during his imprisonment, whether he was going to make it.

For him it was a personal test. He knew people frequently were hurt in prison, and he wondered whether he would be hurt, or whether he would have to hurt somebody else. Pup says that although he had been robbing people for years, he considered himself careful in not hurting anyone physically. He played on people's fear, oblivious to any psychological harm his actions may have caused. Besides hurting someone, there was the danger of being stung with new criminal charges while confined, or falling sick. Pup was entering a world replete with unknowns. The two-year sentence felt like it potentially could evolve into a lifetime of incarceration.

Over fifteen thousand prisoners were confined on Riker's Island. They were separated into numerous different housing units. Pup learned that he had been designated to one of the most notorious, to unit C74, which housed adolescents. Although Pup was twenty-eight at the time, and clearly not a teenager, jail administrators kept a small cadre of older prisoners with the juveniles, likely in hopes that they would bring a stabilizing presence.

Although Pup had spent a relatively short time confined on Riker's Island, he had heard about unit C74. There, it was said, the juveniles cut people for recreation. Some were successful in having street-fighting-type knives smuggled into their dorms. Inmates who did not have imported knives made their own weapons by tearing apart the state-issued plastic razors for shaving, pulling out the blades, and then melting the tiny blades into a toothbrush, using the brushes to conceal the razor and the handle to hold when going about their slashing. The adolescents even had a name for the cuts they inflicted, calling the slice from one's ear to one's mouth a "buck-fifty"; the name signifies the 150 stitches necessary to sew up the wound.

When Pup finally walked into the unit, he was given a bedroll containing a blanket, a pillow, and sheets. He moved to his assigned bed with an air of nonchalance. As he walked, he felt all eyes upon him. The guard sat in a bubblelike enclosure, separated from the prisoners in the dorm. Approximately fifty beds were lined up along the dorm's walls. Most of the others in unit C74 appeared to be between fifteen and twenty years old. Some were sleeping, some were playing cards or table games laid out on their beds. A group stood in front of the blaring television listening to rap music videos.

Pup did not know any of the prisoners with whom he was assigned initially, but within two hours, the guard called his unit for the noon meal. All of the prisoners lined up and followed the escort to the dining facility, the chow hall. During meals, the prisoners in Pup's unit mixed with the prisoners from other dorms in unit C74, and among them, Pup found several in the chow hall who had grown up in his neighborhood. Those adolescents respected Pup from the streets, and inside the adolescent unit C74, they were leaders, feared ruffians. Their approaching Pup and "showing him love" made everyone else in the unit notice. Their affectionate welcome of Pup gave him an image among the others in his dorm, and an image, he was observing, made all the difference in one's quality of life inside.

Pup and his young friends were not assigned to the same dorm in unit C74, but several of the leading prisoners in the dorm to which he was assigned were tight with Pup's friends. By the time they returned to the dorm after lunch, word had spread that Pup was a respected man among the hoods of Harlem and that he was a star basketball player. The references he received and the accolades about his basketball skills made his adjustment easier inside the dorm, or at least less volatile and dangerous for him.

Other newcomers to the dorm were "tried," usually within the first day, definitely within the first week. The potential victims were identified by the clothes they wore and how they carried themselves inside the unit. Anyone who showed the slightest sign of fear when walking through the door was immediately preyed upon. One of the prisoners would walk up to him and ask him for cigarettes. If the new arrival was too accommodating, he would be singled out for extortion. If he refused to provide, verbal abuse would follow. That was his test. His response to that abuse would determine his fate in the unit.

The newcomer might be wearing a pair of sneakers other prisoners wanted. Strong-arm robberies were a common occurrence inside the dorms of C74; anyone who lacked the presence to defend himself, or lacked the backing of others, was certain to endure constant stress. Such a person is so vulnerable that living in such a chaotic facility is tantamount to putting one's head in a hornet's nest. One can hope not to get stung, but that is so unlikely that even the memory of peace disappears.

People who have not been exposed to the complexities of living in confinement among so many violent predators may wonder why a potential victim would not seek protection from the guards who are on duty to oversee the prisoners. Several reasons exist. The first is that one guard may be responsible for watching over two to three hundred prisoners. He or she cannot monitor all the activities in a unit. Opportunities favor the predators. A victim can be found in the shower, on the toilet, or in the black of night, lying helplessly on his mattress.

Besides that, toothbrushes and razors are so easily combined to form lethal weapons that they are virtually everywhere, and the violent residents, many of whom have been living in the same monotonous tanks for months or years, get a charge—bring excitement to their lives—by slicing a man's face as if it were a tomato. The victim may not know who sliced him or even understand why he was cut. But when the blood begins pouring out, cheers follow, as if the home team had just scored a touchdown.

Another option is for the prisoner to ask the guards to place him in protective custody. In protective custody, however, a man is locked in a small cell for twenty-three hours every day with another man. In protective custody, the individual often will not have equal access to reading materials, to showers, or to other amenities of prison life. Besides that, guards may require the individual who seeks protection to provide information on others. The population assumes that anyone who seeks protective custody is, ipso facto, an informant, a snitch, a rat. Those labels, once applied to an individual remain with him wherever he is confined and subject the person to certain, constant abuse.

Whichever choice one makes, protective custody or living in the general prison population, the prisoner who fails to demand his respect among the others with whom he is confined will serve his sentence in terror, incapable of escaping the tormenting thoughts of what could happen at any moment. It is like dying a thousand deaths.

Pup did not have these problems. For one thing, he came from the streets of Harlem, not the gilded suburbs. Although he may not have known the other prisoners when he walked into the dorm, his body movements and facial expressions betrayed no fear. The other prisoners did not pounce on him at once; the manner in which Pup carried himself gave him a reprieve from the predators, and they had cause to wait before he would be tested. Then, when he was embraced openly by other leading thugs in the housing unit, other predators noticed. Eyes inside the dorms are always watching. Finally, when the unit was released for recreation later that afternoon, Pup was able to demonstrate his skills as an exceptional basketball player.

The day began for Pup with turmoil over what he would encounter in the jail. By the end of the day, however, his image had been established, and he had nothing to fear even though he never had been put to the test by others. With this acceptance, C74 became an extension of his Harlem neighborhood.

He had no more thoughts about getting his life together. While he was on The Island, Pup played basketball every day, stayed awake much of the night playing cards, gambling, and watching television. He smoked pot that others had smuggled into the jail through complicitous guards. There was constant disorder around him, but he was having fun, immune to the other, weaker prisoners who lived in terror in the chaotic, upside down world of unit C74.

Pup served the first four months of his sentence in that unit, and he would have been content to remain there among the friends he had made. But he was told to "roll up" one early morning, as he was about to transfer to the state's reception prison, where he would have his head shaved, his body sprayed with a delousing agent, and go through a few days of indoctrination over the rules and responsibilities of living in the prison system of New York State.

UPSTATE TO "REAL" PRISON

After a few days in the state's reception prison, Pup was chained and rode the bus to New York's medium-security prison at Woodbourne. Once he was processed, he looked outside the window and saw the high fences and walls surrounding the facility. He says he remembered bringing his hand to his mouth and saying to himself, "My God! This is really prison."

Pup began to look around him and see how different life was compared to what he had experienced on The Island. Joke time was over. In prison, the men were much more serious. They were built up from lifting weights, had schedules for school, participating in programs, or working. People were not lounging around aimlessly, wearing street clothing, as on Riker's Island. Being confined on Riker's, Pup explained, was a lot like living in the city. Drugs were around and female guards were not adverse to flirting or engaging in affairs with the men. Life in prison, Pup saw, was much different.

By the time Pup arrived at Woodbourne, he already had passed nearly five months toward the completion of his two-year term. Once he was within a year of his release date, he learned, Pup would be transferred to a work-release program where he would be allowed to find a job in the community, work, and return to prison for sleep. Once he made it into work release, Pup could spend weekends at home. The little time Pup had remaining to serve gave him an incentive to stay out of trouble so nothing would interrupt that release.

Pup explained that although most men had ready access to weapons, he found the best weapon to protect himself was his mind, how he thought and presented himself. He respected other people, did not pay attention to what they were doing. If someone was getting stabbed right next to him, he simply would walk by as if he saw nothing. By minding his own business, and showing no fear, he was able to stay in his own world behind the fences.

Pup was not trying to adjust to prison. He did not have enough time to focus on the programs. He was thinking about the racket he wanted to join upon his release. His career as a robber was over. When release came for Pup, he was going to launch himself as a drug dealer. More than a thousand people were confined with him at Woodbourne, and he set out to connect with those through whom he could establish himself in the potentially lucrative world of distributing narcotics.

Many short-term prisoners come to prison with the same ideas as Pup. They express no remorse for breaking the law and expect to use their time in prison as a kind of training ground for their criminal career, making new alliances that can open new opportunities. For them, prison becomes an accepted and expected hazard of their chosen lifestyles; they feel no stigma attached to it. Rather, they eagerly anticipate the enhanced status they will receive in their communities upon their release.

When Pup was released, he used the contacts he had made in prison to begin selling drugs. Within two years, he was apprehended and reconvicted. He is now serving a fourteen-year sentence, but his adjustment to this term has been different. Rather than thinking about more crime, Pup has attended school and has regularly participated in programs. He is certain that his criminal ways are a part of his past, not his future.

During the decade that Pup has served on this current sentence, he has matured in more ways than just physically. He has reflected on the guidance his parents tried to provide when he was a younger man and realized that it would have been more prudent to listen to their wisdom rather than reject it. His mother passed away early in this second term, deeply saddening him, but he has been fortunate to enjoy the continuing support of his father and his sister, Diane, throughout his term. After the arrests for the taxicab robberies, his former accomplice straightened out her life and began living as a law-abiding citizen. Pup wishes he had done the same then.

He will be forty-four when he is released in 2004. Pup says he does not regret his past because he has learned from it. "Sometimes people need to be aggressive." His background has prepared him for this need. Pup explains that although he will not engage in any more crime, he always will be stigmatized as a gangster, which he articulates as "a person who is either loved or feared, and a person who can reinvent the world in his own image." He does not have to be a criminal, but neither will he shy away from criminals as they intersect with his future life. Pup understands what criminals go through, he says.

Like Pup, many of the people in prison are no strangers to violence, and many openly discuss their intentions of reverting to crime upon their release. They freely say that "they will do what they gotta do," and since relatively few spend time in prison preparing themselves for anything else, they do not recognize legitimate opportunities around them. Al Pezlo, the next prisoner, on the other hand, comes from a completely different background. Through Al's story, readers learn how a man who was once a prosperous citizen is cut down to size while serving a Lilliputian sentence at Fort Dix.

EVEN THE AFFLUENT . . . :
AL PEZLO

A former high-level banking entrepreneur describes his medical frustrations in prison.

NEW LAW, OLD LAW, AND PRISON SPACE

When federal judges sentenced offenders for crimes committed prior to 1987, they had a significant amount of discretion available to them. One offender might receive probation as a sentence for his offense, while another offender who was convicted of the same crime might receive a ten-year prison term. The Comprehensive Crime Control Act eliminated much of the discretion in the federal courts. Crimes committed after November 1, 1987, were considered new-law offenses, and sentences were governed by a strict set of guidelines that ostensibly would make all offenders equal under the eyes of the law, at least the law as legislators (rather than jurists) saw it.

Traditionally, most of the people who have served time in prison have come from the lower socioeconomic classes. They are undereducated and have little experience contributing to legitimate society. These offenders were least informed about and least prepared when the federal government began implementing changes in the law resulting from the 1984 Comprehensive Crime Control Act. After 1987, the sentences offenders received were more rigid and less apt to be mitigated by extenuating circumstances.

The new law has been controversial. It eliminated the possibility of parole for all federal offenses and reduced the amount of so-called good time, or credit, that new-law offenders could earn to fifty-four days per year. Judges had been able to take into consideration at sentencing more of the personal circumstances surrounding old-law offenders. Further, old-law offenders who found themselves in prison, theoretically at least, had some control over their destiny. Through program participation and good behavior, most offenders were eligible for early release through a parole board. Even if they did not receive favorable consideration by the parole board, the federal prison system itself could reduce a prisoner's sentence by one-third simply as a result of the prisoner's staying out of trouble.

Since the new law took effect, prisons have become more crowded. Journalists have also attributed crowding to lengthy drug-law sentences. Indeed, when I began serving my own sentence, in 1987, fewer than 40,000 people were serving time in the federal system. Today, the Bureau of Prisons system holds well over 150,000 prisoners. With few opportunities to earn good time, and no opportunities for parole, the prison population is expected to continue growing.

The new law has not only made sentences more difficult for drug offenders, but many white-collar offenders, too, are finding themselves exposed to long terms of imprisonment. Indeed, many people who likely would have received probation or a fine if they were subjected to penalties under the old law now are serving multiyear sentences. Since their crimes were committed after 1987, federal judges were forced to follow the new-law guidelines. Accordingly, the prison population now comprises a segment with backgrounds that are as different from others in the population as a buttoned-down insurance executive's background might be from the regulars at a leather-and-chains biker bar. Al Pezlo is one of these white-collar offenders whose professional background is markedly different from that of most of his new colleagues.

BEGINNING IN A NEW COUNTRY: AL PEZLO

Al came to this country as a poor immigrant in 1962, when he was not yet nine. He was born in Cuba, but after his father passed away, and with Castro implanting a communist government, Al's mother decided that she would make a new start in America.

Because Castro's Cuba had a ban on its citizens emigrating (and especially to the United States), Al's mother had to apply to leave. After a year of waiting, she was forced to renounce ownership of all the family's assets, then work together with Al in a government-operated sugarcane field until papers were cleared for them to leave for New York. They arrived without any money or belongings, but his mother had a brother residing in New York who was working as an electrical engineer. Al says he remembers his uncle helping him and his mother settle in Woodside, Queens.

His mother found work as a seamstress in Long Island City, and young Al began his American education. He excelled in academics and athletics, and after graduating from high school, Baylor University offered him a full athletic scholarship to play football. He turned down the scholarship, however, as he also was recruited by the New York Yankees to play baseball, his first love. Al chose the Yankees, and when he was eighteen, he played on a Yankee farm team in AA ball for one year, and the next year he graduated to play a year of AAA ball. The highlights of his youth, he reminisced, were the two games for which he suited up in pin stripes and played catcher in Yankee Stadium.

After realizing he was not cut out for a career in the major leagues, he joined the U.S. Air Force. Because of scores he had received on his aptitude test, Al was assigned to work as a medical technician. While he was in the Air Force, he studied nursing at the college level, eventually earning a nursing degree. After leaving the Air Force in 1977, Al continued his work as a nurse in New York City. In 1984, however, an opportunity opened for him to begin a career in the financial sector.

Al had neither the experience nor the academic background for finance. What he did have in abundance was charm. A big man, Al stands about six-one and suffers from obesity. He has an easy, charismatic way, effortlessly drawing people close to him. He is the type of person who listens nonjudgmentally, and after brief conversations, strangers find themselves reflexively opening up to him, telling him their secrets. A man he met during his nursing career recognized Al's gift as a listener and offered him a position in his firm, which specialized in addressing the needs of companies in distress.

Al worked primarily in banking, helping large lenders collect or reorganize problem loans. He thrived in his new position, and after two years he found himself working side-by-side with some of the highest-profile bankers on Wall Street, including those whose dot-matrix pictures regularly graced the columns of *The Wall Street Journal*. After helping a large national bank resolve a matter that could have proven embarrassing to management, Al saw an opportunity to break away and embark on an entrepreneurial career.

In 1986, only two years after leaving nursing, Al became one of the founding partners of Capital Finance International. As a merchant bank, his firm provided financing for companies moving into new ventures; assisted companies in accessing equity markets; and provided commercial financing services. Within five years, Al was chairman of a merchant bank that he was instrumental in forming; it had offices in seven countries and annual revenues in excess of fifty million dollars. In no way was Al a typical prisoner.

MONEY PROBLEMS

Al's problems with the law began in 1992 with accusations that his firm was in some way connected with money laundering. He was arrested and held in the prison at Otisville, New York, for nine months before the judge agreed to release him on a bond guaranteeing that he would appear for trial. The criminal proceedings stretched on for two years, but after spending hundreds of thousands of dollars in legal fees, Al finally proceeded through a seven-week trial after which the jury unanimously acquitted him of all charges. Finally, Al was able to concentrate his energy on rebuilding his banking career.

In 1994, when Al's problems with the criminal justice system apparently were behind him, he and his partners purchased the Union International Bank. The offshore bank existed exclusively to provide letters of credit and assist businesses with international financial needs. For approximately five years, Al traveled the world, dealing with businessmen and government officials on four different continents. Then, early one May morning in 1999, twenty-three law enforcement agents arrived in seventeen separate cars at his home in an affluent Long Island neighborhood. In front of his wife and children, agents in bullet-proof vests with guns drawn ordered Al to the floor. He was under arrest.

Al was charged with tax evasion, which could lead to ten years of imprisonment. Despite his dramatic arrest, upon his appearance in federal court, the magistrate judge ordered his immediate release on bond. Al provided a simple explanation for the crime for which he was charged. He filed and paid his taxes for the income he earned in the United States. He also filed income-tax returns in other countries for the money earned in those countries, but he did not mention that income on his American tax return. Although Al maintains that he did not willingly or knowingly violate any American laws, he agreed to plead guilty in order to lessen his exposure to a possible lengthy prison term. He received a sentence of thirty-six months.

THE COOPERATION GAME

The government's investigation began, Al explained, when one of the accountants working at one of the big-eight accounting firms that filed his personal income taxes was busted in a five-kilogram heroin conspiracy. Instead of facing the long mandatory sentence that would have been associated with that crime, the accountant agreed to cooperate in the prosecution of others. Under the new law, one of the few ways offenders can reduce their exposure to confinement is by drawing others into the criminal-justice web.

There is no telling how many people the accountant, who doubled as a heroin dealer, reeled in, but Al's was one of the names he fed to prosecutors as someone who may have filed questionable tax returns. That tip, eventually, resulted in Al being sentenced to thirty-six months of imprisonment. Unfortunately for him, the nine months he previously had spent in prison on the charges for which he was acquitted would not count toward his new sentence.

If Al had been an old-law prisoner, possibly he would have been sentenced either to home confinement or to probation. Not only had he previously spent nine months in custody for a charge of which a jury of his peers had exonerated him completely, but Al also explained that he had a long history of community service. He and his wife had sponsored over fifty foster children; they had built several parks on Long Island; and they had donated to numerous charities. All in all, Al says that he gave away over six million dollars during the five years preceding his arrest. Under the new law, however, a distinguished record of community service has little bearing at sentencing.

A DIFFICULT JOURNEY

The judge ordered Al to report to Fort Dix at 2:00 P.M. on March 26, 2001. For several months, Al and his lawyers tried to persuade the judge to grant him an extension of a few months before beginning his sentence, as Al was in dire need of surgery for a hip-bone fracture that had been deteriorating. At that time, Al weighed over four hundred pounds, and the surgeon explained to the court that he could not perform the operation until Al lost at least 100 pounds. The court was unmoved. The judge said that the Bureau of Prisons system was equipped with a state-of-the-art health system and that the system's medical personnel would attend to all of Al's medical needs.

Al had been married to his wife Sandra for twenty-six years, and together they had two teenage children. On the day when Al was reporting to prison, however, he was unable to ride in with his wife, as she had an important medical problem of her own and had to meet with her oncologist. While he was being driven from his Long Island home to Fort Dix, he received a cell-phone call from his wife at the doctor's office. She had been diagnosed with uterine cancer, and the doctor indicated she needed immediate surgery. Without the surgery, the doctor explained that she had a life expectancy of less than one year.

Instead of continuing on his journey to Fort Dix, Al turned around and returned to New York City where he had a conference with his lawyer. Again they attempted to persuade the judge to grant him an extension before he had to report so that he could care for his children until his wife was released from the hospital. The sentencing judge denied Al's request, explaining that Al should have considered such ramifications before he committed the heinous crime of tax evasion. Al typically had associated so-called heinous crimes with axe murderers and serial killers; now he learned that his judge considered those convicted of tax-law violations to be heinous criminals as well.

After Al realized that there was no getting around his orders to report to prison, he spent the afternoon making arrangements for others to care for the needs of his wife and children, then resumed his journey. It was just after eleven at night when Al walked into one of the Fort Dix offices to turn himself in. Despite the late hour, he said the officers received him courteously. Then they escorted him to the segregated housing unit. The following day he was released from there and assigned to the top bunk in one of the second-floor rooms of a regular housing unit. Weighing approximately four hundred pounds, Al was hardly in a position to be climbing up stairs, much less climbing onto a top bunk. Ironically, no one was assigned to the lower bunk. Al explained the difficulty he would have in climbing onto the top bunk to Counselor Steel, and asked the counselor whether he could be reassigned to the lower bunk. "Absolutely not," Counselor Steel answered. "And if I catch you on that lower bunk you'll receive a disciplinary infraction."

Al had been in prison for less than a full day and did not know what to expect. Being humble by nature, he said that he did not want to make any waves and proceeded to follow orders. In order to access his top bunk, he positioned a metal chair and a table next to the bed, creating a kind of ladder. He climbed onto the chair, then onto the table, and finally crawled onto the bed. Getting out of the bed, however, required a bit more work and assistance from two of the men who also were assigned to his sixteen-man room.

THIS IS HEALTH SERVICE

Three days later Al was paged to visit the Health Services department. Finally, he was going to be introduced to the Bureau of Prison's state-of-the-art health care facilities. The reader should be aware that in my fifteen-plus years of confinement, I have found that no department receives as many complaints from the inmates as health services. I have been blessed in that during my incarceration, I have never required the care of the medical professionals who work in the prison system. In fact, I purposely avoid that department because I know the frustration that comes with any connection to it.

I have read that health care services outside of prison is a controversial subject. I assure the reader that the red tape is no less intense behind the fences. In addition to the bureaucratic policies, however, prisoners also must frequently confront disparaging remarks and should expect the worst in bedside manner during treatment.

As instructed, Al reported to the Health Services building where he was met by Mr. Esposito, a physician's assistant with a notoriously sadistic reputation inside the prison. As Al was waiting for attention, he said he watched as Esposito spoke loudly and rudely to other inmates. Finally, he turned his aggression to Al.

Esposito stood about six inches shorter than Al. He looked up into Al's face, demanding, "What do you want!"

Al said he passed Esposito his identification card and carefully introduced himself. "My name is Al Pezlo. I was told to report to the Health Services department."

Esposito looked at Al's card before responding in his thick Brooklyn accent. "You know, I wish you fucking guineas would stop committing all these crimes. This place is fucking full of youse guys."

Shaken, Al says he did not expect to be spoken to by a representative of the Bureau of Prisons system in such a manner. After a few seconds of collecting his wits, Al responded, "I'm sorry, but with all due respect, I'm not Italian."

"Oh no?" Esposito pondered the complication. "Then what the fuck are you?"

"I'm Cuban."

Esposito looks up at him and sneered. "Cuban? You can't be Cuban. You're too fuckin' tall. Now get the fuck out of my face." Esposito tossed Al back his identification card then locked him outside the door.

Al said he stood outside the Health Services Building for a couple of minutes wondering what had just happened. He did not receive the medication he required for his high-blood pressure or painful hip ailment, and he had not been asked a single question regarding his medical condition. He began to wonder what he was in for as a federal prisoner. It certainly was a world that was different from what he knew in his life prior to confinement, and totally inconsistent with what he knew of the medical profession from his earlier professional work as a nurse.

Al returned to his unit, dazed. He tried to speak with his counselor to get some information about what he should do about his medication. Counselor Steel, he said, told him that medical personnel would see him in due time. Four days already had passed without his medication. In Bureau of Prisons terms, or at least according to Counselor Steel, due time had not yet passed.

On his ninth day at Fort Dix, Al was instructed to proceed through an Admissions and Orientation (A&O) program. During A&O, representatives from the prison's various departments speak to the incoming inmates about their rights and responsibilities. When Mr. Adil, the Health Services administrator appeared, Al went to speak with him and explained that he had been confined for nine days, that he had need for medical attention and medication, but that no one had spoken to him about his medical needs much less examined him. After listening to Al, Adil accompanied him to the Health Services Department. Adil presented Al to Dr. Chung, and asked Dr. Chung to complete his intake examination on Al and to make sure that he received his required medication. Dr. Chung agreed, then told Al to wait while he finished some other paperwork. Adil then left Al in Dr. Chung's able hands.

After Adil left, Al explained, Dr. Chung showed him his list of the patients he had scheduled to see that day. Dr. Chung showed Al that one of the inmates on his list was named Pezlo. "Do you see that?" Dr. Chung pointed to his clipboard. "I already have one Pezlo on my list. I can't see more than one Pezlo in one day. I will reschedule you for another day."

Finally, Al began to object. He said he wanted to serve his time deferentially, respectful of all prison rules and procedures. The treatment he had received during his first ten days of incarceration, however, bordered on the ridiculous. It made no sense to Al as to why the doctor would not see him simply because he shared the same last name with another prisoner named Pezlo. As he was making his argument, another white-smocked representative of Health Services came by and told Al to continue waiting, as someone would see him soon. Al then retreated to the waiting room. Mr. Varego, another physician's assistant, then called for Al. Varego was ready to administer Al's intake examination. Al described the experience to me.

Varego led Al into a hallway that had an eye chart hanging at the end. After ensuring that Al was standing in the appropriate position, Varego instructed Al to cover his left eye and read the chart. Al said that before he responded with even a syllable, Varego spoke.

"That's good. Now cover your other eye and read the chart."

Al did as instructed. He read two letters before Varego interrupted him again.

"Excellent! You have twenty-twenty vision. Now go into the next room and remove your shirt."

Al had no idea of the extent of the farce he was experiencing. He knew he did not have twenty-twenty vision. For over ten years he had worn glasses. In fact, Al explained that his glasses were sticking out of his breast pocket at the time of the examination.

When he stepped into the other room and removed his shirt as instructed, Varego pointed his index finger and then stuck it into Al's belly. "You very fat," Varego observed in broken English.

"Yes, I know," Al responded. "I have to lose weight."

"You must walk. Walk all day."

Al thought about this sage medical advice before answering. "I can't walk because I have a bad hip. I brought papers from the doctor who has been treating me." Al tried to give the physician's assistant his medical papers.

Varego did not accept the papers, wanting to continue with his theory that all Al needed was to walk. "Well, take two or three steps. Then take a rest. And then walk more. If you do this, all your problems go away."

Al sat down on the examination bed.

"What crime you here for?" Varego asked.

"I'm here for tax evasion."

"Oh, that good. That not bad crime. Who you work for?"

"I worked for banks."

"Did you ever work for Citibank?" Varego asked.

Welcoming the conversation, Al spoke a bit about his long relationship with Citibank. Varego indicated that he was from the Philippine Islands and that Citibank had a branch in his village. Al mentioned that he had visited Varego's village, trying to ingratiate himself with the medic, hoping that his charm would entitle him to better medical service. It did not. Instead, after listening to Al for a few minutes, Varego just looked at him. Then he stuck his finger back in Al's belly.

"You know, you very fat. You must lose weight."

"Yes, I know," Al said. "I think I'll start walking a few steps, then taking a rest before I walk again."

Varego then attempted to take a reading of Al's blood pressure. At four-hundred pounds, Al has an arm that measures over twenty inches in diameter and the regular apparatus for measuring blood pressure does not properly fit around his arm. Each time Varego tried to connect the velcro ends of the standard device and start pumping, the arm covering would split apart. Varego told Al that since the velcro would not hold, he ought to hold the strap together around his arm while Varego worked the pump. After rigging the apparatus, Al was amazed when Varego told him that he had normal blood-pressure. This was despite the fact that except for the time since he arrived at Fort Dix, Al had been taking high blood-pressure medication for over two years.

After learning that he did not suffer from a blood-pressure problem—despite not having taken medication for nine days; despite not being able to use the phone; despite not knowing how his wife was progressing through her surgery for cancer; and despite being stressed from his initial exposure to incarceration—Al's humiliation continued. Varego instructed Al to drop his trousers so he could conclude his examination. Al did as he was instructed. Varego looked at him. "Your hip looks fine," he said. "I see no problem."

Al then passed a copy of the letter he had brought from his physician to Varego showing that he was suffering from a bone fracture. Al asked Varego to pass the letter along to a doctor. This time Varego did look at the letter, then at last he agreed to allow Al to receive his medication. He also assured him that he would pass the letter on to a doctor who would see him soon.

THE SAME "NEW" HOUSING

When Al returned to his unit, he learned that he had been assigned to another housing unit at Fort Dix East, which was behind a completely new set of fences and as far as he was concerned might as well have been a different prison.

He met Ms. Rivera, his new counselor. Apparently, he thought, Rivera had received the same training in rudeness as Esposito. She assigned him to the top bunk on the third floor of the building. By then Al had had enough. He told Rivera that he was not going to walk to the third floor and climb onto a top bunk. He asked her where he should wait so that guards could retrieve him and take him to the segregated housing unit. Rivera told him to wait in the hallway and left him standing there with all his belongings. He estimates that he waited there for ninety minutes before another counselor came by and assigned him to a lower bunk on the building's first floor. Finally, Al was able to rest. He also was able to call home, and he learned that his wife's surgery had been a success.

After Al settled into his new unit, he surmised that the best way for him to pass through his thirty-six month sentence was to make every effort to avoid staff members and keep a low profile. He has committed himself to losing weight, and seven months after his arrival at Fort Dix he has managed to shed well over 100 pounds, making it possible for him to undergo the hip replacement surgery he so badly needs.

Al retained legal counsel to see about the possibility of having his own doctors perform the surgery, but he has failed. As the judge said, the Bureau of Prisons maintains a state-of-the-art medical program, and qualified doctors will tend to his medical needs. Because of the experiences he encountered during his first months of imprisonment, however, a cloud of anxiety hangs over him as he waits to be scheduled for surgery.

One thing Al has learned about his incarceration is that his position outside means nothing inside the fences. While wearing the khaki uniform, he is indeed a prisoner.

Roger Ellis, the next Lilliputian prisoner, is another white collar offender, however, his adjustment problems were quite different from those we have seen so far.

FROM BAD TO WORSE:
ELLIS ROGERS

One inmate describes how the passing of his sentence became more difficult as he had to interact with others and face the realities of his life.

In most instances, prisoners serve up to the last six months of their sentences in a halfway house facility. Although a place of confinement, a halfway house usually is a converted hotel or apartment building, managed as a program by adjuncts of the prison system. Administrators designed the halfway house program with expectations that it will help recently released offenders readjust to the community, and it has a goal of providing a head start for prisoners in finding employment and shelter prior to the expiration of their sentences. Prisoners admitted to the program work in community jobs, then return to the halfway house to sleep. In time, they may earn extra privileges, such as weekends at home.

On rare occasions, sentencing judges recommend that prisoners serve their entire sentences in these community halfway houses. Ellis Rogers, a fifty-eight-year-old African American, received a fourteen-month sentence for his mail fraud conviction. He was surprised, but grateful, when he heard his judge recommend that he participate in a work-release-type program while serving his term. Since federal prisons do not have a work-release program, the Bureau of Prisons designated Ellis to report to the Klintock Halfway House on March 20, 2001, to commence his sentence.

A HALFWAY BREAK

Ellis thought a mistake had been made. After his sentence was imposed and the judge recommended a work-release program, he was told that the Bureau of Prisons would contact him within six weeks with orders regarding where he was to report for his term. He had never been confined before, but with a fourteen-month term, Ellis expected to serve at least the first half of his sentence in a secure federal prison. He welcomed the news about reporting to a halfway house near his home, and when he called the halfway house to confirm his assignment, the administrators cordially told him they were expecting him. There was no mistake.

The person who gave Ellis information over the phone explained that residents of Klintock wear their own clothes, and that he should bring a bag of his personal belongings when he reported. The Klintock halfway house, in downtown Philadelphia, holds well over two hundred people, men on one floor and women on another. When Ellis reported, he was led to a six-man room.

Ellis's roommates had transferred to Klintock after having served as long as ten years in prison. They were well experienced in life behind bars; for some, much of their adult experiences had occurred while they were serving time. Ellis was twice their age. But in the ways of confinement, he was the new kid on the block, green with inexperience. Nevertheless, the others were in the final months of their terms, focusing more on living in the community than continuing the behavior patterns that led them to prison.

Ellis, of average height and weighing about 150 pounds, looks fit and young for his age. He sports a closely cropped beard and always keeps his clothes freshly pressed. For the past decade Ellis has been self-employed as a mortgage broker. As a well-spoken, clean-cut professional, the young men immediately recognized that Ellis was out of his element. They began explaining the nuances of prison living. They told him about the rules—which ones were serious and which ones could be overlooked. In exchange, Ellis answered their questions about building credit, finding employment, and other aspects of adjusting to the community that contrasts so sharply with their experiences of living as prisoners.

As most citizens would expect, the majority of prisoners have only a rudimentary education. Many struggle with basic reading, writing, and arithmetic. Even those minimal skills tend to atrophy during incarceration. Prison provides its inmates with their basic needs and requires little from them that presents a mental challenge. They have no experience in opening or maintaining bank accounts, networking, or planning for the future.

Many prisoners simply wait out their time, fill the daily, hourly void by watching soap operas, music videos, or playing table games and sports.

Men and women who led professional lives in the community, like Ellis, represent a small percentage of any prison population. In some prisons, seasoned prisoners identify articulate newcomers with the same system that they feel has been oppressing them throughout their lives. Accordingly, knowing that professionals are unfamiliar with the details and subtleties of prison life, predators frequently target them as easy marks for extortion or abuse. On the other hand, if professionals reach out to other prisoners and offer the benefit of their skills and experience, they may enjoy a symbiotic relationship—one where the thugs and the refined help each other through the struggle of confinement.

Although Ellis experienced the normal nervousness that accompanies the unknown, upon meeting his five roommates, he began to relax. Ellis realized that he could use his time to help others find their way. He saw himself as a mentor to the young men around him and felt that he could make a contribution. Upon hearing of Ellis's career experiences, other residents of the halfway house soon began coming to him for advice on how they could make a new beginning after their release.

One of the first lessons Ellis learned was that although he was required to find employment, the halfway house would not permit him to be self-employed. Further, he learned that he must give twenty-five percent of his gross earnings to the halfway house as a kind of tax to support the program.

In Ellis's search for employment, he avoided businesses that were remotely related to his own. He did not want to explain to colleagues embarrassing questions on why he was caught in the web of the criminal justice system. Instead, he found a job as a caterer, where he would earn nine dollars per hour during his year of quasi-confinement.

The halfway house and job were humiliating for Ellis. That shame, however, was likely a part of the intended punishment. Even so, Ellis knew it was not as bad as it could have been. Instead of living under the rigid rules of a prison, he was in the community every day, interacting with citizens, able to enjoy liberal visiting privileges with his family. He even was allowed to attend religious services with his wife and children on Sundays.

A TEST AND A TRANSFER

The easy time would not last. Less than two weeks after Ellis arrived at Klintock, he was summoned for a urinalysis. The Bureau of Prisons randomly tests at least five percent of its prison population monthly; in some facilities it tests a much higher percentage. Ellis says he did not use drugs, so he had no concern when he was called. The tests came back indicating that Ellis had been using morphine, however, and two weeks later the Klintock administrator had him detained. Two U.S. marshals came to put him in handcuffs, and he was transferred from Klintock to the federal detention center in Philadelphia.

Officers who administer urinalysis tests are required to follow specific procedures detailed in a Bureau of Prisons policy statement. Once the prisoner is notified, he is escorted to a control room where he is under constant observation. The inmate has two hours to fill a tube that stands about three inches high and is about as broad as a quarter. The guard stands directly next to the prisoner and watches closely as the urine leaves the body. After the tube is filled with the specimen, the officer seals the tube with a plastic cap, then places a numbered sticker that the inmate has initialed over the cap so the container cannot be tampered with or opened without breaking the seal.

Despite these precautions, Ellis insists his test results were flawed. He cannot explain where the error occurred, but he says he is certain that he has never used morphine in his life. I tend to believe him. His claims of innocence notwithstanding, Ellis was admitted as a prisoner in the detention center, and all of the halfway house privileges were stripped. He was issued jail clothing and confined to a housing unit holding approximately two hundred other prisoners whom he described as a who's who of the criminal world.

Within the first few days of Ellis's transfer, representatives of the Klintock halfway house came to him for an administrative hearing. Ellis professed his innocence, but the hearing officers said they were not interested. Their sole purpose was to make a recommendation to the disciplinary hearing officer, and they were recommending a finding of guilt on the disciplinary charge that Ellis had used morphine. As a sanction, they were suggesting his permanent removal from the Klintock program, that he be transferred to a low-security prison, and that he lose forty days of good time.

A few weeks later, Ellis was told that the disciplinary hearing officer had found him guilty, that his security level had been raised, and that he was being transferred to Fort Dix to finish his time. He also was told that he had indeed lost forty days of good time, meaning he would remain incarcerated for just under six additional weeks as a consequence of the disciplinary infraction.

While Ellis was detained he was free to mix with the other prisoners. Although he already had spent about one month at Klintock, that experience did not prepare him for the maneuvering that was going on in the detention center. In the halfway house, everyone was focused on doing whatever they could to help prepare themselves for return to their communities. They were eager for any help or guidance Ellis's experience could provide. In the detention center, people were looking for something else.

Unlike the people in the halfway house, who were only a few steps away from freedom, those in the detention center were just coming into the system. They were either being held without bail while their charges were being resolved; awaiting sentencing; or, like Ellis, waiting for transfer to the prison where they would serve out their terms. Many of the prisoners whose cases had not yet become final were cooperating with the prosecutors, providing information on other crimes in an effort to reduce their own exposure to confinement.

Ellis was held in Philadelphia's detention center for approximately six weeks. During that relatively brief time, two separate prisoners approached him. Each had heard that Ellis was in the mortgage business. They tried to engage him in a discussion about the possibility of using his business as a vehicle for laundering money.

Both of the people who approached him, it turns out, had pled guilty to drug charges. Rather than accept the stiff mandatory-minimum sentences that were associated with their crimes, these prisoners agreed to identify others with whom they were active and testify against them in the event of a trial. In exchange for their cooperation, the government agreed to recommend a reduced period of incarceration for them.

Ellis learned about their maneuvering through documents that other prisoners somehow obtained and were circulating throughout the housing unit. It became clear to Ellis that they were not only fishing for information about money laundering, but also trying to ensnare him in a criminal plot they could feed to prosecutors for further bargaining powers. The experience taught him a lesson. He learned that when among prisoners—all of whom were in desperate situations and in a struggle for their freedom—it was best to keep to himself and to keep his mouth shut. The federal detention center was not a place where one should discuss one's personal business.

People in the detention center were tense because most of the men there had only recently been separated from their families and communities, and many did not even yet know what they were facing. Men like Ellis, with relatively short terms, were eating in the same room as the reputed boss of organized crime in Philadelphia, Joey Merlino, who was on trial for alleged crimes that could send him to prison for the rest of his life. Ellis was eager to move on to Fort Dix, where he had heard people were already into their sentences and past the volatile stages of adjustment. Ellis had less than a year of confinement ahead of him, and he wanted to begin his own adjustment.

FINALLY, A DESTINATION

In early June the marshals secured him in chains, then marched him with others in lockstep to a school-sized bus. The bus had no markings on the outside. The windows were blacked out; on the inside they were covered with a steel grill. Ellis did not mind. He was happy to be moving to Fort Dix, his final destination, located about an hour's drive from the detention center.

Unfortunately, the bus did not make a direct trip. Instead, he was driven well over a 100 miles away to the maximum-security prison in Lewisburg, Pennsylvania; few prisons hold as many men who have been convicted of crimes of violence. When Ellis saw the massive wall surrounding the medieval-like fortress, he began to panic, thinking yet another drastic mistake had been made. First he was erroneously convicted of using morphine, and now he was being sent to Lewisburg, a prison holding men who never expect release.

When the bus stopped outside Lewisburg, Ellis heard prisoners taunting from their cells. With its high walls, coils of razor wire, and aggressive occupants, Lewisburg was a frightening place, a morass of evil and darkness contrasting with the brilliant skies of early summer. He was processed in and relieved when he heard it was only a layover. The journey would continue in a few days when more prisoners arrived at Lewisburg who ultimately were headed for Fort Dix.

While held at Lewisburg, Ellis was not allowed to use the telephone. The counselor provided him with paper and postage so he could send out mail. He and the other holdovers were kept in an area of the prison that was isolated from the penitentiary's maximum-security prisoners, so he was quarantined from the regular violence erupting behind Lewisburg's walls. After seven days, the other prisoners had trickled in from their previous facilities, and the bus resumed its trip to Fort Dix. Ellis arrived on June 14, with less than ten months remaining to serve on his sentence.

Ellis and his wife have two children under the age of ten. From a previous marriage, Ellis also has two adult daughters. Once he was processed into Fort Dix, he looked forward to receiving regular visits from his family and hoped that he could find an activity to keep him busy. He approached the education supervisor with a proposal to teach a course on beginning a small business but was told that no staff members were available to supervise such a course. So he tried to settle in, spending his time reading and getting to know his surroundings and the people with whom he was confined.

INSTITUTIONALIZING 9-11

Ellis was assigned to one of the twelve-man rooms. After having been suckered into buying new sneakers for a few guys, he recognized that the youngsters with whom he was living were taking him for an easy mark. They were institutionalized, he explained, and described the term as a label for those who have come to accept that prison is a way of life. Institutionalized people accept the meals, the shelter, and the clothing, then focus their attention on immediate gratification. They are happy to pass years watching television and playing table games and feel a sense of accomplishment in being able to con a newcomer out of a few hundred dollars worth of commissary items.

The alternative to the institutionalized prisoner, Ellis came to observe, was the prison thug. The thugs walk around with a scowl of pure hatred and try to intimidate others. Ellis explained that criminal behavior is an extension of the thugs' makeup, that they never will be rehabilitated because they refuse even to acknowledge responsibility, much less accept it. Instead, they blame others and the government for their actions and rejoice at evil. On September 11, 2001, he was chilled when the extent of their cold hatred revealed itself.

It was just before nine on that sunny Tuesday morning. He was walking downstairs, and he heard two prisoners walking up the stairs jubilantly talking about a plane crash. He walked to the television room, which was tuned to one of the news stations, and watched in horror at what he saw. A live picture showed the second plane crashing into the second World Trade Center tower. Two young prisoners on his left exchanged high fives as if in celebration, and Ellis wondered what kind of person could rejoice when thousands of people had just lost their lives, when their own country had been attacked. Then it struck Ellis. His eldest daughter, Cherise, worked for Morgan Stanley on the fifth floor of the World Trade Center. She was in that building, he realized, as he watched the skyscraper collapse into rubble.

Ellis rushed to the telephone and tried dialing home with hopes that his wife would have some information. The phone system on the eastern seaboard was overloaded, however, and no calls were going through. Hearing the repeating busy signal with each call, he returned to the television room.

By then the room was crowded with concerned prisoners, and the hecklers had quieted down or gathered among themselves. Ellis had been in Fort Dix for less than three months, and he had few close relationships. He could not get through to his family and had no way of obtaining news about his daughter. In the middle of the television room he broke down and started sobbing uncontrollably, realizing that he might have lost one of his children.

Lieutenant Ana Callahan happened to walk into the television room when Ellis was in hysterics. A slim and attractive woman in her late twenties, the lieutenant has a no-nonsense reputation. She presents herself as a strict disciplinarian, perhaps in order to ensure that the female-starved prisoners of Fort Dix do not forget that she holds a position of authority. Given her demeanor, no one mistakes her for someone who invites honey talk from prisoners.

When she saw Ellis grieving, however, Lieutenant Callahan's usually stern outward behavior changed completely. She offered comforting words, even took the extremely unusual step of gently putting her hand on his shoulder and suggesting that he find strength in prayer. Ellis says that her compassion and kindness was completely out of character with what he had come to expect from staff members of the Bureau of Prisons system. How bitterly ironic, he thought, that prisoners who were in the struggle with him were happy to see the devastation, while comfort came from one of the ranking guards charged with incarcerating him.

After the lieutenant left, Officer Susney, who was the guard in charge of the housing unit, called for him. Susney took Ellis for a walk outside the building. He told him how sorry he was for the stress Ellis was going through. Then he gave him some hope. Susney told Ellis his daughter may have made it out of the building. After all, her office was on the fifth floor, and there was a good chance that his daughter was not trapped like some of those on higher floors. It was a possibility that Ellis said he had not considered in his grief; after the experiences he had gone through over the past several months, he had become conditioned to expect the worst. The officer told Ellis to have faith, not to fall apart, and that he was not alone.

Ellis wanted to be with his family during that time of grief. Even at noon he still had not been able to make contact with his wife. He went to speak with his case manager, told her about his daughter, and explained that he had not been able to call through the inmate phones. Ms. Flowers, his case manager, asked him for the numbers he wanted to call; she said she would put them on automatic redial and page him if she got through. An hour later, he still had no news.

Sometime after 2:00 P.M. he was able to reach his wife. She said that she had been trying to reach their daughter ever since she heard of the attack. She had left messages on Cherise's answering machine and with her friends urging her to call home. Although five hours had passed since the building collapsed, there was still no word from Ellis's daughter.

At 11:30 P.M., the inmate telephones are turned off and prisoners are required to report to their assigned rooms. Ellis still had not heard about Cherise, which for him was an ominous sign. He prayed, but since so much time had passed without her sending any word, he was convinced that she had not made it out of the building. He spent the night confined to his bed, lying on top while listening to radio reports and weeping. Just after 5:00 A.M., however, a guard came to his room.

"Ellis Rogers," the guard screamed.

Ellis's heart sank, certain that he was about to receive devastating confirmation of his worst fears. "Yes. I'm Ellis Rogers," he answered.

"Your wife just called. She said your daughter called home. She is fine."

News of his immediate release would not have been more welcome. Tears really started to flow, but this time they were tears of joy. When the inmate phones turned back on at 6:00 A.M., he called his wife. She explained that Cherise had escaped the catastrophe unharmed but had not been able to access a telephone. They both planned to visit him on the next available visiting day.

Those were the most traumatic seventeen hours of Ellis's life. But although his daughter was safe, Ellis explains that the conversations—or arguments—he has had in the aftermath keep him tangled in tension. In his room of twelve men, daily disputes erupt over the validity of America's leading the Western world in its war on terrorism. Eight of his roommates are vociferous in their opinion that the United States brought these problems upon itself.

"Why do you love this country so much?" The dissidents pestered him. Although they were born and raised in the United States, they have no love for it and question Ellis's fealty and patriotism.

"I love it because I'm an American, because my children are American. This country is what I am, it is who I am. It provides my family and me with security, with opportunities, with freedom to choose and express myself."

"You don't look so free to me, Nigga! Why you in here then?" they asked.

"I'm here because I broke the law. I'm paying the price. That doesn't change the fact that I'm an American," Ellis argued. "Let me ask you something," he continued. "Why do you hate this country so much?"

"What do you mean why do I hate it? Look at what they done to me!"

Like many prisoners whom I have encountered over the years, Ellis's roommates have a hard time accepting responsibility for their convictions. Rather than recognizing the role they played in their offenses, many prisoners explain they are serving time not because they did something, but because someone told on them or because the laws are unjust.

Ten out of the twelve people in Ellis's room were convicted for offenses related to the distribution of drugs. Several even pled guilty to the charges. Despite their admission in open court, they insist that they should not be serving such long sentences, and that the government is to blame for their predicament. Some accuse agencies of the government, for example the CIA, of bringing the drugs into the country to fund covert wars that have led to these acts of terrorism. When Ellis scoffs at this argument, they accuse him of being an "upitty nigger," that he is just old and does not understand what he is talking about.

Not all prisoners are so firm in their hatred of the government, of course. Ellis is unfortunate in having been assigned to a room filled with such animosity. Some counselors will not allow an inmate to change rooms simply because he does not get along with his roommates. Ellis has less than a year to serve on his sentence, while each of his roommates will serve a sentence in excess of ten years; indeed, two of them are serving twenty-year terms. Further, few even completed a high school education. They are avowed and proud criminals, eager to discuss their knowledge of weapons and willingness to use them, to brag about their futures in crime upon release. For Ellis, living among such people has become the crux of his punishment. But he cannot escape them.

Since the events of September 11, 2001, and after several arguments with prisoners who express sympathy for terrorists, he has decided to isolate himself for the remainder of his sentence. Instead of continuing to mix with the dangerous, volatile people around him, Ellis tries to withdraw. He eats alone, walks the track alone, and eagerly counts the days that separate him from home, from what he knows of normalcy.

In the next section, Billy Williams, the last of the Lilliputian prisoners, tells us how his difficulties come from the criminal justice system itself, not from other prisoners.

CHOOSING PRISON OVER SUPERVISED RELEASE: BILLY WILLIAMS

One prisoner discusses why he would violate his parole and face five additional years in prison rather than serve time in the community.

I met Billy Williams just before he finished serving his first term of incarceration. He was an electrician at Fort Dix, who arrived to repair a light in an office where I was working. Technically, we are supposed to notify a staff member to initiate a work order when building maintenance is required. Like everything else in the federal government, work orders at Fort Dix unleash an avalanche of red tape, and weeks pass before anything is done. Pete worked in the office with me. Since he was friendly with Billy, Pete ignored the official procedures and simply asked Billy to bring his tools to the office to repair the buzzing light fixture.

With light brown hair that hung halfway down his back, and large tattoos on his forearm, Billy looked like a biker to me. My impression was that he most likely was serving a sentence related to the distribution of drugs, probably methamphetamines. The impression was wrong, however, as I later learned that Billy was neither a biker nor serving a sentence for drugs. In fact, after listening to his story, I thought of Billy as someone trapped in the bureaucracy of laws, someone who never should have come to prison in the first place.

There is some irony in my prejudging the long hair and tattoos. As a long-term prisoner who has struggled to show that I am somewhat different from what my forty-five year sentence would suggest, I should have known better.

Several months after his release, Billy returned to the Fort Dix compound. We hardly conversed during his previous term, so I did not know much about him. After encountering Billy again in the housing unit to which I was assigned, I approached him to find out what happened. During my fifteen years of imprisonment, I have seen many people leave and then return through revolving prison doors. Knowing that Billy had only recently been released from his last term, I asked him to describe the events that brought him back. He told me about his ordeal.

After serving a 100-month sentence, Billy was happy to return home to Iva-Gwyn, his wife of twenty years. She and their five children stood by his side faithfully during the time he served, and the family looked forward to being united again. Billy explained that his previous employer rehired Billy the day of his release.

Thus, I was surprised to learn that instead of keeping his relatively high-paying job as an auto mechanic outside, fewer than six months after his release, Billy made a voluntary and conscious decision to return to prison. Rather than serve time in the community under the strict supervision of a parole officer, Billy explained that he preferred to violate his parole and subject himself to whatever new sentence of imprisonment the judge would impose.

Unlike many of the people in prison, Billy did not live as a criminal outside. Rather, he describes himself as a responsible, hard-working family man. Indeed, at fifteen he dropped out of school to marry Iva-Gwyn, his pregnant teenage girlfriend. Billy took a job as a mechanic in a gas station to support his new family, and ever since then he has worked consistently as an auto mechanic or a carpenter.

FROM CARPENTER TO CRIMINAL

Billy's problems with the criminal justice system began when he was twenty-four. He explained that he had been working as a carpenter. After a power saw he and his coworkers had been using burned out, Billy accompanied his boss to a hardware store to purchase a new one. Assuming his boss had paid for the saw, Billy said he did not think about asking for a receipt when his boss told him to carry the saw from the checkout counter to the car. A store detective, however, followed Billy out to the vehicle, where he determined that no one had paid for the saw. Since Billy was carrying the saw, he was charged with and convicted of theft. He received a suspended sentence of probation. Because the saw was worth approximately three hundred dollars, however, Billy became permanently scarred with a felony, not a misdemeanor.

Billy moved forward with his life, not thinking any more about his problem with the justice system; he certainly did not consider himself a criminal. People who have been convicted of felony crimes in the United States, however, must endure consequences that, for most, remain with them for the remainder of their lives. Felons are not allowed to vote in American elections; foreigners who have been convicted of American felonies are prohibited from reentering the United States; and felons cannot have firearms in their possession. Breaching the firearm stipulation resulted in Billy's second encounter with the criminal justice system.

In 1993, when he was twenty-seven, Billy was installing a new carburetor on a vehicle. After completing the work, he took the car for a test drive. He was pulled over for a traffic violation. After plugging Billy's driver's license number into the police database, the patrolman probably noticed that Billy was a convicted felon. That, and perhaps because he wore his hair long in the conservative state of Virginia, the policeman may have wanted to take a closer look at Billy. He asked for permission to search the car Billy was driving. Not having anything to hide, Billy consented to the search. In the vehicle's trunk, the officer found two hunting rifles. They belonged to the vehicle's owner and were enclosed in their cases; no bullets were present. Billy insists he had no idea the weapons were present in the vehicle.

Explanations notwithstanding, the firearms were in Billy's possession—a federal crime. During the judicial proceedings, the owner of the hunting rifles provided testimony that Billy was only repairing the vehicle and did not have any knowledge of the rifles being in the auto's trunk. Nevertheless, Billy was convicted of being a felon in possession of a firearm. The judge sentenced him to eight-and-one-half years for the crime, and automatically, because firearms were involved, his was considered a crime of violence. Immediately after his sentencing, Billy was taken into custody.

REAL PRISON, REAL VIOLENCE

After the sentencing hearing, Billy was transported to a federal prison in Petersburg, Virginia, where he began serving his sentence temporarily until administrators determined where to send him permanently. During the time he was there, Billy saw two stabbings at close range. Not having been incarcerated before, those violent incidents made him concerned about the type of environment in which he would be living.

Billy had been lifting weights when he saw the first stabbing. One man came walking out of the gym and another rushed up behind him and repeatedly plunged an ice-pick type weapon into the victim's buttocks. A few weeks later. Billy says he was playing a card game with three strangers. When one of the players tried some sleight-of-hand movement at the table, Billy's card partner immediately pulled a shiv out of his pocket and stabbed the would-be cardsharp in the stomach.

Wanting no part of the complications associated with a stabbing, Billy says that on both occasions he immediately walked away from the incident. He had learned this bit of prison wisdom not from experience, but from watching television. Leaving the scene helped him avoid questioning by investigating staff members. After having recently received a sentence in excess of eight years, his hopes were to avoid problems in prison—he hoped to see no evil, hear no evil, and speak no evil.

After several months in Petersburg, which was within an hour's drive of his family's home in Portsmouth, Billy was told to prepare for transfer to Butner, North Carolina. The Bureau of Prisons operates three prisons in the Butner complex. One is a camp, holding offenders whom administrators deem need the least amount of security; another is a low-security prison, where the security is slightly tighter. Billy, however, spent his first six months in the medium-security prison at Butner, which in many ways, is different from most other federal prisons.

Besides housing regular offenders, Butner Medium also has a medical ward where federal inmates from around the country who suffer from psychological disorders frequently are sent for treatment. Those in the psychiatric ward mix relatively freely with those in the regular population. Living in such close proximity with the mentally unstable left Billy concerned for his own well-being. One never knew when a psychopath would "flip out." As he explained, "The prison itself was okay. It was clean and everything. But a lot of the other prisoners were creepy. They had slobber dripping from their lips, a glazed look in their eyes. They walked with heavy legs, like they were auditioning for a part in the movie *Night of the Living Dead.* They talked to themselves, might start masturbating in public, or smearing excrement over themselves. One guy resembled Mr. T (the television character) and called himself Badman. He used to pace himself about ten yards from a brick building, run towards it, then smash his body into the wall. People were crazy."

The six months he spent there were hard on him. Since the prison was overcrowded, most all of the jobs available to inmates were taken. Not being able to find employment, Billy says he just remained in his room most of the day. He did not like walking outside of his unit, he explains, because he was trying to avoid the disturbed inmates whom he regularly saw having loud arguments with themselves.

After his sixth month in Butner Medium, the administrators transferred Billy to Butner Low, the low-security facility, where he finally began adjusting. He found his first job in the maintenance department, where he worked with forklifts, performed electrical work, and installed fences. The work was a relief for him, as it kept his mind off his confinement.

Unlike most prisoners, Billy did not concern himself with finding a prison hustle. A blue-collar worker all his life, he was not financially independent. In fact, his wife was working as a dental hygienist, doing her best to keep up the payments on the family home and support their four children—the fifth had not yet been conceived. Although his wife could not afford to send Billy money to make his life easier inside, he made no attempt to capitalize on his mechanical skills to enrich himself.

Billy not only had been working as an auto mechanic and carpenter since he was fifteen, he also was certified in the state of Virginia to work with heating, ventilation, and air conditioning systems. He was comfortable with tools and working with his hands. In prison, people who have such skills easily can initiate hustles to help ease their confinement. They may modify lockers, build shelving for prisoners to store their personal belongings, or repair headphones and radios. Any one of these hustles can provide an individual with cigarettes or other commissary items. After witnessing those two stabbings during his first weeks in confinement, however, Billy chose to lessen his immersion into the prison community. He applied himself only to his Bureau of Prisons job working in maintenance.

A JOB IS A LIFE

Billy began his work day at 7:30 A.M. and stayed on the job until 3:30 P.M., at which time he had to return to his room for one of the five daily census counts. After the 4:00 P.M. count, he returned to his job and worked until 9:00 P.M. In a prison that holds over a thousand men, the maintenance work is never completed. Billy was grateful for the work. He ate all his meals in the prison dining room, and he used the approximately thirty dollars in monthly earnings to purchase postage stamps so that he could communicate with his wife and children.

After another six months, the administrators transferred Billy to the minimum-security facility at Butner, the camp. The camp has no fence around it, nothing to keep prisoners confined other than their honor—and the threat of new criminal charges for walking away. A new hospital was being erected at the camp, and because Billy had such a strong background in construction, along with the appropriate security classification, he proved an ideal candidate for camp placement. Billy passed the next several years of his sentence living more like a feudal serf than a prisoner.

Generally, prisoners desire to make their time pass as easily as possible inside the fences. Instead of seeking ways to contribute to the system that incarcerates them, they look for opportunities to lessen the pains of confinement. For some, that means not working at all. They play cards, watch television, or participate in recreational activities. Others work to educate themselves or participate in programs they hope will help them in some way upon release. Others long to bring excitement to their time in prison, and this urge leads them to participate in extortion rackets or other subversive activities. Billy adjusted differently. His only concern was staying busy; working hard to build a new hospital helped him feel useful and forget the years that were passing him by, apart from his family.

Living in the camp provided Billy with an extraordinary amount of freedom. He was assigned a construction vehicle to help him transport the tools and equipment he needed to complete his duties. Except for the daily census counts, Billy was essentially unsupervised in the camp. Recognizing his skill, Billy was given long-term assignments. His bosses would issue him a set of plans for a building they wanted erected, and Billy would organize a crew of other inmates and go to work. Supervisors would come by periodically to check his progress, but essentially, he acted in the capacity of an independent contractor performing services for a client. The only difference was that instead of paying Billy for his services, his client provided food and shelter and expected Billy to remain on the estate.

A do-nothing job would have exacerbated Billy's tensions. If he did not have a full schedule to keep himself busy, he would have drowned in depression. Throughout his incarceration Billy has had weekly sessions with the staff psychologists. He is on medication, taking four pills every day to help lessen the intensity of a posttraumatic stress disorder. In 1993, a vehicle he was driving was carjacked. While he was in his automobile, waiting at an intersection for a light to change, an armed gunman opened the passenger door and entered the vehicle. The gunman shot Billy in the knee and then ordered him out. Just then, five others joined the melee, pulling Billy out from the driver's side. They shot him four more times. Doctors could extract only three of the bullets because the other two were lodged in his spine.

Since the carjacking, Billy has suffered regular nightmares of being shot again, of cars blowing up, or of the carjacking event itself. The medication and weekly psychology sessions have helped him cope with such fears. He talks with the psychologist about his work, about his family, and about his adjustment in prison. Those sessions, he says, together with his heavy work load, helped his time pass quickly. Otherwise, he says the nightmares haunt him so badly that he screams in his sleep, waking everyone around him except himself. In order to keep from falling out of bed, he says, he strapped himself in with a large belt. The alternative would be a long fall to the concrete floor from the top bunk to which he was assigned.

Billy's level of responsibility inside the institution spared him the indignity and frustrations of regular shakedowns. Unlike citizens in the community who can expect to walk by policemen without concern about being stopped and questioned, prisoners have no such rights and no such expectations of privacy. They may be stopped, questioned, and searched at any time. Those found with contraband can expect to lose privileges or suffer punishments. They may lose the ability to visit, lose access to telephones, be assigned extra duties, or be sent to segregation. In the camp, Billy regularly carried torches and tools in a vehicle that he was authorized to drive anywhere on the scores of acres that composed the Butner complex.

THE STRUGGLE FOR FAMILY TIES

Iva-Gwyn, Billy's wife, made the four-hour drive from their home in Portsmouth to visit Billy every weekend he was held at Butner. Sometimes she brought the children, sometimes she came alone. Because of the relative freedom at the camp, Billy was able to sneak brief periods of intimacy with Iva-Gwyn, and as a consequence of one of their visits, she conceived a child. Although several state prison systems authorize conjugal visits, those committed to the federal prison system are expected to live in celibacy for the duration of their confinement. All sexual relationships, including those that sometimes develop between inmates and staff members, are expressly prohibited. In camps, however, where supervision is less intense, inmates may find opportunities for physical intimacy.

When Billy came within two years of his release date, he requested to transfer to the prison in Petersburg, Virginia, closer to his family. Despite having worked consistently throughout his sentence—likely saving the government hundreds of thousands of dollars in construction fees—when it came time to consider Billy's request for a transfer, he was reminded of his status as a prisoner.

After having his requests for transfer either denied or ignored for several months, Billy was told to pack his property. He thought that he was on his way to Petersburg. Instead, after he was placed in manacles and leg irons, he was told that he had been redesignated to Fort Dix, nine hours away from home—twice as far as he had been while he was in Butner. Further, instead of the relative freedom he had at the camp, Billy was going to serve his last year inside the Fort Dix fences.

Billy's experience was not at all unusual. Although he was a dependable and hard worker who did not create problems for staff, and even though he was able to establish close relationships with his immediate supervisors, as far as the larger system was concerned, Billy was just a number, one more prisoner. Whether he spent the first six years of his sentence watching television and playing cards or erecting prison buildings made no difference to those staff members responsible for his formal classification and location.

The prison machine has no formal mechanism to reward superior adjustment, a bitter lesson that many positively oriented prisoners eventually learn. Prisoners have infinite opportunities to make their periods of incarceration more onerous. For example, if they are caught adding an unauthorized or contraband onion to their food, they may lose visiting privileges for a three-month period; if they make a three-way phone call, they may lose their telephone privileges for a year. Despite abundant penalties being available for behavior that violates rules, however, no formal means exist for staff members to reward prisoners who distinguish themselves in a positive way—to arrange transfers closer to home, for example. The prisoner may forge positive and reciprocal informal relationships with individual staff members, but the bureaucratic system does not recognize such informal relationships. Despite the work he had performed, when it came time to ask for personal consideration, Billy received none.

Despite his resultant frustrations with the system, after arriving at Fort Dix Billy accepted employment in the prison's electric shop. When he was given the assignment to rewire the prison's education building, he again found some comfort by losing himself in his work. Because he was so far away from home, his wife was not able to come visit him. Instead, Billy wrote home every day. At least he could tell his children about what he was doing and express how much he longed to see them. After a year at Fort Dix, his sentence expired. He was given a bus ticket to return home to Virginia.

Billy had saved the thirty dollars he received each month for his work as an electrician. Before boarding the bus to take him home, Billy says he stopped at a mall to purchase his wife a gift. Since he was fifteen he had never been with another woman, he says, and he wanted to show Iva-Gwyn how much he appreciated her. When his wife met him at the bus station, she was totally surprised by the set of diamond earrings Billy gave her. After having served an eight-plus year sentence, Billy and his wife were optimistic about resuming their lives together. They did not know the complexities associated with his period of supervised release that awaited them.

THE PRICE OF PAROLE

After arriving home, Billy had to meet with his parole officer. Like most prisoners sentenced after 1987, in addition to the time Billy served in confinement, he also was sentenced to serve a period of time on supervised release, meaning he would live his life under the close supervision of a parole officer. When Billy reported to his parole officer, he met a man in his early twenties who said he would be supervising Billy's adjustment to the community.

The parole officer explained the rules to Billy. Billy was to come into the office each month and fill out a written report that would describe his activities during the month. For one thing, he was prohibited from associating with anyone else who had been convicted of a crime. Since he did not make a habit of asking others whether they had a criminal record before associating with them, this technicality concerned him. Billy is a blue-collar guy who does not associate with white-collar-type people. "We have nothing in common," he says. Since he did not know who had a criminal record, he was prepared to spend the five years he was scheduled to serve under supervised release not associating with anyone.

Although Billy was not convicted of a drug offense, another stipulation of his supervised release required that he dial a telephone number every evening to see whether he had been scheduled for a urinalysis. This was a mandatory call. Further, the parole officer required Billy to attend a total of three classes each week. One of the classes was for anger management, one was Alcoholics Anonymous, and one was Narcotics Anonymous. The classes were offered only during Billy's normal weekday work hours, and he was required to arrange his work schedule around the ninety-minute classes. In addition, Billy explained that each participant had to pay ten dollars toward the expense of each class. "The classes were driving me nuts. I didn't need them in the first place, and I hated having to leave my work to attend them. My boss was cool with me and worked my schedule around them. But I was losing income, and on top of that, I was having to pay out thirty dollars a week to sit around in a circle listening to the group rap session that was nothing but bullshit anyway."

Billy and his wife also had to keep a detailed accounting of all their finances. If he went to the local convenience store and purchased a quart of milk, Billy had to save the receipt and turn it in with his monthly report. The parole officer wanted to know how much money Billy earned, how much money his wife earned, how much they were spending, and what they were using their money to buy. The parole officer had a comment for the type of shoes Billy and his wife bought for their children, on whether they paid for cable television, and on their weekly grocery bill.

The parole officer also intruded into Billy's work. Each week he made an unannounced visit to the garage where Billy worked as a mechanic. He would talk with Billy's superior and other employees in the shop. It did not matter whether Billy was with a customer or in the middle of replacing a transmission. When the parole officer made his visit, Billy was expected to stop whatever he was doing and talk with the parole officer.

For the first six months of his sentence, Billy endured the complexities associated with his period of supervised release. His parole officer had visited Billy and his family at his home periodically during those six months, but he usually came at reasonable times. One morning, however, before the sun came up, at 5:30 A.M., the parole officer knocked on Billy's front door. Billy was in the bathroom getting ready for work; his wife and children were sleeping. When no one answered the door, the parole officer started pounding on it. He then started walking around the house, peering in through the windows with his flashlight. It was the light that woke Iva-Gwyn.

People who are serving time on supervised release, or parole, do not have the same constitutional protections that other American citizens enjoy. Their rights to privacy, for example, are restricted. In many ways, their abbreviated freedom is laden with caveats and asterisks. As Iva-Gwyn was learning, the conditions of parole did not affect only Billy, but her and their children as well.

Upon being awakened by the beaming flashlight, Iva-Gwyn rushed to the door to accost the parole officer. She screamed at him for bothering her family at an indecent hour, interrupting their lives when Billy was doing everything required of him. To her, the parole officer appeared to be going out of his way to harass the family, to see how far they could be pushed. This time, she was sure, the parole officer had gone too far, but he insisted that he was just doing his job. Billy's wife was so irate that Billy had to lead her into another room so he could talk with the officer alone. The parole officer said he only stopped by to see "what was going on."

THE LESSER OF THE EVILS

That dawn visit was the last straw for Billy. He called his attorney to find out whether the parole officer had been abusing his authority. The news was not good. As a convicted felon, Billy had few alternatives available to him. The parole officer was within his rights to come by Billy's place of residence periodically at early hours in the morning, or late hours in the evening.

There was a loophole in the laws of supervised release under which Billy was convicted. If he violated the conditions of his supervised release, his attorney explained Billy would return to prison. Although it was unlikely, Billy could then be sentenced to as many as five additional years of incarceration. After his subsequent release, however, he would be free of the parole officer and the criminal justice system unless he committed a new criminal offense. That loophole has since been sealed. Now, individuals who violate the conditions of their supervised release return to prison for whatever term the judge arbitrarily chooses to impose. And now, upon release, violators resume their period of supervised release from the beginning. Thus, making more work for parole officers; it is not only the prisons that create jobs for people. Under the newly revised laws, some people serving time under supervised release will never escape the grips of the criminal justice system. Fortunately for Billy, he had an alternative.

Billy said that he and his wife discussed their options. There was no telling exactly how much time the judge would impose if Billy violated his period of supervised release, but his attorney suggested the range was usually between six and twelve months of imprisonment for those who violate the conditions of supervised release. To Billy and his wife, living under the parole officer's microscope for five years seemed worse than another six to twelve months of imprisonment. The outside risk, however, was that the judge would send Billy back to prison to serve the entire five years of supervised release in custody. In the end, it was a risk Billy was willing to take. "I'd been with my wife since we were teenagers. She stuck with me all through my prison term, even after they moved me so far away from home that she couldn't visit. Our marriage was strong. But the stress associated with supervised release was too much. He wasn't only screwing with my life, but the PO was screwing with my family. The stress threatened to break us up. I just wanted out. And if that meant going back to prison for a while, that's what I was willing to do. It was the only way I could get my life back."

The following week, when his parole officer made his regular unannounced visit to Billy's place of employment, he told his parole officer that he would no longer be reporting for his monthly meeting and that he and his wife had made a conscious decision to technically violate parole so he could return to prison and finish his sentence within the criminal justice system. The parole officer simply said that was his choice.

Billy continued to dial the mandatory number each evening to see whether he was scheduled for a urinalysis, and he continued attending the mandatory classes. He wanted to provide the sentencing judge every reason to impose the low end of the imprisonment range. When Billy missed his next scheduled meeting with the parole officer, he received a phone call. Billy told the parole officer, again, that he would no longer report and wanted to be in violation.

"Very well," his parole officer said. "I'm issuing a warrant for your arrest." Billy then turned himself in and waited for sentencing. The judge issued another year of confinement without the possibility of time off for good behavior.

Billy is serving that year now. He writes home every day and feels good about his decision to incarcerate himself, thereby ending the almost unbearable and seemingly bizarre restrictions imposed on his family.

BANTAM-TIME PRISONERS

The five men profiled in this section are serving terms between five and ten years. Although such terms may seem significantly long to people who have not been incarcerated, those with less than ten-year sentences are still considered short-term inmates by those who inhabit America's prisons. Sociologist John Irwin and gangster Al Capone both served bantam time.

A sentence between five and ten years, although disruptive to one's life, is not so long that it completely alienates an individual from society. Bantam-time prisoners still remember clearly and poignantly what it was like to live in the community and know that returning to their families and communities is not so far in the future. After five years pass, they know that they are more than halfway home. Most never lose sight of that goal, and if they are young enough at the start of their terms, they have adequate time to prepare themselves to lead new lives upon release.

Those serving bantam sentences differ from both longer- and shorter-term prisoners. They come into the prison system with different expectations. They are not anxiously awaiting release, as they know they have substantial time to serve. But neither are they utterly hopeless about returning to the world outside, as are many longer-term inmates. They straddle a period that gives them enough time to reflect on the earlier decisions of their lives, as well as sufficient time to make meaningful changes if they choose to do so.

Bantam-time prisoners may be in the best position to adjust. First, they must successfully move through the initial shock that comes with incarceration. If they succeed, they may adjust in ways that not only fill their time, but also allow them to grow on some level despite the chains that hold them. Such prisoners cling to a degree of optimism. One key, however, is not allowing the initial stages of confinement to pull one under the current, leaving one drowning in the endless eddies of prison problems.

THE BANTAM STORIES

Harvey Ziskis, the first Bantam prisoner we meet, did not adjust well during the initial stages of his ninety-seven-month sentence. In his late fifties, Harvey had lived as a successful businessman. Convicted of money laundering, he was sentenced to a federal prison camp in northern Florida. Harvey did not endure the same type of frustration as Ellis Rogers. He was not confined in a room with men he viewed as thugs. Rather, in a federal prison camp, Harvey was surrounded by men who came from backgrounds much like his own.

Domingo Morales, on the other hand, began his bantam-time sentence by creating a position for himself as a quasi-staff member. In a higher-security prison, such an open alliance with staff members could have exposed Domingo to systematic and oftentimes violent retaliation from other prisoners. At Fort Dix, however, Morales's adjustment resulted in his receiving perks that helped pass his time.

Like Billy Williams, Domingo found solace by working independently during his adjustment to imprisonment. Domingo, now in his seventh year, is reaching the last months of his term. A native of Spain, Domingo had few interests outside of the prison fences. His only concern was completing his term. By moving himself into a full-time job, he accepted responsibilities that most prisoners would avoid. He lived in a manner that he says would have closely resembled the way he would have passed his time if he were in the community. Because of his work and the way he informally distinguished himself, Domingo says he never felt like a prisoner during the seven years he served.

In academia, students distinguish themselves through their grades and activities; professors earn reputations based on their teaching, research, and publications. In the commercial sector, individuals do not start from scratch every time they make a career move, rather, they have incentives to progress because their accomplishments follow them throughout their careers and influence the compensation they receive. Resumes and work-history reports document their contributions to past organizational goals. Not so for the prisoner. Indeed, the correctional system does not identify any goals for the prisoner to achieve other than to serve time and partici-pate in a mishmash of programs.

Regardless of what contributions a prisoner makes to the system, or what the offender accomplishes in efforts to prepare himself for a more successful future, only negative adjustments have an impact on records kept by the so-called correctional system. Iqbal Karimi, the third bantam-time prisoner, found this out when terrorists with roots in his homeland, Afghanistan, attacked the United States.

Early in his term, Iqbal found his passion—and perhaps the beginning of a legitimate career in America—painting. Eventually, his talent led to other prisoners commissioning Iqbal to paint portraits of them and their families from photographs. He describes the prison's underground econ-omy and how some prisoners use it not only to support themselves in prison, but also to support their families outside and accumulate funds that they hope will help them settle after their release.

In the large communities existing within prison fences, it is inevitable that prisoners will enter into agreements with each other. Because prisoner transactions play such a ubiquitous role in every prison, readers will find that several of the men profiled describe how the underground economy contributes to their adjustment.

After living as prisoners for a lengthy period, many men are scarred by the disparaging treatment they endure. Institutional rules, policies, and customs leave the men doubting their worth as human beings. At any given moment, their belongings or their person may be searched; they may be ordered to perform belittling tasks. Years of such conditioning takes its toll, causing formerly confident men to question their validity—unless, of course, one clings to the us-versus-them values of the criminal world.

Iqbal was different. He had expressed remorse for his crime, held a full-time job, educated himself, received no disciplinary infractions, and de-veloped a marketable skill. It would seem as if he had crafted a model adjustment—until the terrorists struck. After September 11, 2001, every-thing changed.

Fermin Martin came to the United States from Cuba. He was well edu-cated before he began his term. Through his profile, readers get a feel for the constant noise that accompanies incarceration, and the cramped con-ditions under which prisoners live. Fermin describes the necessity of adjusting not only to confinement, but also to the peculiar obsessions others adopt in their efforts to cope with the stripping of their identities.

Through Fermin's profile, readers learn about some long-term prisoners who have adopted obsessive-compulsive disorders during their adjustment. Fermin describes what it is like passing years together with such men while sharing a cell not much larger than a walk-in closet. Through Fermin's story, readers also learn about the red tape one must cut through in order to find a compatible cellmate; some staff members refuse to allow prisoners the opportunity to choose with whom they will share their closet-sized space.

Like Iqbal, Fermin discovered an activity to assuage the pains of his confinement. Whereas Iqbal turned to painting, Fermin found his solace in music.

Earlier in his life, Tom was an up-and-coming member of one of the five widely chronicled, New York–based, Mafia families. Those who come to prison with reputations of having close ties to organized crime may serve their terms with a celebritylike aura, surrounded by sycophants trying to ingratiate themselves. Instead of encouraging the flattery that came with his status, however, Tom repelled it. He committed himself to changing his life during his roughly eight-year term.

Tom engineered a highly structured adjustment. As I write this commentary, he is weeks away from his release. Because he began preparing for his life after release as soon as his problems with the criminal justice system surfaced, he is now ready to live in society as a contributing citizen, something he had not envisioned before his incarceration.

AN ESCAPE FROM PRISON FRUSTRATIONS: HARVEY ZISKIS

One federal prisoner responded to the frustrations of confinement by escaping from a federal prison camp and hurting his family in virtually irreparable ways.

As a consequence of my being confined since 1987, I have encountered thousands of other prisoners. This long-term experience inside federal prisons qualifies me in some ways to recognize differences among the prisoners around me. Many assure me that prison walls are important physical barriers, as some people who become prisoners have no intention of ever respecting the laws that contribute to social success. Some inmates, though, strike me as being completely out of place in prison. Harvey Ziskis is one of them.

Harvey has been incarcerated at Fort Dix since June of 2000. He is in his late fifties, stands about five-feet-seven, is slightly built and well-groomed. Harvey wears wire-rimmed glasses, speaks to few others inside the prison, appears reticent and harmless looking at a glance, and spends most of his time writing, typing, or watching television. He is a big fan of old black-and-white films.

A khaki uniform in this environment makes anyone look like a prisoner, but when I look at Harvey, I see someone who belongs to another world, a world far from the grime of prison. Harvey looks much more like someone you would meet on a golf course, and not surprisingly, that is where he would be today had he not escaped from the federal prison camp in Pensacola, Florida.

Most prisoners whom authorities designate to serve their time in minimum-security camps are given the privilege of turning themselves in to the prisons, that is, self-reporting. Harvey was not so fortunate. After he was convicted at trial on money laundering charges, the judge revoked his bond and ordered him taken into custody. After spending four months in various county jails, not knowing what to expect, Harvey was led through the rituals of degradation associated with prisoner transport. In leg irons, chains, and handcuffs, Harvey was delivered to the Saufley Field Prison Camp in Pensacola. He arrived in the fall of 1998 as federal prisoner number 53100-004. He had been sentenced to serve ninety-seven months.

Besides being a first-time offender, Harvey is a man who has operated several successful businesses across America. Although he is proud of his business accomplishments, it is devotion to his family that brings him his greatest happiness. Indeed, family issues were the impetus for Harvey's decision to escape from Saufley Field. He did not adjust well to the tribulations that accompany one's initial months in custody.

Upon his arrival at Saufley Field, Harvey felt relief. Like most Americans, he had heard the rumors about prison life. At the time of sentencing, he was worried about senseless violence and chaos that he might have to face inside our nation's federal prison system. Jokes that he had heard previously about not bending over to pick up the soap when taking a shower suddenly took on a new personal meaning. Anxiety plagued Harvey. As an older, white male, Harvey anticipated being in the minority at his designated prison, perhaps a target of the prison predators about whom he had heard.

When the U.S. marshals delivered Harvey to the prison itself, however, he saw at once that he had been designated to serve his sentence in a federal prison camp, the easiest place to serve time, although Harvey did not know that yet. His attorney had told him that he likely would serve his sentence in a Florida prison because Harvey's residence was in Palm Beach, Florida. Harvey had heard about the overcrowded Florida prisons and was worried about the violence that stirred inside them. At that time, Harvey did not appreciate the difference between prison camps and other facilities. He had no way to make accurate comparisons; prison was prison, or so he thought. "One of the big mistakes the prison system makes, I think, is letting people start off in prison camps. Guys who've never been to prison before have no idea that they're in a privileged environment. All I knew about prison was what I'd seen on television. Then, all of a sudden, I'm in this place with a golf course and easy living. I had no supervision, was really just relaxing. I came to expect that all prisons were easy like this. If I would have started out in a low- or medium-security prison, with all the petty rules and regulations and controls, then after a year or two been transferred to a camp, I would have known that I was in a privileged spot."

Harvey did not actually "start off in a prison camp," as he claims. After the jury returned a verdict of guilty, Harvey was taken into custody. While he awaited sentencing, he was confined in various holding facilities and county jails. Those places of confinement maintain tight security and have stressful environments. Prisoners generally are confined to small quarters with few privileges because they have not been officially classified. Mass murderers may share the same living space with offenders accused of credit card fraud. Although it is true that Harvey had not served time in another prison before he arrived at Saufley Field prison camp, he did serve his initial four months in a restrictive, prisonlike environment. That experience alone should have given him all the information he needed to confirm how fortunate he was to begin his term in a prison camp.

THE APPEARANCE OF CLASSIFICATION

The Bureau of Prisons operates its facilities according to the level of security it determines each prison requires. Each federal prison falls into one of five different security levels: minimum, low, medium, high, or administrative. Administrative-level facilities are designed to hold prisoners from each security level. That means an administrative facility may be holding mass murderers together with people who mailed envelopes with fake postage stamps.

Because administrative facilities hold such diverse groups of prisoners, life inside of them is strictly controlled. The prisoners are usually there for a specific purpose besides serving their sentence. Generally, these facilities serve three purposes:

1. As a facility close to courthouses to hold prisoners who the U.S. Marshal Service needs to transport to court frequently

2. As transit facilities where prisoners are held while en route to other prisons

3. As hospital-like facilities where medical staff members and equipment are available to treat the complicated health concerns of the Bureau of Prisons system prisoner population

Harvey's first four months of incarceration (the time spent between his court dates and his transfer to Saufley Field) were spent in prisons with an administrative security rating. He came to expect all prisons to have this high level of control.

The other four levels of security classification—minimum, low, medium, and high—are designed for prisoners who will be staying for longer periods of time—possibly several decades. As a result of the Bureau of Prisons' complex system of classifying prisoners, those in each classification, and therefore in the same prison, largely have similar security needs.

Seven factors determine an institution's security level: (1) the use of mobile patrols that drive around the institution's perimeter twenty-four hours a day; (2) gun towers located around a prison's outside perimeter from which armed Bureau of Prisons guards monitor the activities inside of a prison; (3) perimeter barriers that separate the prison from the community; (4) the use of detection devices such as metal detectors and sound guns that can intercept prisoner conversations; (5) internal security such as locks on individual doors and bars on windows; (6) housing issues such as whether prisoners are confined in locked rooms, cages, or open dormitories; and finally (7) the ratio between inmates and staff members.

The higher the security level in an institution, the more stringent the security needs. The most secure prison in the federal system is the administrative-maximum unit at Florence, Colorado, where prisoners basically are denied all human contact. Those institutions known as "penitentiaries," as distinguished from "administrative units," "correctional institutions," and "camps" suffer higher rates of violence because they hold prisoners with violent backgrounds in more open settings.

Medium-security prisons also have relatively high security needs, as they generally hold prisoners with sentences of up to thirty years. Exceptions may be made for well-adjusted prisoners serving longer terms, but for the most part, prisoners with more than thirty years to serve are held in penitentiaries. Longer-term prisoners frequently bring higher levels of volatility to an institution.

Low-security prisons still maintain a degree of tight control, but they are more open than medium- or high-security prisons. Prison camps, on the other hand, are designed to hold prisoners whom the Bureau of Prisons has determined need the least amount of supervision or security. Since Harvey was convicted of nonviolent, non-drug-related crimes—financial, white-collar crimes in his case—he was properly designated to Saufley Field, a relatively pleasant minimum-security prison camp.

Taxpayers frequently complain about the system's use of prison camps. Many citizens want prisoners to suffer through long sentences, and they express outrage at what they perceive as the system's coddling of offenders. What these people fail to take into consideration, however, is the extraordinary difference in costs to operate prisons at different security levels; the higher the security level, the higher the cost on a per-inmate basis.

The least expensive prisons to operate are prison camps, where Harvey was designated originally to serve his sentence. Camps do not require a fence around the perimeter of the prison. No gun towers exist. And the staff-to-inmate ratio is the lowest in the prison system. Whereas a high-security facility may have as many as one staff member for each prisoner confined there, a prison camp may require a single staff member for every thirty prisoners assigned to it. Accordingly, the most expensive high-security facility may drain the public coffers of forty thousand plus dollars per year to confine each prisoner that it holds; while it may cost taxpayers less than ten thousand dollars per year to confine each inmate in a federal prison camp. With approximately two million people in American prisons, it is necessary to manage taxpayer dollars by properly classifying prisoners and holding them by the least restrictive and most cost-effective method available.

THE CAMP EXPERIENCE

Once Harvey was processed into the Saufley Field prison, he began to breathe easier. He saw that the other prisoners with whom he was going to live while serving his sentence were not the aggressive predators that he had anticipated. Indeed, they were normal people—no gang members, thugs, extortion artists, or blood-thirsty psychopaths. Even the staff members seemed pleasant. Indeed, inmates appeared rather docile, serving their sentences without the level of tension he had encountered over his first four months while he was moving around from detention facility to detention facility on his way to prison camp. He quickly came to expect that his adjustment and term would pass easily.

Harvey was assigned to one of the prison's dormitories. The entire prison held about 350 people, 100 of whom were assigned to the same dormitory as Harvey. The dorm was divided into two-man cubicles; it was well organized and clean. Harvey took the top bunk in his cubicle and, after settling himself in, began walking the prison compound to acquaint himself with his new surroundings.

Harvey made a few friends—people who came from the background and social circle that he understood—and they walked him around the prison. He saw the prison library from which he could check out books, a recreation area he could use to maintain his health, and a commissary from which he could purchase items that would make his stay a bit easier. Harvey's new friends told him that there was hardly any tension at Saufley Field, and that once one got over the initial shock of being separated from society, a man could serve his sentence with relatively minimal aggravation. These friends even helped him locate a desirable job as a greenhouse gardener on a nearby golf course.

In order to work, Harvey and his two coworkers had to board a bus at 6:30 A.M. each morning in front of the prison. They were driven about a half-hour away to a military golf course. Harvey's responsibilities at work were to maintain the plants in the greenhouse, a very easy, tranquil job. His supervisor was a civilian, not the Bureau of Prisons disciplinarian he was expecting. Harvey learned that as long as he performed his required duties, he would be left to himself.

Essentially, Harvey's worries about prison life were erased after his first week at Saufley Field. He had been assigned to a calm environment and to a job that would not only keep him busy, but would provide some soothing therapy as well. Harvey looked forward to tending the plants; they took his mind off of the pains of confinement. Minor though his sufferings would be, Harvey was still a man in his late fifties who would be separated from his beloved family for eight years. And indeed, as Harvey grew more at ease with his prison sentence, thoughts about remaining apart from his family, of not being there when they needed him, began to torment him. "I began to feel guilty about my situation. While my wife was outside struggling to keep our family together—handling the children, taking care of the house, paying the bills—I was pretty much relaxing. Although I was working full-time as the system required, every day felt like I was avoiding my responsibility to my family. I was spending time in a garden, swinging a golf club. Those activities helped me forget about what I was missing outside, but I didn't feel right. Yet if I didn't work, all I could do was mope around. The punishment was in my head—not because of what I was going through, but because of the complications my own predicament brought to my family."

Harvey had been married to Jackie, a critical-care nurse, for the past ten years. Together they had close ties to Harvey's parents and to Harvey's twelve children. Harvey's mother and father, both of whom were approximately eighty years old, lived in Connecticut, and so they could not easily make the long trip to visit Harvey. But Jackie and several of his children were able to visit him regularly.

Those visits, together with regular phone calls to his parents, helped Harvey begin to manage the distance that had been placed between him and his family. About four months after he had arrived at the prison camp, though, his mother became suddenly ill and died; her death affected Harvey deeply, threatening his adjustment to prison.

THE FUNERAL FIASCO

When Harvey called home on a Friday afternoon his father told him that the family had taken his mother to the hospital. Harvey called back on Saturday morning to see how his mother was feeling, but was given the sad news; she had died during the previous evening. "My brother-in-law told me about my mom's death on the phone. It was such a shock, and I wasn't at all prepared for it. Tears were coming out of my eyes uncontrollably within seconds. It was early in the morning, but several others were around in the phone room. I felt weak, had to hang up. I walked outside looking for a place to be alone. The only place I could find were the bleachers around the softball field. I just sat there, in the hot sun. I cried like a baby, knowing I was alone."

The news of his mother's passing left Harvey distraught and unable to contain his emotions. He went to see his counselor to explain what had happened and requested permission for leave to attend the funeral. The counselor received the news with apathy. She processed it as if he were asking for a pencil. Although her title was counselor, there was no counseling, no sympathy expressed—Harvey's tears notwithstanding. After listening to Harvey's request, she told him to write up the details and see her in a few hours. Harvey was then dismissed.

The faith of Harvey's family requires a funeral to proceed quickly after death. Because Harvey was incarcerated, however, his family agreed to postpone the funeral for a few days if Harvey could be given permission to attend. And, indeed, later that Saturday, his counselor told him that he would be able to attend the funeral if he agreed to pay two Bureau of Prisons officers for all of the expenses they would incur on the trip, including their overtime wages. Also, Harvey would have to agree to attend the funeral in handcuffs and to sleep in the county jail while he was in Connecticut.

Harvey agreed to all of these conditions. His counselor then told him that he would be authorized to travel on the following Tuesday, provided all financial arrangements were completed by Monday afternoon. Although the two-day trip was going to cost Harvey approximately five thousand dollars, he was grateful that he would be able to pay his final respects to his mother, along with his family and friends. His family agreed to hold the funeral services on Tuesday, the day Harvey was scheduled to arrive in Connecticut.

Over the next couple of days, Harvey's family made all of the arrangements to accommodate the Bureau of Prisons officers who would be accompanying Harvey. They purchased airline tickets, paid for the officer's lodging, purchased vouchers for the officer's meals, and sent the Bureau of Prisons a certified check to pay the officers' wages and incidental expenses. All such arrangements had been made and were verified by the Bureau of Prisons late Monday morning. Making the necessary arrangements assuaged some of Harvey's grief. It gave him the feeling that he was doing something useful, something to pay his mother his last respects.

On Tuesday morning, however, when Harvey was preparing to leave, he was called to the counselor's office. He was told that prison administrators did not realize how much time Harvey had remaining to serve when they granted him permission to attend the funeral. Because of that, someone in the prison bureaucracy determined that Harvey would be a flight risk if he were allowed to leave the institution.

This news hit Harvey like an exploding hand grenade. It came at the last possible minute. The funeral already had been delayed, and his flight was scheduled to leave within the next two hours. Unbelieving, Harvey noticed that his counselor was totally indifferent as she gave him the crushing news. Harvey had spoken with his mother every day of his life. Now she was dead, and he was being denied, by a stranger, the opportunity to mourn her death with his family. Not knowing how to respond, Harvey said he burst out of the counselor's office in a frantic and tormented state of emotional distress. "The counselor's telling me that I couldn't go to the funeral was worse than hearing that my mother had died. I couldn't believe it. She poured salt in the wound by telling me that I had too much time ahead of me to serve. Then she had the audacity to say that she would authorize a free phone call if I went to the chapel and made an appointment. I was enraged. I told her that I could pay for my own phone call and stormed out. From that moment on, I knew I had to get out."

Harvey called his family to give them the bad news and instructed them to proceed with the funeral. He would not be attending. He went to sit alone on one of the benches and sobbed as he continued to absorb the loss of his mother.

While he was mourning, Harvey steeled himself to leave the prison, to escape. Not thinking clearly, he became filled with rage toward the Bureau of Prisons, angry at what he perceived to be its illogical and hard-hearted ways. Everyday, he reasoned, the Bureau of Prisons allowed him to travel unsupervised on a public bus to attend a job on a golf course where he was supervised by a civilian. Clearly those administrators agreed that Harvey presented neither danger nor threat to the community. Now, at the last minute, the system had rescinded its permission for him to attend the funeral. "We are not talking Willie Horton," Harvey told me. "I'm nearly sixty years old and I've never had a violent thought, much less a violent action. I'm no danger to anyone."

It just did not make sense to Harvey. Over the next few days, he refused to attend his job detail. He stayed to himself, trying to find solace in his own thoughts. Finally, the following weekend, he received a visit from Jackie, his wife. She told him about the funeral and how everyone was so distressed at Harvey's absence. The more Harvey heard about the funeral, the more he began to realize how totally helpless he was. His father, who was also over eighty years old, could fall ill suddenly, and again, Harvey would be subject to the capricious discretion of a Bureau of Prisons employee. During that visit, Jackie knew that Harvey was not himself. But she could not persuade him to share the illogical thoughts that were whirling through his mind.

THE ESCAPE

After Jackie returned home to Palm Beach, Harvey made arrangements to obtain access to an automobile. The following week, when he had secured access to the car, Harvey walked away from his job detail on the golf course. He got into the car and drove several hours from the prison to his home in Palm Beach. He had no plan whatsoever. Without thinking of the serious consequences of his actions, Harvey decided that he had had enough of prison and was going to take a break from the pressure. In retrospect, the whole idea seemed comical in its simplicity.

What Harvey did not realize is that by choosing to leave prison, he actually was committing a new crime. Specifically, he was violating Title 18 of the United States Code, Section 751 (a), which holds that any individual who escapes from federal prison shall be fined up to five thousand dollars or imprisoned for up to five years, or both.

By driving away from prison, Harvey was subjecting himself (and anyone who assisted him) to significant punishment. Further, he would no doubt be serving the remainder of his sentence—assuming he was caught—in a federal prison with far less agreeable conditions than the federal prison camp at Saufley Field. But Harvey was in no state of mind to think about the ramifications of his actions. He just drove the car south to Palm Beach. He arrived on a Friday afternoon and rented a furnished apartment less than five minutes away from his home. Once he was settled in, Harvey called his wife. He told her that he was in town and that she could come visit him, conveniently ignoring the fact that by implicating her he was placing her in violation of the law as well. The only way she could exonerate herself would be by turning Harvey over to the authorities. No one considered that option.

Again, Harvey had no plan. He simply moved into a furnished apartment and had his wife come visit him every evening. He began making arrangements to have his eighty-year-old father come down from Connecticut to stay with him. "I just wanted to be with my family," Harvey said. He did not think about employment or leaving the country to begin a new life. He was living off his savings, trying to sidestep law enforcement for as long as he could.

Within a couple of days of Harvey's escape, the U.S. Marshal's Service initiated a search for him. They went to visit Jackie at the hospital where she worked, asking her whether she had heard from Harvey. Although she had been spending every possible minute with Harvey since he returned to Palm Beach, she denied to the federal officers that she knew anything about his escape, and thus violated Title 18 of the United States Code, Section 1001, which subjects anyone who makes materially false, fictitious, or fraudulent statements to a federal officer to a term of imprisonment of up to five years.

Despite the U.S. Marshals' persistent surveillance of Jackie, every day she eluded the officers to extend her illegal tryst with her husband. Harvey purchased prepaid cell phones and beepers, giving one of each to his wife and keeping a set for himself. He drove behind his wife as she was leaving her home or work, watching to see how closely she was being followed. As Harvey watched the officers, knowing that they could not see him, he engaged in a cat-and-mouse game, instructing his wife through cell phone conversations and beeper codes as to how she could lose the U.S. Marshals who were following her so she could then rendezvous with him.

Harvey and his wife lived in this manner for about one month. The marshals continued interrupting Jackie at her work to ask about Harvey. She continued to tell them that she did not know where he was. Nevertheless, Jackie spent part of every day with Harvey, and they did not confine their newly charged romance only to the apartment Harvey had rented. They dined out. They went to movie theaters. They went to the beach. For a fugitive, Harvey was leading a rather open life. Thirty days after his escape, however, Harvey's vacation from prison came to an abrupt end.

The evening began routinely enough, with Jackie's departure from her apartment. She was followed, a few cars back, by the marshals. After about thirty minutes, and with Harvey's instructions, Jackie was able to break free of the surveillance. She then parked her car in a shopping center and joined Harvey in his car. They drove off together to enjoy the evening. What Harvey and Jackie did not know is that the marshals had spotted Jackie's car in the parking lot; they placed it under surveillance for the remainder of the night. Early the next morning, when Harvey was returning Jackie to her car, the marshals swarmed around him and shattered his make-believe world.

THE CUFFS AND CONSEQUENCES

After trying to apprehend Harvey for the thirty days, the marshals on his case were visibly upset. Three marshal vehicles came to a screeching halt around his car from three different directions. Six marshals then jumped out of their cars, weapons drawn and pointed at Harvey's head. They ran to Harvey's car door and forcibly removed him from the car, throwing his 150-pound frame on the ground, pinning his head under one of the marshal's boots. Harvey was pleading with them, "I'm not armed. Be careful. Don't shoot!" The marshals restrained him in handcuffs, then lifted him into one of their vehicles and drove him to the local jail. He was placed in solitary confinement, given no access to a telephone call.

It was not only Harvey who found new problems with the law. His wife Jackie also was arrested. Jackie's apprehension changed everything for Harvey, sending him into a sinking depression and making him feel even more helpless than he had before. Harvey was not so concerned with his own problems. He was despondent because he was just beginning to realize that his actions helped enmesh Jackie in the criminal justice system. She was suffering only because Harvey could not stand to be without her; that was the thought that paralyzed him. He was alone, in solitary confinement with nothing to occupy his mind but his worries about Jackie. Harvey felt as if he were serving time in hell, tormented by his own thoughts.

Eventually, Harvey was transported back to northern Florida, and Jackie was moved to a local jail for women that was not far away from where Harvey was held. They communicated through letters, but both were frightened.

Harvey hired an attorney who was able to structure a guilty plea that resulted in Jackie's being charged with conspiracy to commit escape; she was sentenced to four months imprisonment, which she served at the Coleman Prison Camp for Women near Orlando. She also must serve three years of supervised release, during which time she must report to a U.S. Parole Officer on a regular basis. But Jackie's sentence also had a more difficult aspect: she is prohibited from having any contact, either direct or indirect, with Harvey.

Harvey also was charged with new criminal conduct. He pled guilty to escape and received a sentence of just over one year, which was added to the ninety-seven months he already had been serving. Besides the additional time, Harvey also had to accept the fact that as a consequence of his escape, the Bureau of Prisons would ensure that he served the remainder of his sentence at a low- or medium-security prison.

After his second sentence, Harvey was sent to Beaumont, Texas. The Beaumont prison was as different from Saufley Field as apple pie is from pig fat. Within a month after arriving there, Harvey ignorantly walked into the middle of a scheme where gang members were collaborating with staff members to extort money from other prisoners. Harvey was placed in segregation, where Bureau of Prisons investigators left him waiting for several months before authorities finally arrested several staff members at the Beaumont facility for corruption. After the arrests, Harvey was released from segregation in Beaumont, but he was not allowed to settle in. Within weeks he was transferred again, this time to the federal prison at Fort Dix, New Jersey.

Since Harvey's escape from Saufley Field, he has been transported in chains on eleven buses and seven different airplanes. He has been processed through fifteen separate prison facilities since the time of his recapture. Once he was caught, it took the Bureau of Prisons eighteen months to transfer him to Fort Dix; even now, Harvey says that he does not know whether Fort Dix is his final destination. He says that he is going through what the prison system calls "diesel therapy," a tacit punishment for recalcitrant prisoners. Harvey has spent thirty-nine months incarcerated thus far, and nearly half of those months have been in solitary confinement. Worse yet, he is being deprived of the one thing in this world that matters to him: contact with his wife.

I asked Harvey how this experience has affected his life. Clearly, he remains devastated over his actions. "I cannot believe I did it," he says. "I just wasn't thinking about what I was doing. I had no concept of the seriousness of my actions. Especially, I didn't know that I'd be putting Jackie in danger." In retrospect, Harvey says he knows that he made a foolish move, one that not only he, but his entire family, is paying for. He is one prisoner who visibly lives in deep regret.

At Fort Dix, Harvey has had a difficult time adjusting because he is prohibited from contact with his wife. He says he lacks the concentration to read anything longer than magazine or newspaper articles. He tries to abandon his problems by watching television. As a prisoner, Harvey says he feels like "a cousin of the dead." He has not been successful in connecting with others outside prison fences; consequently, he is forced to live among strangers with strange behavior. One of his acquaintances, he says, is a rabbi who was convicted of selling the drug ecstasy. The rabbi now supports himself in the prison by stealing vegetables from the kitchen and selling them to others in order to feed his nicotine habit.

Ironically, Harvey escaped from prison because he could not stand to live apart from his family. As a consequence of his escape, however, he is separated further from them, and he will be apart from them much longer. It is, to paraphrase Shakespeare, a tangled web that we weave, and nowhere more tangled than in the nation's prisons.

Rather than exacerbating his criminal problems after arriving in prison, Domingo Morales, our next bantam-time offender, adjusted by aligning himself closely with staff members and accepting a position of responsibility.

AN INMATE-STAFF HYBRID:
DOMINGO MORALES

Working as a head orderly brings one prisoner extra privileges.

MAINTENANCE MATTERS

Maintaining control and security of the institution represents every prison administrator's most important responsibility. Maintaining cleanliness and sanitation, however, comes in a close second. Orderlies are essential to achieving this goal.

Prisons are crowded. They concentrate thousands of people together into a relatively small space, most living within shouting distance of others. In order to prevent the spread of disease and the invasion of rodents, administrators must implement policies to ensure that the thousands of pounds of garbage inmates generate weekly does not accumulate.

This garbage comes from a variety of sources. Inmates receive mail every day, creating an enormous accumulation of paper. Inmates may shop in the commissary each week, purchasing such items as canned or bagged foods, and other products that come in packages that need discarding. They share bathrooms, microwaves, telephones, and living space, all of which need constant cleaning. And, with well over three-hundred men living together in a single building, it receives constant physical abuse. Staff members do not clean, inmates do.

The federal prison system, administered by the Bureau of Prisons, employs a bureaucratic system of management. It falls under the umbrella of the Department of Justice, led by the U.S. Attorney General. The Director of the Bureau of Prisons, a presidential appointee, reports to the Attorney General on the system's operations and policies. With well over 150 prisons in the federal system, the director obviously is not involved in each prison's daily operations. Instead, the system is divided into regions, each of which is led by a regional director who oversees the wardens who, in turn, serve as chief executive officers of their respective prisons.

The wardens make use of associate wardens in the management of their institutions, and the associate wardens rely on department heads to oversee the day-to-day operations. All housing units fall under the direction of the associate warden of programs, who delegates immediate authority to the unit managers. Unit managers are like mini-wardens for the inmates assigned to their housing units. They, too, have a cadre of staff members who report to them, including case managers, counselors, and unit correctional officers (all of whom are referred to as guards by the prisoners). Among other things, the unit manager delegates the responsibility of unit cleanliness to a counselor. The designated counselor then supervises a work detail of inmates (who prefer to be called prisoners) to perform the actual cleaning duties.

At Fort Dix, staff members emphasize unit cleanliness. Each week, a representative of the Safety Department inspects the housing areas and assigns a numerical score to each in order to determine which units on the compound are cleanest. Top scores begin at 100, but the representative from Safety will deduct points for deficiencies in cleanliness or for safety hazards. For example, points may be lost for dirty showers, cigarette butts found on the floor, or cleaning supplies inappropriately stored or labeled.

Because of space limitations, the single chow hall at Fort Dix East receives only one unit at a time. Units that score highest in the weekly cleanliness rating are released first in the weekly meal rotation. With approximately 350 people in each housing unit, it frequently takes as long as two hours to serve the entire population. The difference between eating first and last may be the difference between receiving food that is steaming hot and food that is lukewarm, or having access to a salad bar with fresh lettuce or a salad bar with no lettuce at all. Eating first is a privilege, and the unit's cleanliness score determines which units receive that privilege in any given week.

At Fort Dix East, which has six regular housing units, unit 5702 regularly receives the highest cleanliness score. Counselor Hood takes great pride in her supervision of the orderlies and makes an extra effort to ensure that the orderlies assigned to the work detail that she supervises take pride in their work as well. This is not an easy task.

Few inmates have much motivation to work at all, or to work in more than a perfunctory manner. Pay scales in the federal prison system are low; with average monthly earnings among inmates hovering at less than twenty dollars per month, there is no incentive system for inmates to work hard. Counselor Hood is limited to paying the orderlies who work for her twelve cents per hour, so a full-time orderly earns approximately twenty dollars for a full month of work. Without constant supervision, it is difficult for a counselor to distinguish between those who loaf on a job and those who work diligently.

Nevertheless, some counselors attempt to micromanage their orderly details. They fail to recognize that although staff members generally work eight-hour shifts, a prisoner's shift does not end until the expiration of his sentence. Whereas the counselor may be working toward the advancement of his or her career, most prisoners interest themselves only in passing their time as easily as possible. For many, that means not working. Counselors perceived as abusing inmates who work for them do not receive much cooperation from their unit orderlies, and as a consequence, their units frequently come in at the bottom of the Safety Department's scoring range. Although this means the inmates assigned to that housing unit may come in last in the meal rotation, it also reflects poorly on the counselor's ability to manage his or her work detail.

Counselor Hood maintains a work detail of over seventy orderlies who are assigned to keep her unit clean. Recognizing the virtual impossibility of providing direct supervision to all of these orderlies, while at the same time keeping current with her other administrative responsibilities, she relies on a head orderly. Since 1997, inmate Domingo Morales has served in this capacity.

THE ROAD TO PRISON

Domingo Morales is a native of Spain and speaks only broken English. In 1996 he began serving an eight-year sentence for a conviction related to the distribution of cocaine. He describes himself as having been a hard worker all his life but was caught up in the criminal justice system when federal agents found cocaine in a trailer he was hauling as a long-distance truck driver. He later pled guilty to charges that he was working as a courier. After sentencing, Domingo was transferred to Fort Dix, where he accepted a unit orderly position for his required work detail.

Like most federal prisons, Fort Dix has a large Hispanic population. Most of the Spanish-speaking inmates come from the Caribbean islands or South American countries; fewer than a handful come from Spain.

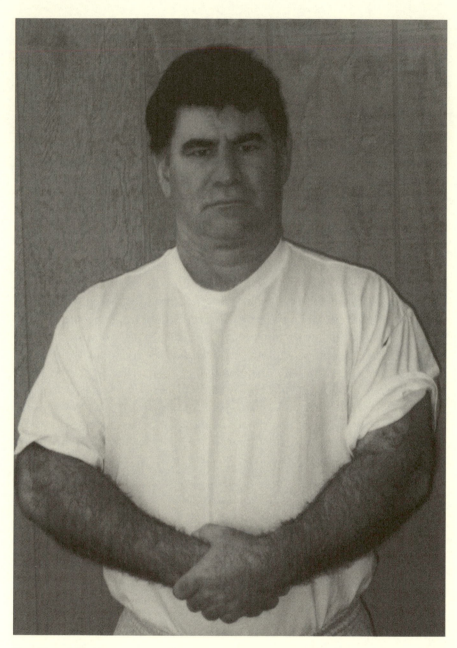

Domingo Morales

Many of the prisoners assigned to unit 5702 have national origins in the Dominican Republic, and one of those inmates, Oro-Negro, held the position of head orderly. Counselor Bridges was in charge of the orderly detail at that time, and when Domingo arrived, unit 5702 held the reputation of being the filthiest unit on the compound.

AN ORDERLY LIFE

Being an orderly offers certain privileges. For one thing, inmates who work as unit orderlies are assigned to the unit all day. Once they finish their work assignments, few of which take more than ninety minutes to complete, the orderlies are allowed to spend their time freely. They may watch television, use the recreational facilities, play table games, or sleep. Besides that, some orderly positions do not require work until after midnight, which allows those who hold such positions to watch late-night television.

The hours and responsibilities of unit orderlies contrast with those of other, more demanding work details. For example, inmates who are assigned to the building maintenance departments are required to report for work before 7:00 A.M. each morning. They are issued tools and may be required to perform duties such as mixing cement, digging ditches, mowing lawns, or repairing plumbing systems. Some work-detail supervisors do not allow their inmates to bring books or radios to their job details, so they frequently are left waiting around with nothing more exciting to occupy their time than watching paint peel. Sleeping on the job, however, may result in disciplinary action. Time spent in an uncomfortable job adds significant frustration to an inmate's time in prison.

The reason unit 5702 was so dirty, Morales explained, was that Oro-Negro was selling orderly positions to people who wanted the privileges of being an orderly but did not necessarily want to work. Instead of issuing cleaning supplies that were rationed out to the unit on a monthly basis, Oro-Negro sold the supplies to inmates who wanted extra wax for their floors, or cleaning solvents for their personal use. For perhaps a one-time hundred dollar fee, followed by another twenty dollars per month, Oro-Negro also arranged for well-heeled inmates to be assigned to do-nothing jobs in the unit. As a consequence, the unit deteriorated.

As his first job, Morales was assigned to clean one of the large bathrooms. The room had seven toilets and sinks, three urinal stalls, and one large shower room. With over 350 inmates sharing the few inmate bathrooms, those who were assigned to their daily cleaning suffered through perhaps the worst of the unit orderly jobs. When Morales was given the assignment, he said he took pride in doing the best job that he could.

Domingo explained that other bathroom orderlies made it their mission to complete the job as quickly as possible. They poured some cleaning solvent in a bucket, splashed the bucket on the walls and floors, then sprayed water over the area with a garden hose. The rooms were constantly filthy, worse than the uncleaned public bathroom of a downtown park. They had scum buildup on the toilets and sinks; it was spread across the shower walls and floor as thick as the mud and muck that covers the underbelly of a truck that had traveled for seasons over a dirt road in the rain. Wearing shoes in the shower was mandatory, and even then, one had to be cautious of what might splash up from the floor.

Since Domingo recognized himself as having to use the same shower that he cleaned, he explained that it was necessary to sanitize it completely. Instead of going to Oro-Negro for supplies, he went to Counselor Bridges and asked for rubber shoes and rubber gloves, scrub brushes, and extra cleaning supplies. After six hours of work, Domingo explained, he had all of the stains scrubbed off the porcelain, and years of scum buildup removed from the walls. He then applied several coats of wax to the tile floor, giving the erstwhile center of filth a look, smell, and feel of startling cleanliness.

Each regular housing unit has a total of nine bathrooms (including thirteen shower stalls) that the 350 inhabitants must share. Once word spread about the cleanliness of Domingo's bathroom, few people in the unit were showering elsewhere, and the staff began to take notice.

The representative from Safety was so impressed with Domingo's bathroom that instead of deducting points, he awarded the unit three bonus points on his weekly inspection. The associate warden toured the unit and commended Domingo for maintaining the cleanest prisoner bathroom at Fort Dix. After that visit, Counselor Bridges paged Domingo and asked him whether he would assume the duties of head orderly.

RESOLVING A DIRTY DILEMMA

Domingo explained the problem. Although he was confident he could clean the building thoroughly, there was the practical problem of offending Oro-Negro, the current head orderly. It would be a breach of prison etiquette to cut Oro-Negro out of his job, as the head orderly job was the source of his lucrative hustle. Domingo explained that while there were several hundred Dominican prisoners on the Fort Dix compound, there were fewer than ten Spaniards like himself. His taking the job, he explained, could expose him to problems with other prisoners who were supportive of Oro-Negro.

Bridges asked Domingo what he would need to accept the position, as he wanted to lift the unit's sanitation scores. He felt confident that Domingo had the skill to deliver. Domingo told me that he thought about the proposition Bridges had made and struck a bargain with him. He had been assigned to the top bunk in one of the unit's third-floor twelve-man rooms. If he were going to accept the position of head orderly, Domingo asked Bridges to assign him to one of the two-man rooms on the first floor. Further, he asked for carte blanche in hiring and firing the orderlies who worked in the unit. Counselor Bridges agreed to Domingo's proposition. Bridges told Oro-Negro that he had been reassigned to another detail.

Domingo's proposition was certain to expose him to scores of regular problems in the unit. In a higher-security prison, his actions probably would have led to an act of extreme violence on his person, like a knife being thrust into his back or his room being set on fire. Prisoners do not look kindly on inmates who enter into such chummy agreements with staff, especially to the detriment of other prisoners. Domingo was treading dangerously close to the label "prison rat" or snitch.

Since Fort Dix is a low-security prison, the probability is high that at least half of the people confined within its fences have cooperated with the government in some form or other. That may explain why such minor repercussions followed Domingo's assumption of the head orderly position; with so many informants in the compound, an orchestrated attack on Domingo could not have been kept secret. In addition, Domingo has the physical presence of a fire hydrant. He stands about five-feet-eight and weighs a solid 210 pounds. With a chest like a keg of beer, and forearms that look like Popeye's, Domingo walks around the unit with the grace of a pit bull. His gruff manner of speaking is one that might be appropriate on an oil rig or in the trenches with an earth-moving crew. His was the language of other prisoners, and that, too, may have contributed to the relative ease with which he took over the head orderly position in unit 5702.

But his situation was not trouble free. Domingo says that he began his work by giving the unit a thorough cleaning. He began his cleaning duties at 6:00 A.M. each morning and worked straight through, as if he were a private contractor, until 6:00 P.M. I would estimate the housing unit's square footage at between thirty and forty thousand. Picture a medium-sized, three-story office building.

Domingo applied the same gusto to cleaning each room as he had to his originally assigned bathroom. He collected other hard-working orderlies to work with him as he stripped the old wax off the floors before applying heavy layers of new wax. He removed the covers of light fixtures to clean out the dead bugs; he made sure that even the grounds around the building were free of cigarette butts and orange peels. Within a month, the unit was in tip-top shape and placing first in the weekly cleanliness competition. Although other prisoners assigned to unit 5702 were happy with the removed cobwebs, shinier floors, clean bathrooms, and first access to the chow hall, Oro-Negro and the other orderlies who had lost their coveted jobs as a consequence of Domingo's diligence were fuming. Someone wanted revenge.

DROPPING A NOTE

Instead of confronting Domingo directly, on a Friday afternoon after he had orchestrated the turnaround of unit 5702, someone sent an anonymous note to the lieutenant's office indicating he was going to kill Domingo. Without explanation, Domingo was rounded up, his belongings were packed, and he was sent to segregation until the lieutenants could complete an investigation. Domingo spent the weekend in the hole, not knowing what was going on.

On Monday, when Counselor Bridges came in, he went over to see Domingo and explain. When Domingo learned that he had been confined as a result of a threat, he agreed to sign a paper indicating that he was not in need of protection and would not hold the institution responsible in the event that someone took violent action against him. Domingo said he was confident he could take care of himself. When asked whether he had any ideas on who would write such a threatening note, Domingo said his response was that only a coward would do such a thing.

Domingo returned to the unit and resumed his methodical cleanup program. Over the next several months he was able to rebuild the roster of inmate orderlies completely, replacing malingerers with those who wanted to work. Whereas others had a hard time finding good help, Domingo says he found no shortage of workers who eagerly accepted the responsibilities that came with an orderly position.

Domingo's method of getting rid of an orderly who was not performing, he explains, was rather simple. As head orderly, Domingo assigned the men their duties and shifts. He expected each man to clean his assigned area thoroughly at the beginning of each shift and then monitor it once an hour until the shift was over. Several times each day, he walked around the unit with his clipboard inspecting the orderlies' performance. If an area was clean, he made a note of it. If an area was dirty, he made the orderly who was responsible aware of it. Orderlies who did not respond to Domingo's admonitions soon found themselves out of a job. He tested them regularly, he explains.

PERFORMANCE CHECKS

One way Domingo checked on an orderly's performance, he says, was by dropping a napkin or an orange peel in a given area. If he came back an hour or two later and the planted refuse was still there, he would have all the confirmation he needed that the orderly was not doing his job. Domingo said he would then call the unit officer and ask him to check out the particular area. When the unit officer came back and reported to Domingo that the area was dirty, Domingo says he asked the officer to accompany him to see Counselor Bridges and report on his findings. When Bridges asked Domingo what he wanted to have done, Domingo said, "Fire him."

Most prisoners would consider Domingo's actions treasonous to the prison community. He does not see it that way, does not consider his actions inappropriate at all. He believes that he has been given a job, and he strives to perform it to the best of his ability in the same way he would if he were working in the community. It is a responsibility he welcomes; keeping busy in this way helps his time pass quickly and gives him a feeling of accomplishment. Domingo actually takes pride in his work, even though he may be identified derisively as almost an inmate-staff hybrid, or a rat.

The orderlies who worked under Domingo's leadership also were limited to wages of twelve cents per hour. That did not stop him from recruiting hard workers. He scouted employees who were assigned to food services, building maintenance positions, or other less desirable prison jobs. If they were unhappy with their job assignments, and they lived in unit 5702, Domingo could, through Counselor Bridges, arrange a job change for them. Domingo cautioned them before beginning, however, that he expected them to perform their assigned duties. The pay was not so good, he explained, but the benefits of being assigned to the unit all day were substantial.

Many of the inmates who agreed to work for Domingo were grateful for the jobs. After they completed their assigned duties, many were able to perform domestic services for other prisoners living in the unit. They might wash clothes for three dollars per load; they might iron clothing for a negotiated monthly fee; they might clean rooms or even cook for others. With the free time that comes with an orderly position, a true prison hustler may generate an extra two to four hundred dollars per month in income. And Domingo was not averse to taking a cut for helping prisoners arrange and secure these lucrative contracts.

As a result of Domingo's passionate acceptance of responsibility as head orderly, staff members began depending on him to help them with their duties. He explains how inmates once had disassembled a fire alarm on the third floor of the housing unit. At the time, arson was a big problem in the prison, as inmates were known to set inmate beds aflame or initiate garbage-can bonfires in an effort to victimize or vandalize. When the unit officer explained that the third-floor fire alarm had been disassembled, Domingo volunteered to stand sentry on the third floor to make sure nothing happened. Since no staff member was available, Domingo agreed to remain on the third floor until someone arrived to repair the alarm. Because his newly accepted duties as a quasi-staff member would have resulted in his missing dinner, the guard agreed to have it delivered.

An unwritten rule exists that prisoners must never work against each other to assist staff. If someone is stabbed or being beaten, regardless of how close a witness is to the incident, the inside rule holds that no one should have seen anything. Even if an individual is the direct victim of a stab wound, the convict code holds that he should have no idea how, why, or who inflicted the wound. If someone wants to set the building ablaze, no other convict is supposed to interfere. Domingo's agreeing to watch over the third floor is an example, many would say, of an inmate who has grown far too close to staff. Yet he saw it as a responsibility; he certainly saw no shame in doing so. Although he says he would not have turned anyone else in, his presence alone lessened the likelihood of any misconduct.

I'M NO SNITCH

Other staff members took notice of Domingo's willingness to help out. When Langer, a new case manager, was assigned to unit 5702, he attempted to recruit Domingo into working as an informant for him.

"Morales," Langer said, "I understand you're the head orderly in this unit. I want you to bring me any type of information you have about what's going on in the unit. I don't care whether someone is using a stinger to heat water, using drugs, or selling tomatoes from the kitchen. I want to know about it."

Domingo says he was offended at the suggestion. "I'm no snitch," he told Langer. "If I wanted to tell on other people I would have been home with my family."

Domingo explains that he accepted full responsibility to work as a head orderly. He agreed to make sure the unit was put in tip-top shape and to manage its maintenance to the best of his ability. That is why, he says, that he was willing to stand sentry in the event of a fire, and to ensure that all orderlies performed their duties. But there is a line he would not cross, he explains, and turning in other people for activities that had nothing to do with the unit was one of them. Langer was not pleased with Domingo's categorical refusal to act as his rat. Repercussions would follow.

In order to facilitate the cross-training of staff, unit managers rotate counselors every couple of years, and after a while, Counselor Bridges was rotated to a different post. Counselor Hernandez took over the orderly responsibilities of unit 5702. Instead of using Domingo as her head orderly, she chose to revise the arrangement and assume the duties herself. Domingo no longer had control of hiring and dismissing orderlies, or ordering and allocating the cleaning supplies.

Counselor Hernandez was a by-the-book counselor, meaning she refused to rely on an inmate to perform duties to which she believed staff members should attend. During the time Counselor Hernandez was in charge of the unit orderlies, Domingo says he slacked off. He explained that if she was going to assume control of which orderlies were assigned to which jobs, he could not assume control of their performance. As a result, the unit's sanitation scores began to fall back into decline. After six months, much of the work that Domingo had done during his years under previous counselors was damaged or destroyed, as the orderly roster had changed completely.

For whatever reason, seven months after she started, Counselor Hernandez was replaced by Counselor Hood. Hood quickly reinstalled Domingo in the head orderly position. As a result of Counselor Hood's leadership, unit 5702 returned to being the cleanest unit inside Fort Dix's fences.

Domingo explained that as long as a counselor allows him to work closely with him or her, he is able to make certain the work is complete. It is essential, he says, that as head orderly he has input into who is assigned to which work details. The counselor has too many responsibilities. With well over 100 inmates assigned to each counselor's case load, his or her time is thinly stretched with, among other things, time-consuming tasks such as updating visiting and approved telephone lists, handling disciplinary matters, bed changes, and arranging outgoing package mail. There is no way a counselor can check on who is doing which job effectively. Since the head orderly remains in the unit even when the counselor's shift ends, he can assume responsibility to ensure that all work is done appropriately. But why would a prisoner accept such a job?

It is an open secret that Domingo receives extra privileges for his work. While every other orderly in the unit receives approximately twenty dollars in monthly pay, as head orderly, Domingo receives the maximum pay of eighty-two dollars. Further, he has enjoyed the privilege of living on the first floor in a two-man room. Only one time has that privilege been taken away from him, and it was only for a brief period.

OLD ISSUES ROCK THE BOAT

McKinnon was the assigned unit manager when trouble arrived, but he either had been given a special assignment or vacation for an extended period. While he was away, he appointed Case Manager Langer as the acting unit manager. Soon after McKinnon left, Langer marched into Domingo's privileged quarters and ordered him to pack his belongings, as he was being moved to the second floor of the unit. Technically, the first floor of the housing unit is supposed to be reserved as the unit's medical ward. Whereas over 150 men live on the second and third floors, the first floor holds no more than twenty inmates. It is cleaner, and it is quieter than anywhere else in the building. Domingo was not ill, so his being assigned to one of the coveted first floor two-man rooms was indeed a privilege.

Perhaps because Domingo had refused to work as Langer's personal informant, Langer decided that Domingo did not deserve the privilege of first floor quarters—the extra duties he had performed over the years notwithstanding. With Langer acting as unit manager, Domingo says he knew that he had no room to argue. He simply moved into his newly assigned room. Although there is no way for Domingo to ever know exactly why Langer moved him, it is the type of action petty bureaucrats frequently take to demonstrate their power over inmates.

Not knowing how long Langer would be his supervisor, Domingo says he looked for another job. By then, he already had worked several years as the head orderly and had cultivated a reputation as being a trustworthy, responsible inmate who could be depended upon to perform his assigned duties with minimal supervision.

When he approached the manager of the prison factory, the manager eagerly agreed to hire Domingo as the factory's head orderly. Jobs in the factory were desirable because the pay was better than anywhere else in the institution; there was a waiting list of more than a hundred inmates who wanted employment. Domingo says that the factory manager used his authority to place him at the top of the list, rendering him available for the next open position.

Unit Manager McKinnon returned to the institution before that job opened. When he received a call from the factory manager gloating that he had hired away McKinnon's top orderly, Domingo says that he was paged immediately to McKinnon's office and asked why he was quitting. Domingo explained that he had lost his first floor room and was wary of working for Langer. Domingo explained that McKinnon then berated Langer for his actions. He reassigned Domingo back to the first floor and ordered Langer not to interfere with Domingo again.

In addition to receiving a two-man room on the first floor of the building, Counselor Hood arranged for Domingo to receive a special privilege as a result of his contributions to the unit. Whereas the other three hundred plus inmates assigned to unit 5702 must share one of the three microwaves that are provided for inmate use, a fourth microwave has been assigned to Domingo for his own personal use in his cell. Others may wait in lines for up to an hour to heat up water or cook food they purchase in the commissary. To my knowledge, Domingo is the only inmate at Fort Dix who has received such a privilege. It is indicative of the unique status he holds inside unit 5702.

Others may derisively refer to Domingo as "El Capitan" or "The General." He says that he is not interested in what other prisoners say about him, or what they think about how he serves his time. He is nearing the end of his eight-year sentence, and his busy schedule has given him a feeling of responsibility. He never has been depressed. Instead of whining about his time, he says, he describes himself as putting forth his best effort to make the time work for him. In doing so, he has indeed found some extra privileges as a prisoner in Fort Dix.

Iqbal Karimi, the next bantam-time prisoner, describes how his privileges and reputation were stripped away one day by tragic events that took place miles away.

LIVING WITH THE UNKNOWN: IQBAL KARIMI

A former Freedom Fighter from Afghanistan describes his adjustment to prison.

No staff member at Fort Dix had ever experienced a disciplinary problem with Iqbal Karimi. By all accounts, during the seven years of his imprisonment, Iqbal had served his time as a model prisoner. He voluntarily attended educational programs, participated in programs sponsored by psychology, held a full-time job as a clerical worker for the chaplain, and spent hours each day working independently to develop his skill as an artist. None of that mattered on the morning of September 11, 2001, when a lieutenant escorted him from the compound to segregation.

Iqbal has led a difficult life when measured against the standard of most Americans. Born and raised in Kandahar, Afghanistan, Iqbal attended school until the fifth grade, after which he was forced to drop out so he could help his uncles. They were Freedom Fighters (so termed by the American media) engaged in a vicious war with the Soviet-supported government of Afghanistan.

Because his uncles were leaders in the Freedom Fighter movement, they were forced to live in hiding. They constantly plotted tactical maneuvers against the Soviet war machine in an effort to oust the invaders. Iqbal, an innocent twelve-year-old, dropped out of school so he could join other youngsters to work as couriers for his uncles and their comrades. The children delivered messages to supporters or took money into town to

Iqbal Karimi

purchase clothing, food, and staples that would sustain the hundreds of warriors living in hiding under his uncle's command.

In the early 1980s, Iqbal explained, the American and British governments supported the Freedom Fighters financially and with weapons so they could combat the Communists from the north. Living as a Freedom Fighter, a necessarily covert group, meant dwelling in caves and abandoned mud houses. With a constant sense of imminent death, there was no thought of preparing for a career, building a family, or anything besides fighting for a way of life. An hour never passed, Iqbal explained, without the sound of bombs exploding or the staccato rat-tat-tat of nearby machine-gun fire.

COMING OF AGE IN WAR

When Iqbal was fifteen, while he was in the Freedom Fighter camp with compatriots listening to the government radio station, he heard that his uncles were killed with several others in a Soviet helicopter attack. That day marked the end of Iqbal's work as a courier, and the beginning of his work as an actual Freedom Fighter.

As a Freedom Fighter, Iqbal explained, he began living like the others. They were marked men, never knowing whether they would live to eat another meal. Like nomads, he and his fellow soldiers had no home or possessions. They did not know where they would sleep from one night to the next. "We knew that we could be killed at any minute," he related. "But my only concern was overthrowing the Communists who were taking over my country."

As a young Freedom Fighter, Iqbal explained that he would work in three- to four-man teams. They would dwell in ditches alongside well-traveled roads. When they saw Soviet military vehicles approaching, Iqbal and his team would hold their shoulder-mounted rocket launchers, point them at a vehicle, and fire. After a vehicle exploded, the group would cautiously approach the ruins to ensure all occupants were killed. Then they would run into hiding. Today, he is unable to recall the number of deaths he caused during his service as a Freedom Fighter. He remembers only blood.

Acquiring the weapons themselves was a dangerous mission. Iqbal explained how he and six to eight other Freedom Fighters had to drive four hundred miles to Pakistan in a standard American pickup truck. They could not travel on regular roads, but rather had to drive over rough terrain. In order to lessen the chance of detection, they drove only in the black of night, without lights of any kind. The men riding in the back of the pickup were armed with machine-guns to defend themselves in the event of attack. Besides the danger of encountering the enemy, Iqbal explained that they were in constant danger of being blown up by driving over a land mine. Despite the pervasive danger, Iqbal made the twelve-day journey to Pakistan on three separate occasions to retrieve American-supplied weapons.

By the late 1980s, the Soviet economy had begun to collapse, and one of the new government's first adjustments was to withdraw from Afghanistan. Without the Communist threat, Iqbal explained, the American and British governments also withdrew their support for the Freedom Fighter movement. The result was anarchy. Men who formerly fought as Freedom Fighters began acting chaotically. Millions of dollars worth of weapons were left over from the long-time war; renegades were stealing the equipment and selling it to raise money for themselves. Afghanistan, Iqbal explained, was no safer for him than it had been during the war. At nineteen, he moved to neighboring Pakistan.

In Pakistan, Iqbal met with family and other former members of the movement. They convinced him that he ought to leave the war-torn region and pursue a new life, either in America or Germany. Iqbal was fluent in the languages of Pashto, Persian, and Urdu, but he spoke neither German nor English. He had fond childhood memories of an American family who lived in his native city of Kandahar, however, and based on those memories, he elected to make his life in America. Those in his support group then raised the four thousand dollars an airline worker wanted in exchange for putting him aboard an airliner without a passport or other documentation. He was headed for New York. When he boarded the plane, Iqbal said he had less than thirty dollars to his name, and no identifying paperwork whatsoever.

He arrived in New York, and as a result of some dumb luck and deficient airport security, he was able to maneuver his way through the maze of gates without once being checked for his nonexistent entry papers. He found himself on the sidewalk standing in front of the ubiquitous Yellow Cabs. He opened the door to one, found a driver who was fluent in his native language of Urdu, and eventually was able to negotiate a ride to a distant cousin's home in Brooklyn.

DESTINY IN THE DRUG DEAL

During the five years that Iqbal lived in the United States prior to his arrest, he held a series of odd jobs and spent time learning English. In August of 1994, when he was twenty-four, Iqbal was arrested. A package containing heroin was sent to an address where he was living. The package was sent from Afghanistan and had been intercepted by the DEA. The agents initiated a controlled delivery, meaning they would maintain surveillance as the package made its way to its final destination. When Iqbal signed for the package, he was arrested and charged with violating federal narcotics laws. He pled guilty to the offense and was sentenced to ten years in prison. Soon after his sentencing, he was transported to Fort Dix.

When Iqbal began serving his sentence he hoped not only to improve his English but also to educate himself. As a child, he had been forced to abandon his formal education in the sixth grade because his family and country needed him to fight in the war. Assuming he did not lose any time off for good behavior, Iqbal realized he would serve just over eight and one-half years. That would be enough, he reasoned, to learn some new skills and perhaps even obtain some educational credentials.

THE STRUGGLE FOR EDUCATION

Soon after settling in, he went to the education building where he met with Jan Tenor, one of the Bureau of Prisons staff teachers. Iqbal explained that he had only a fifth-grade education and wanted to learn. He asked for permission to participate in one of her Adult Basic Education classes. These classes are remedial courses that teach basic skills such as reading, writing, and arithmetic. Students who pass a test indicating they can function at the eighth-grade level may move on to pre–general education development (GED) classes, and eventually into GED classes that prepare them to take the high school equivalency test. Although teachers administer the courses, many inmate tutors work closely with the teachers to help students struggling to master the required information and concepts.

Recognizing that inmates without the high school equivalency certificate have a more difficult time finding employment upon release, the Bureau of Prisons has made it mandatory for all U.S. citizens in prisons who lack a high school diploma to attend the GED program. Because Iqbal was not an American citizen, John Bellantoni, the supervisor of education, would not allow him to participate. Although space was available in the classes, Bellantoni said he was reserving it for American inmates who were compelled to attend. Because Bellantoni was her supervisor, Tenor said she could not allow Iqbal to enroll without his permission. Recognizing him as a student who wanted to learn, however, she provided Iqbal with a study book that would help him prepare for the GED exam.

Over the fifteen years that I have served in prison, I have encountered many administrators like Bellantoni. They exclude all human considerations from many of their decisions. Instead of using common sense, for example, allowing Iqbal to sit in one of the vacant chairs and participate in an ongoing class, Bellantoni refused to make this judgment call, to respond affirmatively to pleas both of Iqbal and Tenor for an exception to the guidelines. In the bureaucratic method of management, the printed policy most frequently prevails; the objective trumps the subjective. On the other hand, on the few occasions when I have succeeded in developing personal relationships with staff members, small windows of opportunity open, like the one Tenor opened for Iqbal.

In 1997, Bellantoni transferred from Fort Dix to the only super-maximum-security prison, at Florence, Colorado. It is a prison that holds the federal system's most notorious prisoners, like the Unabomber, and Timothy McVeigh before he was executed. When Bellantoni transferred out, Tenor was able to allow Iqbal into her classes. Two years after enrolling, in 1999, Iqbal passed his GED exam and was awarded his high school equivalency certificate. Since then he has completed courses taught by instructors from a local community college, and he hopes to earn an associate's degree prior to his release in 2003. In addition to studying, Iqbal also has a full-time job working as a chaplain's clerk, facilitating activities for the various religious programs. His passion, however, has been developing his skills as a painter.

FINDING A PASSION

Soon after Iqbal arrived at Fort Dix, he walked through the area dedicated to hobby-craft programs. Some of the available programs include leather craft, bead work, toothpick art (participants construct models out of toothpicks and glue), drawing, and working with acrylic, oil, and water paints. Iqbal toured the art studio, where hundreds of paintings in various stages of completion were hanging on the walls, and perhaps thirty inmates were working in front of easels supporting canvases with paintings in progress. To Iqbal, the paintings looked like the art he would expect to see in a museum. Wanting to deal positively with the years of incarceration he had ahead of him, Iqbal became interested in learning how to paint.

Iqbal spoke with Ricardo, a former drug smuggler from Peru who had been incarcerated for fifteen years. In all those years, Ricardo focused on learning to paint, and he was one of the most accomplished artists among the four thousand prisoners confined at Fort Dix. Besides painting, on Saturdays and Sundays, Ricardo led a twelve-week class to help novices learn the fundamentals of painting. Iqbal enrolled enthusiastically.

Like most activities in prison, the art program had a long waiting list. After an approximately three-month wait, Iqbal was allowed to participate in Ricardo's art class. The institution provided the participants with the paints, brushes, and canvases they would need to complete the educational program; thus, Iqbal's first three months of art work did not cost him anything. He took to the program, realizing that although he had never drawn anything more complicated than a stick man before, he had a natural talent as a painter.

After completing Ricardo's class, Iqbal asked some friends to help him financially so he could purchase his own brushes, paints, and canvases in order to begin painting on his own. He needed three hundred dollars for supplies to start, and as soon as he had received the money he needed, Iqbal purchased his materials through the prison's recreation department. He then began the independent painting program, which is distinguished from the art classes in which Iqbal had been studying.

Inmates then were not restricted in the extent of free time that they could spend in hobby-shop or recreational programs. Except for the relatively brief census counts that took them back to their assigned rooms or work details, inmates were free to leave their housing units between 6:00 A.M. and 9:30 P.M. During those hours, as long as a prisoner was not scheduled to be working on a job detail, he could choose a way to pass the time.

A few years later, a new supervisor began to restrict hobby-shop participation to two hours per day. Such is a perfect example of how the Bureau of Prisons bureaucracy functions. Prisoners develop routines, then new employees take over a department and introduce new rules that disrupt those routines. In many instances, no reasons are provided, nor are appeals from disgruntled prisoners considered. The hobby-shop participants were dismayed over the change, but the only explanation provided was that the new supervisor of recreation had determined that two hours was enough time for hobby-craft activities in any given day. End of story. There may have been some technical, advanced correctional-science explanation for the change, but not having an official need to know, administrators provided no explanation to inmates.

In the beginning of his new-found infatuation with art, when participants were allowed to paint during their free time, Iqbal passed between six and ten hours each day in the painting room developing his skills as a painter. Over that first year, he estimates that he could complete up to ten paintings a month, frequently working on several paintings simultaneously. He painted landscapes, seascapes, wildlife scenes. Iqbal's specialty, however, was painting portraits. Other inmates were free to tour the painter's area and admire the work of the talented artists.

CONFIDENCE AND COMMISSIONS

After about a year, one of the inmates was taken with Iqbal's work and asked Iqbal how much he would charge to paint a portrait of his mother. By that time, Iqbal says he felt confident in his work. He had invested between five and six hundred dollars and about a year in developing his craft. He did not feel that it was unreasonable to ask for two hundred dollars to complete the portrait. The negotiated price was one hundred fifty dollars, which the inmate would pay in prison commissary. It was Iqbal's first commission.

The prison system does not make it easy for inmates to make transactions among each other. In fact, one of the disciplinary infractions available to guards specifically prohibits one inmate from giving anything of value to another inmate; another prohibits inmates from conducting businesses inside the fences. I expect the reason for these rules is that business transactions between prisoners possibly could lead to violence and administrative problems. For example, if one prisoner makes a financial agreement with another, and one of the parties does not perform, it is unlikely that the dispute would be resolved before a judge, as would be expected outside the fences. Rather, it is more likely that the aggrieved party would take the matter into his own hands and resolve it with force or the threat of force. In order to discourage this possibility, staff members try to enforce rules against business transactions inside the fences.

Despite such rules, it is common for inmates to come to private agreements. In Iqbal's first transaction, he accepted fifty dollars worth of commissary to begin the painting. Since hobby-craft program participants are authorized to send their work only to people on their approved visitor's list, when he completed the painting, Iqbal sent it home to his cousin. His cousin then forwarded the painting to the address given by the purchaser. When the painting arrived at its final destination, the purchaser paid the balance owed on the work.

That transaction launched Iqbal into a career as an artist in the Fort Dix compound. He began accepting commissions regularly from prisoners who wanted to purchase his art work. As word spread that he was available to complete portraits for others, he was able to establish a firm price of two hundred dollars per person in the portrait. Since 1998, when Iqbal began accepting commissions for his work, he says that he has averaged three hundred dollars per month in commissary earnings. In addition, his cousin, who receives his paintings outside, has sold several, enabling Iqbal to earn approximately ten thousand dollars over the years.

The money has been particularly helpful to Iqbal. He has been saving it with hopes that it will help him begin a new life upon his release from prison. At the conclusion of long terms of confinement, most prisoners are financially destitute. Few have enough money even to purchase clothing, and far fewer have the means to rent an apartment. Through the money he was able to earn and save from his hobby, Iqbal foresaw the possibility of leaving prison with enough money to help make his adjustment easier.

Besides that, the money he had earned had an immediate use. His family relocated from Afghanistan to Pakistan, and on two separate occasions he was able to send them substantial amounts of money to help their adjustment. Once he sent four thousand dollars and another time he sent two thousand dollars. In a country where residents have annual average earnings of less than four thousand dollars, the gifts he was able to send as a result of his artistic talent made a significant difference in their lives. He hopes to do more, as Iqbal currently is painting a family portrait from a photograph of one inmate, his wife, and two children. With four people in the picture, the purchaser has agreed to send eight hundred dollars to Iqbal's cousin once the painting is complete and delivered. Although doing so is a violation of prison rules, that money will go a long way in helping Iqbal's family, he says. To him, that is more important than observing a seemingly silly rule that prohibits him from preparing for his future.

THE RELATIVITY OF RECOGNITION

It is not only inmates who have appreciated Iqbal's work. The institution's warden, Nancy Bailey, was touring the art studio one evening in early 2001, and she took particular notice of several of Iqbal's paintings. She then had the supervisor of the art program page Iqbal, as she had a proposition for him. When he responded to the page he heard over the loudspeaker, Iqbal was surprised to learn that it was the warden who had summoned him. Wardens act in the capacity of chief executive officer of their prisons and, therefore, rarely deal with inmates directly. Of course, they may make themselves available to listen to inmate grievances (perhaps in the dining room). But after listening to prisoners vent, they generally assign the problem or request to an underling who may or may not respond directly to the inmate. Iqbal wondered with a bit of anxiety why the warden would want to speak with him.

When Iqbal walked into Warden Bailey's office, she told him to relax. She explained that he had been paged because she appreciated his paintings. She asked him whether he would be willing to donate some of his talent by painting some landscapes, seascapes, and wildlife paintings that could be displayed around the institution; there was no discussion of a fee.

In the nearly seven years that Iqbal had then been confined, he never had received a single compliment from the system or one of its representatives on his adjustment to prison. When the warden singled him out to tell him that she found his work beautiful, he says her compliment was worth more than all the money he had earned as an artist. She had provided him with validation, made him feel like he was something more than a prisoner. In recognition of the warden's praise, Iqbal says that he immediately agreed to paint for her. She then instructed the art director to purchase whatever materials Iqbal would need, and over the course of the next few months, Iqbal painted a total of ten pictures for the warden. The warden arranged for the framing of the pictures, and they now hang in the room where inmates meet their visitors.

On the morning of September 11, 2001, Iqbal was in a television room with hundreds of other inmates who resided in his housing unit watching the coverage of the terrorist attacks on the United States. At approximately eleven that morning, a guard notified him that he was to report to the lieutenant's office. There is rarely any good reason to be summoned to the lieutenant's office; rather, it is like seeing a policeman's flashing lights in the rearview mirror. Iqbal had no idea what was wrong. When he walked into the office and identified himself, the lieutenant on duty gave him an order.

"Cuff up. You're going to the hole."

"What for?" Iqbal said. His heart dropped to his feet, and he felt his legs shaking. He had to pee.

"I'll tell you that when I'm ready," the lieutenant answered.

After Iqbal was fastened in leg irons and handcuffs, he was escorted to a van and driven to the segregation building; it is the prison's equivalent of the county jail. Being processed in was a new experience for him. Iqbal described how he was instructed to sit on some type of X-ray chair. With his hands cuffed behind his back, he was instructed to bend over forward, apparently so the chair could x-ray his rectum from the seat to ensure that he was not smuggling anything into the segregation unit. Once that picture was taken, Iqbal said he was ordered to stand up and place his chin on another camera so a picture could be shot of the inside of his mouth; then, X-ray shots were taken with him placing both sides of his face against a camera to examine the ears. Only by looking into each of the body's orifices could guards be sure that prisoners were contraband free when being processed into segregation.

After the photographs, guards ordered Iqbal to strip naked for a visual inspection. They then issued him an orange jumpsuit to wear in place of the khaki uniform inmates wear in the general population. As he was being led to a single cell, a guard gave him a piece of paper indicating that he was being placed in administrative detention pending an investigation. Since he could not think of having done anything wrong, Iqbal says, it began to dawn on him that he was being placed in confinement as a consequence of the terrorist attacks on America. That frightened him.

For the next twenty-one days, no staff member would provide Iqbal with any information other than that he was being held administratively pending an investigation. He was not allowed to receive or send mail. When he asked why, the staff member told him he was on mail restriction. He asked to make a phone call but was told that he was on telephone restriction. He wanted to receive a visit, but his visiting privileges had been suspended, too. He was not even allowed access to his property, as the lieutenant had placed him on property restriction.

Being put in such a situation left Iqbal with his imagination running wild. He still had not been given confirmation that his detention had anything to do with the terrorist attacks, but that is what his gut told him. He said he heard guards talking outside his cell.

"We've got one a them Afghan terrorists," he would hear one of the guards tell others working in the segregated housing unit.

"Where is he?" Another voice would inquire.

"Up there. The cell by the bathroom."

Footsteps would approach his cell, and soon two eyeballs would peer into the small cut-in window of the cell's steel door to have a look at him. Whenever he asked for information, guards who had known him for years spoke to him harshly, as if he were a terrorist himself. They told him he would have to wait to speak with a lieutenant.

On Saturdays a guard and an orderly would wheel a book cart around carrying about thirty novels. As an occupant of the hole, Iqbal was allowed to choose three books to hold him over until the following Saturday. There was not much reading material, but it did not matter, he said. His thoughts were too scattered to read.

Not knowing what to think, his thoughts went so far as to worry that because he was an Afghan, the government might attempt to pin terrorist actions on him. He was neither militant nor religious, but in the world in which he grew up, a world torn by war, the government in power would look to pin the blame on someone just to appease the people. The whole episode was bringing back memories of his childhood, where allegations and rumors could result in imprisonment or death. He was fearful that something of this sort could be happening to him. Not being able to turn to anyone for information, he was tormented by his anxious, cascading thoughts.

To a rational person, Iqbal's imaginings might seem to be those of a deranged person. When one is living in a concrete box, on the other hand, and being held incommunicado and without stated cause, there is no thought too fantastic. One is simply tormented by the possibilities of what can happen. Iqbal was helpless, and he worried that the only explanation for the silence was that he was being framed. Not sleeping well, Iqbal said he lived in a perpetual state of fear, sometimes unable to stop his body from shaking. He did pushups to calm himself.

After three weeks, Lieutenant Marts came to his door to speak with him. Lieutenant Marts's pleasant, avuncular manner puts people at ease. In this way he contrasts with the stereotypical lieutenant who snarls and intimidates, as if all prisoners are rodents, incapable of ever telling the truth. When Iqbal saw the lieutenant through the window of his cell, he says he jumped up to speak with him.

"Why am I being held here?"

"You've been under administrative investigation," the lieutenant calmly told him.

"But I haven't done anything wrong," Iqbal tried to clear himself.

"We know that," said Marts. "We've been in some extraordinary times, and we just had to do some checking. I need to ask you a few questions. Okay?"

Iqbal says the lieutenant then asked him whether he knew Osama bin Laden and whether he thought bin Laden was involved in the attacks. Iqbal said he did not know bin Laden, but from what he had read he thought that he certainly was capable of being involved in the attacks. But Iqbal added that after having been in prison for so many years, he really had no more information than anyone else. Marts told Iqbal that his investigation was over, and, as far as he was concerned, he should be returned to the prison's general population.

"So I'm being released?" Iqbal was optimistic.

"It's not up to me," the lieutenant said. "I'll make my recommendation to the warden. But it's up to her."

DEGREES OF FREEDOM

Iqbal said he felt certain that the warden would release him. After all, he had a personal relationship with Warden Bailey after the paintings he provided at her request and with her support. Clearly his record reflected that he was not a problem inmate. Unfortunately for him, however, after Lieutenant Marts left, another lieutenant told him that he was not going anywhere.

Since Lieutenant Marts had indicated that his investigation was over, Iqbal's restrictions on mail and access to property were lifted. He wrote to his cousin and informed him what was happening, that he was being held indefinitely in segregation. His cousin wrote him back and told him that he was going to contact a senator from his state to seek assistance on the matter. In the meantime, Iqbal was taken out of the cell to retrieve property to which he could have access while in segregation. Several guards were present to inspect the property Iqbal was retrieving. Once he had it all, one of the guards informed the others that Iqbal was "one of them Afghans."

"Is that true?" the second guard asked him.

"I was born in Afghanistan," Iqbal answered.

"If I would have known that I wouldn't have given you your property."

"Why not?" Iqbal asked.

"Don't you know we're at war with you people?" The guard informed him. In truth, Iqbal said he did not know anything, as he had been held without information.

"How tall is bin Laden?" another guard asked him.

"I have no idea," Iqbal answered.

"Oh, you know, you know."

The following week Iqbal saw the warden walking through the segregated housing unit. He asked for permission to speak with her. She approached the door of his cell and peered in through the window. "Warden," Iqbal said. "Lieutenant Marts said he was finished with his investigation, and he said I could be released to the general population. He said it was up to you to release me." He had hoped that her memory of the contribution he made to the institution would persuade her that he was not a threat.

"Yes." That was her entire response.

"Well, have you made a decision?" he asked. "Can I go back to the compound?"

"You're not going anywhere," the warden responded, and then she walked away.

For the next several weeks, Iqbal sat despondently in his cell. He did not know what was happening, but then some encouraging news came from his cousin. His contact with the senator resulted in a staff member from the senator's office writing a letter to the Bureau of Prisons inquiring about Iqbal's condition. Although he received no news from staff members at Fort Dix, he felt some relief in learning that although he was being ignored, he was not forgotten. After fifty-four days, Iqbal was released to the general population, without explanation. He assumes the senator's inquiry helped. The lieutenant simply told him to gather his belongings, that he was returning to the general population—to his room, to his job, and to his beloved painting. Returning to the compound, he said, felt like being freed.

There is a possibility that the warden made the decision to isolate Iqbal for his own safety. The media reported frequently about attacks on Muslims, Arab-Americans, Afghans, and others from those regions of the world living in the broader American society. Perhaps the warden was concerned that Iqbal, as an Afghan, needed protection against possible attacks or abuses from inmates or staff members. He has no way of knowing, of course, because no one deemed him worthy of that information.

Whatever happened, the incident has affected Iqbal's adjustment to prison. Instead of looking for ways to contribute, now he lives in fear and wants to live anonymously inside the fences. I asked him whether he intended to donate more paintings to the institution. "Probably not," he said.

Instead of painting, Fermin Martin, our next bantam-time prisoner, found the beauty of music helped his prison adjustment.

LEARNING TO APPRECIATE CLASSICAL MUSIC IN PRISON: FERMIN MARTIN

A prisoner passes his time studying and then teaching the piano while serving his nine-year term.

Fermin Martin, a native of Cuba, came to the United States in 1989. It was not a direct flight from Havana to Miami. Seeking more opportunities than were available on the island of his birth, Martin sought to emigrate despite the Communist government's ban. He took a tourist visa to Panama, then worked his way north through Central America and into the United States.

When he left Cuba, Martin was twenty-five years old and held a degree in chemical engineering from the University of Havana. After several years of odd jobs, he settled in Chicago, then enrolled in a graduate program at the University of Illinois at Chicago with aspirations of obtaining his masters degree in engineering. Martin married, had a child, and seemed poised to establish himself as a hardworking and successful refugee.

In the fall of 1996, however, Martin made a decision that set his life on a different path. In an effort to supplement his income, he agreed to participate with a coworker in a scheme to distribute twenty-five ounces of cocaine. His coconspirator, it turns out, was a government informant working off a previous sentence by setting up others for prosecution. Martin was arrested in the sting operation his coworker had set up. He plead guilty to the charges against him, and since it was his first offense, received a sentence of 108 months.

Fermin Martin

Martin's advanced education set him apart from many of the people with whom he was going to spend the next nine years. Fewer than fifty percent of the approximately two million people now incarcerated in American prisons (federal and state) finished high school, and a substantial subpopulation is functionally, if not completely, illiterate. Martin was about to find that his new community did not formally encourage people to advance themselves or their skills beyond rudimentary levels. Rules and programs, Martin sensed quickly, seemed designed to confine not only men's bodies, but their minds as well.

ADJUSTING TO THE TONE

Martin spent several months in county jails and holding facilities before he finally arrived at the medium-security prison in Allenwood, Pennsylvania. Those initial months came like a wicked stepmother's slap in the face, waking him up and letting him know that his life had changed.

Instead of polite conversation, all dialogue was punctuated with a battlefieldlike aggression. "Please," "thank you," "good morning," and "hello" were replaced with malicious stares and hostile phrases. While squeezing past each other in cramped quarters, for example, people outside of prison might say and expect to hear, "Excuse me." In the cages, however, "Watch your back!" is more commonly heard if anything is said at all. In prison, voice tones are colder, and it is frequently said that kindness, in any form, is taken for weakness.

Besides adjusting to the malevolent tones that come with nearly every verbal exchange, for Martin, learning to live in confinement also meant growing used to the level of noise. A holding tank or cell block may confine hundreds of men in what amounts to a concrete shell. There are no windows and poor acoustics. Nothing absorbs sound that bounces off the hard surfaces of concrete and steel. It is like living ringside before a title fight. Thick clouds of smoke and a restless excitement permeate the air. Even in the dead of night, silence or privacy seem as far away as freedom itself.

Martin's problem with the law led rather soon to his divorce and forced separation from his young daughter. The rest of his family lived in Cuba. Prior to his confinement, Martin spoke with his relatives regularly over the phone. Because telephone access would no longer be available to him, his family ties dissolved.

Like many people who are caught breaking laws and are subsequently incarcerated, Martin was disappointed in himself for letting down those whom he loved and respected. He hoped to adjust to his confinement by finding some activity to which he could devote the expected nine years of his imprisonment, and to substitute correspondence with his loved ones for the telephone calls they would miss.

HOW DO YOU DO?

When Martin arrived at the Allenwood prison, he was assigned to a two-man cell that already was occupied by a long-term prisoner. Like most two-man prison cells, his was about the size of a standard bathroom in an American home. Against the far wall was a free-standing bunk bed instead of a bathtub, but the white porcelain toilet and wall-mounted sink were securely in place. The cell came equipped with two waist-high metal lockers that were supposed to hold all personal property. No clothing, books, or papers were allowed outside the lockers when the room was not occupied. The cell had a wooden desk that Martin and his roommate were supposed to share.

In confinement, most accouterments of life that citizens take for granted are stripped away. Administrators impose limits on what an individual may keep in his possession. Institutional numbers replace prisoners' names, and guards determine the movement of the confined. Gray, white, and khaki are the only shades of clothing prisoners may wear, and rules prohibit prisoners from altering the clothing in any way—even writing one's initials on a sweat shirt to deter theft subjects the clothing to confiscation. Every aspect of the institution must remain homogenous, of a uniform nature, with no colors or markings. Ostensibly, this is done to discourage possible signs of anyone's gang affiliation.

Clearly defined lines demarcate prisoners from staff, but in this community of control, some prisoners latch onto idiosyncratic behavior that helps establish their identities. They look for ways to distinguish themselves from others as a response to the monotony of prison life. Many choose to join gangs or cliques, others fixate on an activity with singular, almost fanatic, focus. Cleanliness and control of the cell, Martin learned at once, had become an obsession for the stranger with whom he had been assigned to live.

Carlos, Martin's first roommate, had been incarcerated since 1981. A native of Cuba himself, Carlos had come to the United States as a Cuban refugee on the Mariel boat lift during the Carter administrataion. Not having family or sponsorship in the United States, Martin told me, Carlos has been confined in one facility or another as an immigration detainee ever since he arrived in America. Carlos spoke no English, nor could he read or write Spanish, his native language. Although they both had come from Cuba, Martin explained that he had nothing in common with Carlos other than the cell to which they were assigned.

Martin explained that Carlos began his day at 6:00 A.M. every morning by rising for breakfast. He then would return to the cell by 7:00 A.M. and begin his cleaning routine with the fervor of a religious fanatic; it did not matter whether Martin wanted to sleep later. The cleaning had to be done.

At approximately eleven feet deep by seven feet wide, the cell had less than eighty square feet of living space. Despite its small size, Carlos spent no fewer than three hours cleaning his cell every day of the week. Corners were scrubbed with a toothbrush. The toilet and sink were highly polished after each use; not one water drop could remain on the porcelain. Lockers were buffed and arranged with military precision, bed linen was washed every day. Carlos brought the room's small floor to a mirrorlike luster by buffing it for no less than an hour after the morning cleaning, and another fifteen minutes in late afternoon. This was a daily ritual for Carlos, as important as brushing one's teeth. He would not permit anyone to enter the room with shoes that had been worn outside the housing unit. The room was his shrine, his source of identity.

Martin lived in Carlos's cell during his first six months at Allenwood, tiptoeing around his eccentric quirks. Recognizing that he had served nearly two decades already, Martin accepted Carlos's hypersensitive devotion to the room. It was his space. That cell was the only thing in the world Carlos could think of as his own, and he seemed to have developed an affection for it, like it was a small child, or a treasure that needed protection. When he was not cleaning the room, Carlos carefully laid on top of his tightly made lower bunk and either listened to the radio or narrated stories about his experiences of prison living. Sometimes he told the stories to himself, sometimes to Martin.

I have been confined since 1987, and during those years I have come across many prisoners who fit Martin's description of Carlos. Obsessed with their cell, it becomes like a tomb for them or a casket, a place where they retreat from the world. If no one is available for a conversation, they talk to themselves. Even here at Fort Dix, a low-security prison, I know at least two people who pass hours in deep conversation with themselves. It can be disconcerting, because one never can be sure what is going on in those people's thoughts. Who knows if they are going to flip out?

Sometimes, while walking around the track, I have tried to narrow the distance between myself and these soliloquists. My proximity does not interrupt their vibrant dialogues. One of them seems to hold an imaginary telephone to his ear and screams into his air-built mouthpiece. I have no idea how long those people have been incarcerated but cannot help but wonder whether their condition is a result of prolonged incarceration—or perhaps a poor adjustment to whatever time they have served.

Carlos rejoiced in describing the best two weeks of his life, which was when he and the more than two thousand other prisoners rioted while he was held in the Atlanta penitentiary. After seizing control of the prison in November 1987, the rioters took nearly a hundred staff members hostage. That small window in his sentence was the closest Carlos had been to freedom since he left Cuba, and the riot brought him a welcome reversal of roles, where staff hostages were required to ask permission of the rioters for everything from food to blankets to movement.

With the enthusiasm of an athlete describing an old moment of glory, Carlos liked to illustrate how he and the others made spears out of the metal springs they pulled from bed frames, and how their unrestricted access to all areas of the prison enabled them to accumulate and walk freely with the weapons they manufactured. They broke into the hospital to steal drugs, as well as into the kitchen and commissary to steal food. They had free reign.

His only regret, Carlos explained, was that he and the others tried to negotiate with the authorities during the riot rather than brutalize or even kill the staff members they were holding hostage. While Carlos reminisced about his participation in the riot, he boasted about looking for opportunities "to set it off again" as an act of revenge for the spiteful way he felt that Cuban prisoners had been treated since the 1987 riot.

COMPATIBLE ROOMMATE SEEKS SAME

Recognizing Carlos's volatility, Martin looked for an opportunity to move to another room. The prison system is crowded, however, and finding a new room is not always easy. An available room must first be located, then the prisoner must submit a written request for a room change to a counselor, and the counselor must agree to make the change. Finally, the counselor must enter the change into the computer database.

It would seem that administrators would want inmates to find compatible roommates. The possibility for tension and prison disturbances increase dramatically when incompatible people are forced to live together. For some obscure reason, however, room changes or requests to be assigned to a particular bed annoy many staff members. At least one counselor in Fort Dix will not even accept a request for a bed change unless the prisoner has spent at least one year in the bed to which he was randomly assigned. It makes no difference to her what reason the inmate provides for wanting to change; before she will consider the request, the inmate must have been in his assigned bed for at least one year, and during that year he must not have received a disciplinary infraction. Oddly enough, this same counselor is very accommodating in other matters. Bed changes, however, seem to be a pet peeve of hers.

After several months of trying, Martin finally was able to move in with a former gang member and recovering heroin addict who then was describing himself as a born-again Christian. Martin was moving up. Carlos felt betrayed because Martin moved out and quit speaking with him. Martin was not deterred. He felt the room change would offer him more freedom to pursue his own goals because he and his new roommate had different schedules and would only be in the room together at night. During the day, while Martin was working, his roommate would use the room. In the evenings Martin would have the space to himself.

A TUTOR'S LIFE

Martin took a job as a tutor in the education department. Initially, he was enthusiastic about the full-time job because he expected it would bring a purpose to his time. By helping others develop reading and writing skills, Martin hoped to experience the satisfaction for which all educators strive. Being one of a few men available who was both bilingual and college educated, Martin found that his skills were in high demand.

Prison parlance described Martin's job as a tutor. His immediate supervisor was a staff teacher. In the classroom, however, the teacher's only role was to record attendance and issue disciplinary infractions to students who were absent. Once the teacher took roll, she left the classroom with Martin in charge to administer the assignments and help the men on an individual basis. In everything except title, Martin was teaching the class, not tutoring.

Although Martin began the job with enthusiasm, it quickly began to drain his energy. Many of the people who were enrolled in Martin's courses, which included English as a second language, remedial learning, and a course to prepare students to pass the high school equivalency exam, participated in the class only because prison rules compelled them to enroll. With no motivation to learn, many students did not want to study and resented Martin for the quasi-leadership role his position gave him in the class. What he hoped would become a modest prison career deteriorated into a cesspool of conflict with others. When Martin realized that his job assignment was bringing him more stress than satisfaction, he reduced the amount of effort he put forth to the same level invested by the students.

Although Martin's work assignment disappointed him, he did learn about the Adult Continuing Education program, which offers qualified inmates an opportunity to design their own course on a volunteer basis and administer it to those who enroll of their own volition. Since the courses are not compulsory, the only people who enroll are those with an authentic desire to learn. Accordingly, the stress accompanying the other courses he taught would not exist in the Adult Continuing Education courses. With hopes of fulfilling his need to bring some meaning to his life, Martin sought to help others progress by designing an introductory Spanish course and a course to help students learn to write personal letters.

Despite no shortage of people enrolling in Martin's introductory Spanish course, learning a foreign language requires a diligence and persistence for which few prisoners have sufficient commitment. His course on how to write personal letters, on the other hand, proved not only popular, but practical as well. Martin kept a waiting list of those students wanting to participate in future courses, and all students who enrolled remained with the course for the full six-week session.

Prisoners who lack the skills to write personal letters lead lonely lives inside the fences. They are left with the alternative of retaining others to write letters on their behalf or communicating only with the felons around them. Those who choose the latter alternative frequently become completely alienated from the world outside. All of the students enrolled in Martin's class had one objective in mind. They did not care about anything other than how to carry on a written correspondence with a woman. Martin, therefore, designed his course to help students compose introductory letters that would elicit a response. It was a sensible course for prisoners wanting to improve their communication skills. Helping others find pen pals and seeing how grateful the students were for the guidance Martin provided gave him the gratification he hoped to find from teaching.

APPRECIATING MUSIC FOR THE FIRST TIME

Teaching also provided Martin with an introduction to other instructors who had specific skills and who had designed their own courses. In a community holding well over a thousand men, some are bound to have extraordinary knowledge or talents they can share with others. Martin enrolled in Arthur's music appreciation course. He had no expectations when he signed up for the weekly class and had no knowledge of music other than the kitschy popular songs he heard on the radio. After his first class with Arthur, Martin felt himself opening up like a desiccated plant that had just been given water. The exposure to music brought color to his otherwise ascetic life and had an immediate effect on Martin's adjustment.

Arthur had been a cultured and accomplished professional musician before his incarceration, gifted not only in reading and writing music, but also in playing the piano, violin, and guitar, among other instruments. Fluent in English, Russian, French, Italian, German, and Spanish, Arthur had an equally impressive knowledge of ballet, opera, classical music, and paintings.

Twenty people signed up with Martin for Arthur's class, none of whom had any previous exposure to classical music. A less inventive and insightful instructor might have lost the attention of the felons in the room as soon as it became clear they were not going to discuss rock or hip-hop music, but Arthur grabbed their attention at the start of the class by dazzling the group with his impressive knowledge of musical history. After his lecture, Arthur played a video recording featuring Placido Domingo in George Bizet's famous opera *Carmen.* After listening to Arthur's mesmerizing lecture, and watching his first opera, Martin became infused with a passion to learn more about music.

Because of Arthur's unique skills, the prison's recreation department authorized the purchase of twenty-five videos to help him teach those interested in opera, ballet, and classical music. The videos were available for inmates to watch on monitors in the institution's library, but in his music appreciation class Arthur provided indispensable commentary before each video that helped participants understand the background of the particular piece and its meanings. Through Arthur's instruction, the students became familiar with the operatic works of famous composers such as Verdi, Puccini, and Wagner, and all the ballets of Tchaikovsky, including *The Nutcracker, Swan Lake,* and *Sleeping Beauty.*

It is not unusual in prison for the recreation department (or perhaps other units) to sponsor an inmate like Arthur. Administrators have the constant challenge to reduce inmate idleness. Their experience suggests that when prisoners have nothing but time on their hands, they frequently find trouble. The unique skills that Arthur made available provided the administrators with an opportunity to present an inexpensive program taught by an inmate volunteer, and the program not only would contribute to the reduction of inmate idleness but also help participants focus on a constructive activity—developing knowledge.

Arthur received a quid pro quo for his contribution to the recreation department. By volunteering his time to teach the music appreciation course, Arthur simultaneously was exposing his myriad talents to the community of the confined. Although participants in the class gained the benefit of Arthur's instruction, and the staff reduced inmate idleness, Arthur was not left out of the bargain. His class was an infomercial of sorts, an advertisement for his extraordinary skills, which, presumably, he could teach to others. Anyone who wanted more specialized instruction, however, would have to pay; the class gave Arthur a forum through which he could showcase his gifts, and that in turn helped him find clients for individualized lessons.

For a negotiated fee, Arthur would tutor a prisoner struggling to learn a foreign language. Musicians in a prison band might want to play a particular song they heard on the radio. They could come to Arthur. For a fee, he would listen to the song, then write out the score for however many instruments were played in the band. Or, if someone wanted to learn how to play a musical instrument, like Martin, he could pay Arthur for private lessons. Officially, no prisoner is allowed to give another prisoner anything of value. Despite the rule, however, paying for services rendered is common behind the fences.

After being duly impressed with the talents Martin witnessed in Arthur's music appreciation class, Martin became one of Arthur's piano pupils. Arthur designed a musical study course for Martin that not only helped him learn how to play the piano, but also taught him about musical theory, progression, and harmony. Studying and practicing music provided Martin with a mental escape from his confinement, gave him a vehicle to sublimate the frustration that came with living inside fences. Music became the nucleus of his adjustment.

During the thirty months that Martin remained in Allenwood, he spent at least one hour each day playing the piano. Arthur coached him for the first year, then Martin made enough progress to study on his own. He had piano books sent into the prison and learned to play the works of Beethoven, Bach, and other classical artists from memory. As his skills improved, Martin began playing the piano for chapel services.

FROM STUDENT TO TEACHER AGAIN

Martin's security level eventually dropped from medium to low, and he was transferred to Fort Dix, where he is scheduled to serve the remaining years of his sentence. The piano skills he developed persuaded the recreation department to employ Martin as a keyboard instructor. Martin's time now passes easily, as he has brought a purpose to his life in leading five classes each week through which he teaches hardened felons the beauty of classical music.

James, one of the other prisoners, introduced me to Martin. James was assigned to a room across the hall from me, and I heard the melodies of an electronic keyboard coming from his room. I walked over, and when I went in the room I saw him playing a familiar piece by Beethoven, *Für Elise*. I asked James if he had learned to play the piano during his incarceration. He told me that he had and that he now was studying under Martin's tutelage. I then met with Martin to see whether I might be able to learn.

When Martin heard that I was interested in learning to play the piano, he came by to speak with me. He was very professional, explaining that he led a keyboard class in the recreation department. Only five keyboards were available, however, and scores of people wanted to participate in the class. Accordingly, he explained that he was forced to limit his classes to ten weekly sessions, during which time he expected successful participants to learn to play at least one song. Because of space limitations, after those ten lessons, students were not allowed to continue studying.

I explained that I was interested in learning a bit more, like how to read music and actually play the piano with a level of competence; I wanted to play with the grace that I saw Martin playing. He explained that developing such skill certainly was possible, but like anything else, it would require thousands of hours of practice. Since so few keyboards were available, it would not be easy.

I took a one-hour private lesson with Martin. During that hour he helped my understanding of music considerably. We were able to play on James's keyboard.

Up until 1996, inmates were allowed to use their funds to purchase electronic keyboards, guitars, and other musical instruments. Public perception, however, was running against inmates, and the federal prison system began implementing rules calling for no-frills prisons. One of the casualties of the new rules was limiting inmate access to personal property; among other things, federal prisoners no longer were allowed to purchase musical instruments.

Although I thoroughly enjoyed learning from Martin during that one-hour lesson, and even asked James to allow me to practice a bit on my own after the lesson, I came to realize that it would not be practical for me to take on such a massive project as learning the piano at this stage of my confinement. I anticipated that it would be too frustrating. James had purchased his keyboard before the new rules had taken effect, and as of this writing, administrators have not confiscated it or ordered him to send it home. Accordingly, he was able to practice regularly.

Had I chosen to continue with my lessons, I would not be guaranteed free access to a keyboard unless I could come to a private agreement with someone like James who still had personal access. Such an agreement would be possible, but it also likely would have violated a prison rule and given me more potential for problems. Writing has been my obsession, and this activity has given me enough problems with staff; I was not looking for a new headache.

Prisoners like Martin, who are able to find an activity that holds their interest, tend to have fewer adjustment problems in prison. They are less likely to engage in disruptive behavior because they do not want to lose access to the activity that has been carrying them, like a magic carpet, over the hassles associated with confinement. An activity like Martin's piano playing is a privilege, one that provides an island of relief and sustenance for him in this ocean of stress. He not only escapes the frustrations of prison by teaching the keyboard to students through the Recreation Department, he also passes his time by helping students like James privately, and playing the piano for the chapel. His piano playing gives him a respite, a kind of mental escape from the prison.

It does not seem to matter what the activity is—playing a musical instrument, attending educational courses, painting, or even the obsessive-compulsive cleaning of one's cell. When prisoners focus on a particular pattern of living in prison, they tend to refrain from activities that could lead to a disruption in their living patterns.

The personal importance a number of inmates attach to their particular, specific activities validates the administrators' position that reducing inmate idleness contributes to the security of an institution. Whereas gang members and predators view segregation as just another part of the penitentiary, punishment as an expected and accepted part of the prison stretch, those who focus on constructive activities try diligently to avoid problems that could lead to disciplinary sanctions. They realize their activity as being helpful; it helps them through the days, months, years, and decades. They adjust positively, as they do not want such patterns disrupted, however briefly.

Martin currently has three years remaining to serve. He has requested that the Recreation Department at Fort Dix purchase a series of videos that would allow him to teach a music-appreciation course similar to the one he completed at Allenwood; he also continues lobbying for more keyboards and at least one upright piano on which he and his students can practice. He expects to continue introducing others to the piano, improving his own playing skills, and writing music. Music has carried him through the term, he says, and he expects that it always will be a part of his life.

In the next chapter, Don Pappa describes how he began planning for his future adjustment as soon as he learned about his imminent incarceration.

MAKING A NEW START:
DON PAPPA

One former Mafia associate uses his time in prison to make a
clean start by turning away from crime.

In almost every prison in America, inmates divide themselves into a lay-
ered social structure, much like citizens do in communities throughout the
United States. The difference is that behind prison fences, qualities such
as morality, temperance, and integrity are not a factor in determining a
prisoner's place in the social hierarchy. Instead, influential attributes include one's ability to mix and move freely among those committed to the
criminal way of life. Those with reputations associated with organized
crime—particularly the Mafia—move within prison societies as if they are
part of a Brahman class.

Long-time members of these confined communities frequently test
those who come in without some type of criminal reputation. Someone
may rob a prisoner who does not appear to have any allies inside, to see
how he responds. If he runs to the guards for protection, he has failed the
test. Such inmates suffer the label of rat, or snitch, ensuring that the wider
prisoner population will ostracize them and perhaps target them for further, more regular abuse. If the man who has been robbed quickly makes
it known that he intends to pursue the matter and exact revenge, he begins
to establish a reputation as a standup convict.

THE WAYS OF THE WISEGUYS

Those whom others consider to have close ties with the Mafia, on the other hand, are immune from such tests. Wiseguys, as they are called, generally enjoy automatic respect from both inmates and staff. Genuine wiseguys are like celebrities in a restaurant, with an entourage of servile hangers-on and others who are obsequious in their presence. Instead of being tested upon his entrance into the community, a wiseguy will be embraced and accorded an almost reverential status.

The ambassador-of-crime status associated with Mafia affiliation insures that many inmates of lesser status suck up to wiseguys. Like groupies, they seek status by association. One prison ritual common among those affiliated with organized crime is the ceremonious greetings and partings. Although everyone is confined in a relatively small space, and all prisoners see each other several times throughout any given day, organized-crime affiliates emphasize relationships by shaking hands and embracing each time they meet. It does not matter whether they see each other at breakfast, again after lunch, in the afternoon, and again after dinner, each new meeting warrants a warm shaking of hands for others to see, or perhaps an embrace. It is as if they are family members just united after a long absence.

Because prisoners perceived as being close to wiseguys—no matter how close the bond—enjoy a kind of free pass inside the fences, many prisoners trip over themselves trying to become a part of the handshaking ceremonies. Those who succeed may actually get a kiss on each cheek. Much more unusual, however, is the prisoner who was an authentic and well-documented intimate of organized crime leaders before his confinement, but instead of pursuing sycophants and their phony attention, takes affirmative steps to distance himself from the Tony Soprano way of life. At Fort Dix, Don Pappa is one such prisoner.

THE ORGANIZATION OF ORGANIZED CRIME

Don was raised in Bensonhurst, an Italian American enclave in Brooklyn where, allegedly, the Colombo crime family has a strong presence. According to prosecutors, the Colombo family is an organized criminal group that operates in many parts of the United States but is headquartered in New York. Members have been accused of engaging in activities that affect interstate commerce.

Theoretically, all Mafia families, including the Colombo crime family are organized hierarchically, with a leader (also known as a "boss"), an "underboss," and a "counselor," also known as the "consigliere." Beneath these three positions are the "captains," who are also known as "capo-regimes" and "skippers." The captains are responsible for "crews," which consist of "made" members. A made member is an individual who takes an "oath of omerta," vowing never to reveal any information about the organized crime family to which he belongs. Made members may also be known as "soldiers," "good fellows," and "associates" of the Colombo Family.

The crews produce funds from a variety of illegal activities, and these funds are distributed throughout the family's hierarchy. In return for a percentage of the illegally derived funds, the highest-ranking members in the family provide services such as protection and the negotiation of disputes between organized crime members.

The principal purpose of the Colombo family was to generate money through various criminal activities, including illegal gambling, extortion, and credit collections. Among the methods and means by which members operated were threats of and the actual use of violence, including murder.

Like many youngsters raised in Bensonhurst, Don gravitated to the wiseguy lifestyle. Unlike most, however, by the time he was in his early twenties, he was considered a potential leader. He traveled in the company of the upper echelons of organized crime while being groomed for leadership. At twenty-five, he was arrested with several others in an indictment charging that during a dispute within the Columbo organization, several crimes were committed, including extortion and murder. Don had never been convicted of a crime before, and his attorney succeeded in negotiating a relatively light sentence that included fewer than eight years of imprisonment. Because of his known status as a highly respected associate of one of the nation's five leading Mafia families, when he arrived at Fort Dix, many hardened criminals fawned over Don as if he were a rock star walking into a crowd of teenagers.

BECOMING UNCONNECTED

By the time Don was convicted, however, he had made a categorical decision to sever his ties with any type of criminal behavior. Instead of courting the flattery that prisoners around him wanted to bring, Don purposely distanced himself from other Mafia figures and wanna-be Mafia figures inside the prison. Although he could not escape his reputation of being a so-called connected guy, like a leader in exile, Don did his best to isolate himself from the committed criminals within the inmate population. His adjustment in prison singularly focused on abandoning his past and making a clean start of his life upon release.

Instead of being incarcerated immediately following his arrest, Don spent over one year under house-arrest while he awaited the outcome of his criminal proceedings. He was confined to his residence except for closely monitored absences authorized for visits to his attorney. Don used that time to focus on the future of his life after prison.

Such an attitude among the newly incarcerated is exceptionally rare. Usually, people who are facing long stretches of time trapped inside the far-reaching web of the criminal justice system pass through extended periods of denial. Not knowing that they are ensnaring themselves further, those in denial not only proclaim their innocence, but also make specious arguments about why the government cannot succeed in its prosecution. Even after such prisoners are convicted and sentenced, they cling to hopes for what they call justice, which for them is synonymous with a reduced sentence or outright exoneration.

Don, on the other hand, took a more objective look at his situation. Long before he was even convicted, he accepted the inevitable, that he was going to prison. He therefore assessed the behavior that brought him his legal problems. As a result of a twisted value system, he realized that he had made some bad choices as a young man; if he continued, he would likely be a target of law enforcement for the rest of his life, going in and out of jail, never being able to enjoy a normal existence. Accordingly, he decided to use the time he felt certain he would spend in confinement to prepare himself for a brighter, more socially acceptable future. "When I was under house arrest, I decided to work with my brother in forming a business. We knew that we needed to start something legitimate, something to support our mom, something to build on. We started a pest-control business. Since I was going to prison, my brother got all the licenses and certificates needed to work. I worked the telephone trying to stir up business." During his imprisonment, Don hoped and expected to contribute to the business in any way possible. Without free telephone access, however, both he and his brother expected that he would be of limited use. What is significant, nonetheless, is that Don had a plan for how he would serve his time before he even entered the prison. Instead of focusing on what they will do upon their release, most incoming prisoners focus on what they can do to make their time pass in the easiest manner.

In the federal prison system, inmates who reach the final months of their sentences are required to participate in a prerelease program designed to help them prepare for the challenges they will face once they leave the prison community. Prerelease classes, sponsored by staff members from the education department, generally are basic. They provide information about obtaining a driver's license, interacting with parole officers, and finding a job. After serving years in prison, however, such classes are about as effective as using a Band-Aid to close the chest after an open-heart surgery operation. Preparations for release ought to begin at the start of one's sentence, not at the end. Prescient individuals, like Don, begin thinking about their lives after confinement even before bars enclose them.

Being in a world that is cut off from the wider society, news within the prison system circulates rather quickly. If there is a fight, someone is stabbed, or anything unusual happens, within hours the grapevine carries the information to all corners of the institution. Similarly, when a high-profile inmate is admitted, people begin to talk. In a low-security prison such as Fort Dix, when those who are reputed to have close ties to the Mafia come into the compound, others take notice. For instance, soon after Don arrived at Fort Dix, another high-profile alleged Mafia member showed up—Nicky Corozza, whom newspapers described as the de facto leader of the Gambino crime family after the infamous John Gotti was incarcerated. Although Don and Nicky were so-called colleagues prior to their confinement, their adjustments differed.

THE GODFATHER

With scores of obsequious prisoners around him every day, Nicky was perhaps the most visible prisoner at Fort Dix. Prisoners frequently exercise by walking around the track, and Nicky walked for over an hour every day. When he did, several others were around him constantly, eager to laugh at his jokes or open doors for him. When he came to the dining room, others would reserve a table for him; he would not wait in line for meals but would instead wait for kitchen workers to bring the meal to him and those with the bestowed privilege of eating at his table. His large following attracted the attention—and perhaps enmity—of certain staff members, at least one of whom targeted Nicky and his followers for harassment.

Lieutenant Nesbitt, who strikes prisoners as the kind of man who began aspiring to work as a prison guard in kindergarten, took a special interest in Nicky Corozza. Little inside the fences escapes Nesbitt's notice, but with Corozza he seemed to have an insatiable desire for information. He frequently interrogated inmates, asking questions about who was on Nicky's payroll and what types of services they were providing. Other prisoners inside Fort Dix were engaged in the distribution of drugs, the operation of gambling pools, or other unauthorized behavior. All deserved close scrutiny by the authorities. Few, however, received as much of Nesbitt's attention as Corozza.

Prisoners who were eager to curry favor with Nicky used their influence to help him secure a choice room and a cushy job. Quarters and job assignments are perhaps the most important aspects of living in prison. One can never find peace or comfort if one is forced to sleep within a few feet of someone persistently incompatible, and a bad job exacerbates the tension of being separated from one's family and community. Nicky's friends were able to orchestrate a twelve-man room that held only his allies and minions—those who waited in lines for him, performed laundry services on his behalf, or prepared food for him and his friends. His celebrity status simply could not escape Nesbitt's notice.

After regular shakedowns yielded no more contraband than an extra onion or tomato, Nesbitt ordered the breakup of Nicky's room, assigning the Mafia don to the top bunk in a room with eleven immigrants, few of whom spoke English. He changed Nicky's job assignment from one with few duties to a position in one of the maintenance departments that required Corozza to report for his tool-carrying job at 6:30 A.M. each morning and remain there until 3:00 P.M. each afternoon. He continued the regular shakedowns, thereby rendering Nicky's time at Fort Dix a punishment within a punishment.

On the other hand, despite Don Pappa's heavily documented Mafia affiliation, he has succeeded in moving well below the radar screen of Nesbitt and other guards who make it their business to focus on high-profile inmates. During the nearly five years that he has been confined, he has never been singled out by Nesbitt or other guards for harassment.

BEING THE SUBMARINE

Don moves through the prison like a submarine. His periscope is up, so he knows what is going on around him, but he moves well beneath the surface to avoid complications with others. In a population of over two thousand prisoners, his circle of associates inside the fences consists of five people. He leads an independent, highly structured life inside. It is arranged with the singular purpose of helping himself prepare to overcome the challenges he will face upon his release.

It will be a struggle, he recognizes, to leave his past behind him and begin a business career. Don put a plan together when he began his sentence. Knowing that he would serve approximately six years, he evaluated himself, then projected what he could become in six years time. Don considered himself at least thirty pounds overweight. He lacked formal educational credentials; his experience as a reader was superficial; and he had a weak vocabulary. In order to facilitate his plans to succeed upon release, he determined to structure his time in a manner that would permit him to address each perceived weakness.

Like Nicky, Don was assigned to a twelve-man room. Instead of bringing attention to himself by using underlings to manipulate a favorable living environment, Don took a quieter, more subtle approach. "I knew that there was some turnover in the room. At least one or two beds would open because someone would get transferred, released, or go to the hole. So I kept an eye open for people who wouldn't get on my nerves. There were lots of noisy rooms. I wanted mine to be a quiet, clean room. I looked for people who didn't have visitors, didn't play their headphones so I would have to listen to their music. Then I invited them into my room to fill the vacated beds."

Surprisingly, in a building holding over 350 men, there is a dearth of those who cherish silence. Every room seems to have at least a few people who enjoy loud table or card games that render silence the rarest of commodities; it is difficult to find a room where all twelve people respect each other's needs, activities, and space.

After little more than seven months, Don unobtrusively had rearranged the human quotient in his twelve-man room to his liking. It now allows him to work more effectively toward the goals he has set for himself. He purposely solicited people from different racial and ethnic backgrounds, so as not to draw the attention of staff. The only criterion he looked for when soliciting room occupants was that the prospect respect "the rules of the room," which included few visitors, cleanliness, and above all, silence.

Instead of keeping a cadre of minions, Don compensated one trusted prisoner to clean the room daily and take care of his other needs. The inmate keeps the floor waxed and buffed to a glossy polish. For a few cans of tuna each month, Don's maintenance man keeps the lockers and walls painted white, touching up scuffs or marks regularly. Each occupant makes his bed in a uniform manner with tightly stretched white linen. The room looks like a hospital ward, and despite its twelve occupants, it is as quiet as a monastery's library.

Through regular procedures, Don was able to secure a favorable job assignment, requiring him to sweep and mop a section of the building's floor after midnight on weekends and holidays. The job is desirable because the responsibilities require no more than one hour of work and even that only a few times each week. Because his scheduled work hours are late at night, Don is free to spend his day in any way he chooses. This contrasts significantly with the far less desirable job assigned to Nicky. Further, Nicky's demanding job meant his access to the telephone was limited because inmates are not authorized to use the phone during their assigned work hours. Don did not have this problem.

Don's job assignment may not have required much time, but that does not mean he sat idly. Focused on developing skills during his confinement, Don designed a formidable schedule that kept him working toward his goals. His days inside the prison are as routine as the rising and setting of the sun. His mornings begin at 8:00 A.M. Four times each week he begins with a ninety-minute exercise routine that includes push-ups, chin-ups, dips, sit-ups, and a five-mile run. As a result of his constant exercise routine, Don has shed the extra thirty pounds he was carrying prior to confinement; now he is fit, with an athletic build. On Thursdays, Fridays, and Sundays—the days when he does not exercise—Don spends the first four hours of his mornings reading the *New York Daily News,* the *New York* magazine, and whatever book he may be interested in at the time.

Don was not a reader prior to his incarceration. Since he began serving his sentence, he has become a voracious consumer of literature. Keeping a pen in hand, he reads with a purpose. Not only does he take steps to remain current with the community he left behind, through his reading material he also hopes to develop his vocabulary, spot opportunities that may benefit his family, and prepare himself so that when release comes he will have more than prison stories to tell.

Generally, when people come to prison a kind of myopia sets in, prohibiting many from seeing any way they can make a difference in their lives or in the lives of their loved ones. They are prisoners in their minds as well as in their bodies. The system itself conditions this dependent thinking, usurping so much control over each prisoner's immediate fate. The structure of the prison dictates when they will eat, with whom they will share a room, where they will work, and what contacts they will have with the outside community. Although any number of factors can render their time more onerous—for example, involvement in a fight, being caught with contraband, or violating some obscure rule—few opportunities exist for them to enhance their status formally.

From the perspective of the inmate, the prison community bears a strong resemblance to the plight of the worker under Communism. Behind the fences, administrators design rules to eliminate individuality, replace names with registration numbers, require all enforced inhabitants to wear uniform clothing, assign jobs according to institutional need, censor reading materials, and ration portions of meals and spending. Only the strongest minds find ways to flourish in these societies of deprivation.

Instead of thinking about the communities to which they will return, and thinking about ways to prepare themselves for the obstacles they will encounter, for the most part, prisoners occupy their minds with steps they can take to lessen the frustrations of imprisonment. Some will look for hustles inside that will provide them with food or commissary items. Some become expert malingerers, avoiding work so that they can experience their soap operas, music videos, and table games as if they were narcotics. Others devote years of their time to sports, or nurturing hope for some magical legislative or judicial relief to come their way. The institution encourages this fantastic, fatalistic thinking, leaving few with any sense of their own efficacy, any hope of having the power to make an appreciable difference in their lives.

THE POWER OF PRAGMATISM

Recognizing that his incarceration was an inevitable, but temporary, period through which he would pass, Don welcomed every day as an opportunity to prepare himself further. In his reading, he circled every unknown word he encountered, then wrote it in a notebook that became his own lexicon. Each Sunday evening, Don would work through his word lists, exercising his mind to enhance his vocabulary, with hopes of becoming a stronger communicator. Whereas the vocabulary of most long-term prisoners degenerates into primers of vulgarity and profanity, after years of practice, Don estimates that his efforts have added well over a thousand words to his repertoire.

In addition to collecting words, Don also has taken the unusual step of making efforts to familiarize himself with the many restaurants of New York City. In addition to circling words, he circles the name of every restaurant mentioned in the articles he reads and keeps a separate notebook of the ones that he wants to visit. A company called Zagat publishes a guidebook each year that lists and ranks thousands of restaurants. Don has a new Zagat guide sent to him each year; he uses it to obtain a reference for the restaurants that appeal to him. Although he will not be able to visit any of these restaurants until his term expires, he says that he studies them because he does not want his years of imprisonment to render him a stranger to New York. When he leaves the gates behind, he says, he wants to hit the streets running, as if he never left.

The Education Department at Fort Dix sponsors a program together with Mercer Community College where professors come into the prison and teach classes in which inmates may enroll for college credit. Because of the demand, the program limits each student to taking one to two classes per quarter. Despite its long-term and intrinsic values, relatively few people in prison take education seriously. Many enroll in courses but find the work too demanding. Study interferes with other more exciting activities, such as watching television, gambling, or playing sports. Study frequently is the first activity to be abandoned.

Don has been an enthusiastic participant in the college program, which eventually led to his earning an associate's degree. After his morning exercise or reading, Don regularly spent his afternoons in class or studying independently to absorb the material. Once he earned his degree, he enrolled in correspondence courses, studying business, accounting, and English in order to sustain his afternoon study routine and to expose his mind to disciplines that he expected would help his transition to the world of legitimate commerce upon his release.

To that end, Don also subscribed to the *Wall Street Journal* and to a periodical that featured nothing but classified advertisements for commercial real estate. As a prisoner, Don could not engage in business. However, he astutely recognized that the one commodity he had in abundance was time. While his brother kept busy building his family business, Don devoted two hours each evening after dinner to dissecting the dense information available in his business newspaper and scouring through the hundreds of properties advertised for sale in his periodical.

INVESTING IN THE FUTURE

When Don began his term, he had no knowledge of investments or the power of compounding growth. Neither did his brother. They both were tempted by what they then perceived as the glamorous life of the Mafia. But that vision has been altered substantially. His brother began a legitimate business from scratch, and Don studied independently to educate himself in the ways of business and investment fundamentals. He has learned about leverage and about evaluating an investment's potential for growth or return on capital. But Don has done more than learn about it. He also has contributed to the lives of his family members by teaching them what he was learning. From behind the razor wire, Don has become an effective mentor. Instead of being a liability to his family, Don has proven himself an asset by turning his incarceration into a Horatio Alger story of self-reliance.

Don began his study of investments immediately upon his confinement. After a year of scrutiny and reflection, he began developing more confidence in what he was learning and started making suggestions to his brother and his mother on how they could use the stock market to help their savings grow. Not knowing anything about investments, or how to put a value on the seemingly complicated world of obscure symbols and numbers, they initially were reluctant to follow Don's advice. But he was undeterred. After reading his newspapers, Don entered the closing prices of the companies' stock shares that he was tracking, building a series of daily charts that illustrated the opportunities. Each week he sent home copies of his work, and during visits Don would spend time explaining the risks and rewards of a long-term investment program. Instead of gangster talk, Don began to sound like one of the talking heads on CNBC; since his incarceration, he has been all business, literally and figuratively.

In addition to persuading his family members to begin making small weekly deposits into a brokerage account, Don also convinced his brother that he ought to begin using whatever proceeds his business generated to accumulate real estate. He combed through hundreds of classified advertisements each week and, being in no hurry, when he found an advertisement that appealed to him, he sent a letter in search of more information. He kept a detailed list of his work, and he estimates that each month of research yields up to ten properties that may prove of interest to his family. Generally, they are what he calls "don't wanters," meaning the owners want to dump the properties for whatever reason. If the owners or agents responded to his requests for more information, and if the properties still looked appealing, he brought them to the attention of his brother, his mother, or an acquaintance who might be in a position to make an offer on the property.

Over the years since he has been incarcerated, Don has advised his family members to pursue the possibility of acquiring over a dozen separate properties that he has located through his unusual, but diligent research. On most occasions, no deal was consummated. But over the past three years, Don's family was able to purchase two pieces of commercial real estate that his work recommended, and he continues looking for more. Whereas most prisoners talk about the careers they want to begin upon release, over the period of time that Don has been incarcerated, he has invested the energy necessary to obtain experience in the complicated world of business. He has reason to believe that he can continue making himself useful upon his release.

Don never diminishes the obstacles he expects to encounter when his term expires. He is now in his early thirties and he recognizes that he will begin his life as not only a convicted felon, but one who has a past that is tainted with allegations of his being on intimate terms with organized crime and its leaders. Understanding and accepting the obstacles that will confront his life has made all the difference in his adjustment.

Instead of walking through the prison accepting the accolades and homage that others pay to upper-echelon Mafia types, Don purposely and noticeably stays away from the hype. When asked directly about his affiliation with organized crime, he acknowledges that his seduction by organized crime and his participation in it was the most foolish decision of his life, and one that he will spend the rest of his years trying to overcome and move beyond. Rather than whining about the years he has lost to incarceration, however, Don has chosen to use his time practically, not only to prepare himself for the future, but to lead a life of discipline and hard work in one of the most difficult and least supportive environments in American society.

ELEPHANT-TIME PRISONERS

LOOKING PAST LONG SENTENCES

Here, in the elephant-time section, readers learn about five prisoners serving ten- to twenty-year sentences. They came into prison with different perceptions than the lilliputian or the bantam prisoners. Their sentences made it clear that unless something changed, at least a decade would pass before they returned to the lives they once knew. Of the men whom I profile here, not one began thinking about what would follow release until a significant period of time had been served. In the beginning, without exception, their adjustment focused on settling into prison.

A well-worn cliche suggests that those who fail to plan, simultaneously, plan to fail. The first three men whom I profile make it clear that after having been sentenced to lengthy terms in prison, they began adjusting in ways that certainly would bring them further problems not only with prison administrators, but with the criminal justice system as well. They did not care. They were leading lives behind walls, indifferent to or rebelling against the values of American society. As far as they were concerned, they had too much time to serve and no reason to think about life after confinement.

Although the other two prisoners serving elephant-time sentences did not continue their criminal behavior after their arrest, in the beginning they were not thinking about preparations that would help them succeed upon release—and here I define success as simply staying out of prison. Instead of beginning their terms with ideas about what they would do to develop personally or redeem themselves during their terms, they were looking for legal loopholes that would open the gates quicker.

JOE, DORIAN, AND HECTOR

For Joe Black, prison may have been a blessing. Had he not been arrested and sentenced to an elephant-time sentence, like a lot of inmates, he suggests that his activities either would have led to his own death or his being convicted of a crime with an even longer term—or a death sentence. Prison was something he expected to experience at some point in his life. When he came in with nearly twenty years to serve, his only interest was in making the best of it. He was not, however, willing to allow anything to tarnish his image or reputation. Any form of violence was more acceptable to Joe than allowing someone else—staff member or fellow prisoner—to believe that he had broken Joe.

Dorian also believed that a defensive attack was the only way to defend his manhood in prison. His involvement with weapons, drug dealing and in a dangerous love-triangle inside was a formula for disaster. Instead of being released after three or four years, Dorian is now in his twelfth year and expects to serve two more before release. Despite some last minute changes in attitude and lifestyle behind bars, Dorian still does not seem to have his release plans grounded in reality.

Hector has also served twelve years, and like the others, was consumed with establishing a reputation as a defiant prison thug. Not only did violence provide him with a kind of therapy, it kept other predators from focusing on him as the potential target suggested by his slight size and boyish appearance. Hector describes his reliance on weapons to solve problems, and how he came to embrace the ways of the penitentiary. It was not until late in his term that he began to focus on self-improvement, and the reader may wonder if his positive adjustments are too little, too late.

ANDREW AND BYRON

As we will see, different prisoners take different approaches to the prospect of long-term incarceration. Some turn to the law library, spending hundreds of hours in search of the elusive argument that will overturn a conviction or reduce a sentence. Others commit to strict exercise routines to pass the days, while still others pursue pardons and clemency petitions based on various strategies of self-improvement and remorse.

In contrast to those described early in the chapter, Andrew and Byron wanted to use their time in prison to improve their life chances for the future. Through various job assignments at different facilities, Andrew tried to piece together some marketable skills, while Byron turned to religion to bring meaning to his time. Both paid little attention to other prisoners' perceptions of them, their reputation or image. They were looking inward and toward the future rather than at the harsh realities of the cold concrete world around them.

Longer-term prisoners shape the culture inside the fences. They provide advice to less experienced prisoners on how to cope with problems or frustrations and have a stabilizing presence that is surely related to their interest in maintaining the status quo.

PRISONIZATION AND THE U-SHAPED CURVE

One of the first studies of inmate subculture was conducted by Donald Clemmer at Menard Prison in Illinois in the late 1930s (Clemmer, 1940). For Clemmer, prisonization was when inmates took on the folkways, mores, and customs particular to life behind bars. How strongly one identifies with the other prisoners and prison ways, according to Clemmer, depends on the housing area one is assigned to, the strength of relationships or ties one has on the outside, and the vulnerability of one's own personality— whether the prisoner joins groups, accepts the codes and values of others, and will change to suit peers. Back then, he assumed that most inmates do not join groups.

Yale sociologist Stanton Wheeler tested Clemmer's ideas at the Washington State Reformatory around 1960 (Wheeler, 1961). He found that as prisoners move through their terms, their behavior follows the pattern of a U's curvature. The values and culture of the outside community, friends and family, influence an inmate's positive adjustment early on, but as time passes, the prisoner sinks into a trough, adopting the negative values and subcultural attitudes of those around him. This middle portion of the term, means one's thoughts are far from respect for administrative authority and rule-abiding behavior. However, as an inmate moves closer toward release, he begins a movement away from the influence of prisoner cliques and climbs back up the U-curve, mirroring the values of the outside community. While not realizing it at the time, many long-term prisoners look back on their experiences and see the U-shaped curve, as do I.

As anyone living through the pains of imprisonment (as Gresham Sykes [1958] and many other prison writers have referred to it) can attest, it is difficult not to fall into the prisoner subculture. One might also agree with Amitai Etzione, another sociologist, who wrote that doing time is not enough. Byron describes his commitment to God as a source of peace despite the years he is serving. Andrew, on the other hand, remains frustrated with his sentence even though he is busy preparing for release. Although Joe, Dorian, and Hector adjusted to the early phase of their sentences by embracing the prison culture, now that they are emerging through the final stage of their theoretical U, they strive to prepare for the outside community.

GOIN' HARD IN FEDERAL PRISON: JOE "BLACK" REDDICK

For Joe Black, prison is just another part of life.

For some people, coming to prison is a terrifying experience, like being caught at sea in a hurricane without a life raft. Prisoners are ripped away from their families, routine experiences, and comfort zones, and the system also plunges them into a chaotic world where authoritarian guards control their movements and living habits, where they will live within a whisper's distance of ever-changing strangers who often prowl the prison like hungry, vigilant sharks. Many who endure incarceration find the experience among the most stressful events of their lives, and their initial adjustment is the worst part. But this is not the case for all prisoners, and it was not the case for Joe Reddick.

Joe was raised in the Bronx. Crime had been a part of his life as far back as he can remember. He described his mother as an expert poker player who did not take notice when Joe, as a preteen, began hustling marijuana in the neighborhood for extra money. Her only admonition was that he "take the heat like a man" if he was apprehended. Prison never held any stigma or negative connotation for him. It simply was a natural part of life and one that he expected would someday be his.

By the time Joe reached his early twenties, he was leading what he considered to be a rather uncomplicated existence. He supported himself through his own drug distribution network. His group purchased kilogram-quantities of cocaine in New York, converted it to crack cocaine, and then had it transported to North Carolina where it was sold in smaller quantities for huge profits. A real assembly line. The racket provided him with enough money to live as lavishly as the hip-hop artists with whom he cavorted, and equally important, it gave him enough time to spend hours each day playing basketball, a skill that would, curiously, prove useful in his adjustment to prison.

In 1993 Joe turned twenty-three. He says that as a young, street-savvy black man, who admittedly lived in constant violation of the law, he was fortunate to have avoided arrest for so long. He knew his days were numbered. The prospect of incarceration, however, did not stress him out. Joe was not losing sleep.

Not long after his twenty-third birthday, a state trooper in North Carolina stopped Joe for a traffic violation. The trooper learned that Joe had an outstanding warrant for conspiracy to distribute crack cocaine in the state of North Carolina; he was arrested and taken to a county jail for trial.

The large county jail crowded hundreds of prisoners into several different housing units. Three men were assigned to rooms built for a single man, and many more scattered their flimsy vinyl mattresses on the filthy, nicotine-stained floor in the unit's common living area. Except for the confinement and the guards, however, things were not too much worse than the urban conditions Joe had grown up with in the Bronx.

PLAYING GAMES AND PLOTTING ESCAPE

Within hours of being admitted into the county jail, Joe joined a pickup basketball game. As a gifted athlete, he became known quickly as Air Black or Joe Black, and those nicknames have followed him throughout his prison term. After playing a few games and making several acquaintances on the basketball court, he returned to the housing unit and was invited to play poker. By the end of his first day in the jail, he already was a solid member of a clique of guys who had him spending his time playing ball and gambling. He knew he was facing a possible life sentence, but Joe says he was not bothered. "Whatever happens, happens," he said in resignation. "They can do what they gotta do, and I'm gonna do what I gotta do."

Joe was in jail for seven months awaiting the conclusion of his criminal proceedings. He became close with two acquaintances he had met in the jail. Rayford already had been sentenced to a life term, and Malik, like Joe, was waiting for trial and expected to receive a long sentence. Both Rayford and Malik also were natives of New York. The three played basketball and poker, games that Rayford and Malik had been running in the housing units. Gambling is not allowed in any jail, as guards view it as a precursor to problems. With so much time on their hands, prisoners easily find ways of getting around such rules. Since poker chips are not sold in the commissary, the men make their own by clipping used cards into squares. Many pass several hours each day trying their luck at the poker table. Because his mother had sponsored poker games in Joe's child-hood home, he grew up around cards and gambling, and his luck seemed to run better than most.

Rayford, who already had served six years of his life sentence, was the most experienced prisoner of the three. One day during a meal, he told Joe and Malik that he had been casing the jail and had spotted a hole in the security, a place from where the three could make a break. "How we gonna do that?" Joe asked.

The windows were covered with a steel-mesh screen. Rayford said that he had checked it out up close and noticed that the metal was corroded. All they needed was a hacksaw blade to saw through the bolts and they would be able to pull the screen off. Once the screen was off, the three could slip through the sliding window in the dead of night. He expected that no one would notice their absence until the next census count after their hiatus.

Most prisoners who are waiting for trial have hopes that they will be exonerated. Accordingly, they do not look for further potential problems with the law. Some, however, like Joe and Malik, consider themselves hardcore and easily make their own rules. If there was a way to bust out of the jail, they said they wanted in, just as Rayford expected they would. No one questioned what would happen if they succeeded, and no one considered what would happen if they failed. Joe and Malik were inter-ested only in what was necessary to move forward with the plan.

"The only thing we need is someone to get us the hacksaw blades," Rayford told his crew.

Joe said that he knew a "white boy" had been smuggling marijuana into the jail and selling it. Joe had been locked up for less than three months, but in those ninety days he had established himself as a leader of the jail house, making it his business to know as much as possible about what was going on. Joe suggested that the three put pressure on the white boy to use his contact to bring in a pack of hacksaw blades. They figured if the guy had such a reliable pipeline to bring in marijuana, a little pressure would persuade him to bring in the blades in order to preserve "the sweet little operation he had going." The trio had a plan and moved forward with it.

After locating their prey, Joe says he and the others cornered the drug purveyor. He was a college student serving a one-year sentence in the jail, but somehow he had developed a connection to bring in his marijuana. Like most jails, the one where Joe was confined had an overwhelming population of minority inmates, mostly black and Hispanic. The prisoner they had targeted was no match for Joe, Malik, and Rayford, three hardened criminals who were masters at the art of intimidation. They told their victim that either he would get the blades into the jail or they were going to hurt him, and badly. They did not have to specify what that meant, as they could see from his face that he was petrified. "The cat's eyes was watering and his lips was shakin' when we pulled up on him," Joe explained. Not wanting problems, he delivered the blades to them a week later. If he had been unsuccessful in procuring the contraband blades, Joe says their target either would have had to check in to protective custody or face a severe beating. Either way, his drug operation in the jail would have come to an abrupt end.

With the blades in hand, Joe, Malik, and Rayford took turns sawing the bolts off the screen whenever they had an opportunity. Two would stand as sentries, observing everything they could while the other sawed away. The jail was so crowded that they were not locked inside a room, but had been assigned to sleep on the floor of the housing unit. This gave them access to the targeted window during the day and evening hours. One would simply sit next to it while others were eating lunch or playing table games. The person responsible for sawing would drape a blanket across himself to shield his activity from view, then file through the corroded steel bolts a little bit at a time.

Once they had the blades, their biggest problem was not cutting through the bolts, but hiding the hacksaw blades in a safe place when they were not in use. They found a lip on a drinking fountain and hid them there. All had been going well, and on the third day, they were certain that the last bolt was about to be severed, meaning they could remove the screen. They planned to remove it that evening, bust through the glass, and make their way to freedom after lights were turned out. Rayford had woven a rope together out of pillowcases and sheets he had been collecting; he hid it under his mattress. They knew the window led outside of the jail, but they did not know much more than that. They concerned themselves only with breaking out.

As it turned out, lack of a follow-through plan did not matter. Before the lights went out that evening, a guard went to take a sip from the drinking fountain that was their hiding place. As he was sipping his water, he heard a piece of metal drop from the bottom of the fountain. The machine must have been shaken, and one of the thin blades made a ting sound as it bounced on the concrete floor. The plan was foiled.

Joe and Malik stood watching as the guard bent down to pick up the blade. He held it up, looked at it in the light. After noticing the teeth on the blade had been worn, he ran his fingers along the bottom lip of the fountain and found two other blades. The guard returned to his desk, and minutes later a cadre of guards had come to the unit to begin a massive shakedown.

One guard found the bolts the trio had cut through, another found the makeshift rope Rayford had been storing under his mattress. He was taken away to segregation, but neither Joe nor Malik was apprehended. Apparently, Rayford was not providing the guards with any information on his accomplices.

NO FAIR FIGHTS

Joe then abandoned his plans to escape and simply continued playing basketball and poker every day while waiting for trial. Four months later, he was found guilty and sentenced to a term of just under twenty years. As a first offender, he was transferred to a medium-security prison. A few days before he was to be transferred, however, he found himself in a jailhouse brawl that resulted in his being redesignated to begin his term in a maximum-security prison.

The fight began, he explains, because someone "disrespected him" while he was using the phone. He says he was talking to his mother, explaining that he was about to be transferred from the jail to prison. A table was near the phone where five people were playing cards. One of the guys at the table was a newcomer and talking loudly. Joe says he asked him politely to quiet down while he was on the phone. Instead of obliging, the guy paid Joe a flip remark about his being in jail and not at the Holiday Inn; he ought to get used to the noise.

Not liking his tone, Joe says he did not hesitate. He ripped the phone's handle and cord out of the blue wall-mounted telephone. While wrapping the metal coiled cord around his hand for grip, he walked over behind his victim and repeatedly began smashing the phone handle down on the guy's head like it was a weighted bullwhip.

There is no such thing as a fair fight in prison. When the guy fell to the floor, Joe explained that he kicked him several times in the body and head, wanting to make sure the guy thought twice before disrespecting him again. Joe says that after just having received a twenty-year sentence, he was not about to allow another prisoner to talk to him "any kind of way" without responding, consequences be damned. Joe explained that his victim was certain to have lifelong scars on his face as a result of the beating, and that whenever he looked in the mirror, he would think of Joe and regret the disrespectful way he had spoken to him.

Responding with lethal violence to what people outside of prison might consider trivial encounters is not unusual. Speaking with someone in a condescending manner might be construed as a challenge to one's manhood. For a person like Joe, one who chooses to present himself as "going all out," meaning he will respond aggressively to any type of behavior considered offensive, the way other prisoners perceive him is of paramount importance. For prisoners choosing to go all out, no cost is too high to maintain one's image.

As a result of Joe's fight, he passed a few weeks in segregation. Although he could have been, he was not charged with new criminal conduct for the fight. Instead, Bureau of Prisons administrators simply reclassified Joe from requiring medium security, to maximum security, and soon he was on his way from the county jail in North Carolina to the federal penitentiary in Atlanta.

GOIN' HARD

Just after Joe arrived, in 1994, the *New York Times* published an article identifying the federal penitentiary in Atlanta as the most violent penitentiary in the federal system. Joe recognized that one of the first things he needed when he arrived at Atlanta was to get himself "strapped." Accordingly, as soon as possible after he was processed into the institution, he went to the gym, started shooting baskets, and managed to participate in a game. It was the quickest way to immerse himself in the population, and within hours he had bonded with several other prisoners from New York.

Uptown, a prisoner whose roots are in Harlem, was playing on the same team with Joe. After the game Joe told him that he needed a joint. Uptown, immediately knowing that Joe was referring to a weapon and not a marijuana cigarette, said that he would have one for him after the dinner meal. When they met again, Joe said, Uptown delivered him a shank, or knife. Because prisoners must regularly walk through many metal detectors, the shank Uptown gave Joe was made of a hard clear plastic. The piece, he estimates, was about fourteen inches long. One end had a tapering point like an ice pick, or a stake that might have been effective in pitching a tent; the other end had a handle fashioned out of a cloth tape with a looped rope that could be secured around the wrist.

When Joe was admitted, like all prisoners, he was issued a pair of heavy leather work boots. Except for when he was playing basketball, he wore them everywhere. The boots were useful not only for their sheer weight in the event he found himself in a fight, but also as a hiding place for his shank; he kept the sharpened fiberglass weapon nestled between his leg and the boot, accessible to him at all times. Joe said that he never had to use it but felt it was necessary to keep it on his person in the event of an altercation, saying he would stab a man in a second if he felt threatened by him.

Being in possession of a weapon is a disciplinary infraction. If caught, the prisoner may be charged administratively with sanctions ranging from time in segregation to loss of good time. If the prisoner is considered a problem, the administration may instead refer the matter to the prosecuting attorney and seek new criminal charges. Neither threat concerned Joe. He explained that he would rather have his mother visit him in jail than visit his grave, and he elected to stay strapped at all times.

After a year of basketball and cards, and not having accumulated any new problems in the penitentiary, Joe's security level dropped. He was transferred to a medium-security prison in Allenwood, Pennsylvania, which had a larger population of New York prisoners. Upon arriving there, he followed his same pattern, playing basketball and cards and procuring a knife for himself. While in Allenwood, however, his knife came into use.

RESPECT AND RETALIATION

Joe, who considers himself "a grimy street fighter," had a problem with one of the players on his basketball team. During a game, B. K., his teammate, complained that the men were playing "like a bunch of bitches." As one of those players, Joe said he took offense at the remark. After the game he approached B. K. and told him he would not stand for anyone referring to him as bitch, even if the reference was made indirectly. Essentially, he was "calling B. K. out." Instead of apologizing or trying to clarify what he said, B. K. said he stood by his words. "Word," Joe said. "It's like that? I'll see you back at the unit."

B. K. was from Bedford-Stuyvesant, a rough housing project in Brooklyn. He shared a cell with Jerome, another prisoner from the same housing project. Prior to the game, Joe had been casual friends with both prisoners, but Jerome and B. K. were close friends. When Joe returned to the housing unit, he said he went to B. K.'s room and told him to step out. Joe considered his honor challenged, and he wanted to fight B. K. in the television room.

"Naw, go 'head wit that bullshit," B. K. said. "That shit is dead."

"Naw, fuck that," Joe said. "You could've deaded it on the court. Don't bitch out now."

"It's dead!"

Jerome had been sitting on his bunk laughing at the encounter. When he heard B. K. backing down from Joe's challenge, he intervened.

"A-yo hold up. Air Black calling you out, B. K. Get up and fight, you betta represent."

"Man, I ain't tryin' ta do nothin'," B. K. said.

"Then you better pack your shit and bounce," Jerome said. "I ain't havin' no punkass muthafucka livin' in here with me."

Just as all the commotion was going on, with B. K. and Jerome hollering at each other inside the cell, and Joe standing on the tier waiting for B. K. to come out, T-Money, one of B. K.'s friends came by to see about the problem.

"What up?" T-Money wanted to know.

"A-yo, we got this," Joe responded, not wanting any visitors or anyone else around.

"Ain't nobody talkin' to you, man. I'm here for B. K.," T-Money responded.

"Word?" Joe answered. "Well I'm 'bout to tear that cat out the frame. And if you wan' it, you can git it too."

"Shit yeah. I ain't duckin' no wreck," T-Money responded.

The two then went into the television room to settle the matter. The encounter occurred during dinner time, and the unit was empty. Joe explained how he landed several successive blows to T-Money's head. Realizing he had been beaten, T-Money then left the room. But Joe said he knew it wasn't over, as not only had he beaten T-Money in a fight, he also had humiliated B. K.

Joe expected there would be repercussions, and he prepared himself for battle. He returned to his room and began taping some large paperback books to his torso to shield against a potential stabbing. While he was taping himself up, two guards came in his room. Instead of wanting to do battle, Joe suspects that either T-Money or B. K. furtively passed information on to the staff. As a result of being "snitched out," guards not only found Joe in the act of taping himself up, they also found his shank. He was charged administratively, found guilty of committing a disciplinary infraction, and sent to segregation, or the hole.

Joe was released from the hole sixty-eight days later. Within thirty days after returning to the unit, Joe was sent back to the hole. This time for investigation purposes. He had been in the laundry room washing his clothes. Two other prisoners were also there when a guard walked in to conduct a random search of the room. During the search, he found a shank hidden in the ceiling. Although Joe insists he did not know anything about it, the lieutenant ordered him and the other two prisoners to segregation, where they would be confined to small cells for at least twenty-three hours a day. On that charge, Joe spent ninety days in the hole before he was released; ultimately, he never was charged with a disciplinary infraction.

THE HOLE

The hole is formally known as the segregated housing unit, or SHU (pronounced *shoe*). The prisoners are handcuffed during any movement inside the unit except when they are locked in their cells. They are restricted to as little as one shower per week, whereas in the general population they may shower daily. They do not have access to newspapers, television, or radio, and only limited access to books. Prisoners in the hole cannot smoke, and they are restricted to one five-minute phone call per month. In the hole there are no cards or table games. With mental stimulation absent, all one has to occupy his time is one's mind.

Prisoners may check in to the more onerous living conditions of SHU voluntarily for protective custody. Or, they may be placed there for administrative reasons, for investigation, or as a sanction for disciplinary violations. Whatever the reason, all prisoners confined to the hole live under the same conditions, exacerbating the difficulties of confinement. Joe says he got used to it, that it was just another part of the penitentiary, and his sentence was still running. He tried to hibernate through the time, occasionally sleeping for as many as twenty hours a day.

Not long after Joe was released from that stint in segregation, he inadvertently found himself enmeshed in another problem. Joe explained that he was standing in a line to use the telephone when an argument erupted. A Jamaican prisoner who had thirty days remaining on his sentence was using the phone when another prisoner accused him of jumping ahead in line. They argued, but the Jamaican did not hang up. Minutes later, the accuser returned and plunged a shank into the Jamaican's back. The Jamaican stumbled back to his cell, where he bled profusely and died.

During the subsequent investigation, a guard said that he had seen Joe in the line and assumed that he must have witnessed the murder. When questioned, Joe said that he did not see anything. The investigating officer pressed Joe, asking him whether he would tell him in the event that he had witnessed the murder. Joe categorically told him that no, he would not. Joe says that as a result of his answer, he was taken to segregation yet again for another investigation. By then he had gotten used to doing hole time.

The investigating guard's question of whether Joe would provide information in the event that he saw a murder was a simple question. Joe could have answered yes, that he would tell them anything he knew, while still maintaining that he did not see anything. I asked Joe why he would not avoid problems by taking that course.

"Man, I don't ever want them to think about it, that I would help them in any way," he said. "I just can't stand making them feel good, like they turned a muthafucka."

CHANGING OVER TIME

After Joe had served the eighth year of his sentence, the guidelines that measure an offender's security level changed. Prison space is a limited resource, with higher-security facilities costing much more to operate than lower-security prisons. Accordingly, administrators periodically revise the guidelines to enhance the probability that only the most dangerous offenders will be placed in the higher-security institutions. Under the new guidelines, Joe was eligible for camp placement. The only obstacle holding him back was the disciplinary infraction for possession of a knife that he received early in his sentence; high-level disciplinary infractions count against a prisoner's custody rating for ten years. Although his classification indicated he was ready for camp placement, because of those weapons charges, Joe's case manager indicated that he ought to first pass a year in a low-security prison with clear conduct before his request to transfer to a minimum-security camp be approved.

Joe was transferred to Fort Dix in 2000. He still had nine years remaining to serve on his sentence, but realizing that he now has the possibility of moving to a prison camp, he has decided to avoid activities that could bring him potential problems and threaten such a move. He plays basketball much less seriously, no longer plays poker, and most importantly, he does not keep a knife with him. Indeed, since learning that his security level has dropped, Joe's complete outlook about doing time has changed.

Joe recognizes that in a prison camp his level of freedom will increase significantly. After nine years of living in the midst of tension, Joe expects that a transfer to a minimum-security camp would make the second half of his sentence pass easier. So instead of putting himself in the middle of the action, he spends his time in his room writing, staying free of conversations with the men around him.

Now, instead of living a life on the edge of lethal violence, he spends his time writing about it. He has completed a manuscript he calls *Movin' Violation*. The story describes the fictional escapades of two young drug dealers from New York who make a living selling drugs and murdering those who get in their way. He now is working on a second manuscript and is making connections with publishers to market his urban stories. This diversion keeps Joe out of trouble and focused on avoiding disciplinary charges.

Joe explains his early adjustment to prison as being a consequence of his sentence. With twenty years ahead of him, and no chance of parole or anything to look forward to, he says that he had no reason to live any other way. He did not want to serve two decades as if he were walking on egg shells, but instead chose to confront his environment. Now that he sees the possibility of moving into an easier setting, he readily has readjusted; Joe makes every effort to avoid problems and focus on developing a skill he expects will help him upon release.

Dorian Jones, our next elephant-time prisoner, went through the unusual experience of becoming a father during his lengthy imprisonment. With the responsibilities of parenthood, Dorian exchanged his tendencies toward violence and vice for a commitment to furthering his education.

CATCHIN' TIME WHILE DOIN' TIME: DORIAN JONES

This prisoner could have been released after three years. Instead, he expects to serve nearly fifteen because of decisions he made early in his prison adjustment.

In 1989, Dorian was charged with armed robbery in the District of Columbia. In order to avoid a life sentence, Dorian agreed to plead guilty to charges of robbery, without a gun, which carried a sentence of between five and fifteen years. He was nineteen at the time, and had things gone well for Dorian in prison, he stood a good chance of being released at his first parole hearing, which was scheduled to come after three and one-half years. Things did not go well.

Dorian was cast into the notorious Lorton prison complex, which historically has confined all prisoners convicted in the District of Columbia. The penal code there may be similar to that of the federal justice system, but it represents a separate body of laws, applicable to citizens of the District of Columbia who commit crimes and are sentenced to prison.

The Lorton complex is located about twenty minutes from downtown Washington, D.C., in Fairfax, Virginia. Lorton is not a single prison, but rather a half-dozen different institutions with various levels of security. At its peak, Lorton confined close to fifteen thousand prisoners, many of whom had long histories of violence. In the late 1990s, Lorton had a reputation as a violent and corrupt prison system. Escapes were frequently in the news, and citizens in nearby communities did not feel safe with so

Dorian Jones

many violent prisoners within walking distance. Community leaders were successful in their efforts at having the Lorton complex closed. Now, District of Columbia prisoners are confined in the federal prison system.

SURVIVING: HIGH WALLS AND REPUTATIONS

Dorian had never been confined before, although he grew up in some of the roughest housing projects in Washington, D.C. Dorian says that he was not intimidated by the high walls around him or the thousands of predators with whom he suddenly was living at Lorton. "It didn't matter where they sent me," Dorian said. "I was gonna run the cell house just like I ran my projects." Standing about five-feet-ten, weighing close to two hundred pounds, Dorian is built like a linebacker. In fact, with the scars on his face, he looks like he played the sport on asphalt, without a helmet. At first sight, Dorian looks tough, unable to conceal his stocky frame. Still, at nineteen he was one of the younger prisoners assigned to Lorton, and he was determined to establish a reputation that would ensure he would not be mistaken for prey.

I asked Dorian whether he considered the possibility of that early parole date. He said he thought about it some, but other people whom he met in the system began with small numbers, too. They all became enmeshed in activities that left them in prison for decades, some with no hope of ever going home.

Perhaps surprisingly to the average observer, many prisoners confined in violent penitentiaries think only secondarily or in the abstract of release or the world they have left behind. The here and now—what they taste, feel, hear, smell, and see—is what concerns them on the inside. Dorian told me, "I'd a liked to get out on parole and all that. But it ain't easy. Everyone be trying to take advantage in here. I ain't with that. I don't care if I got ten years or one day left. Ain't no one gonna disrespect me. I'll put a knife in him, leave him with his guts hangin' out." Dorian explained that as a younger prisoner in an adult facility, others were always looking "to get over" on him.

His first altercation came within months of his arrival at Lorton. A prisoner in his dorm, he explained, was making skullcaps that Dorian liked because a cap would help his hair grow in waves. He called the cap a "doo-rag." Dorian approached the prisoner and asked him what he charged to make the caps. The inmate told Dorian to provide him with the materials and three packs of cigarettes. Dorian complied and waited patiently for his new head piece. A few days went by, then a week. Yet Dorian saw that the hat maker had delivered doo-rags to others, and the material looked suspiciously like the same material Dorian had provided.

Tired of waiting, and sensing that he was being had, Dorian says he approached the inmate and asked him how long it was going to take before he received his hat. The guy came off a little too aggressive for Dorian's taste, telling him that he would get to it at his convenience. If he didn't like it, he told Dorian, he could take his material back and "go fuck himself." Dorian noticed the material had been cut into pieces, and his antagonist did not offer to return the three packs of cigarettes Dorian had given him already.

Prisons leave thousands of men together for years at a time. They never escape each other's presence, as they share the same chow hall, the same living units, the same showers. They have very little of value in their possession. What prisoners do value is their reputations. People outside of the fences may choose to avoid each other, but in prison such an option does not exist. If one allows another to take cigarettes, or anything that belongs to another, soon thereafter, Dorian explains, others will be looking for "ass," or to exploit one sexually. His altercation convinced him that the man was trying to bully him, to take advantage of Dorian's youth and inexperience in the Lorton system. Being a product of Washington, D.C.'s streets, Dorian says that kind of situation was right up his alley.

RETALIATION AND NATURAL WEAPONS

Dorian left the living area and let a few hours pass in order to lull his oppressor into a state of complacency. Later that day, when he figured his target had forgotten about the situation and was no longer expecting anything, he walked to the supply room and grabbed a steel mop wringer by its handle.

At that time, Dorian was still rather new in the system and did not have ready access to a shank or a pipe, weapons that prisoners frequently use in violent altercations. Shanks are pieces of metal or spikes that prisoners collect from old desks, chairs, radiators, fences, or wherever they can find them. Prisoners moisten the concrete floors, then grind the metal piece against the abrasive surface to file down the edges and point of the metal. When the weapon is ready to penetrate flesh, prisoners wrap the other end in heavy tape to fashion a handle. No prison in the United States is without a large supply of such weapons.

Dorian did not have access to a shank at that moment, but he always kept himself close to what he called natural weapons, anything that he could put his hands on in a hurry when violence called. One alternative might be filling a pillowcase with canned foods, padlocks, or heavy metal objects that would enable him to use the pillowcase as a kind of club to beat his opponent across the head. Another alternative is a metal folding chair, which, he explained, can be quite effective in bringing down an opponent.

Dorian chose the mop ringer as his weapon because it was made of metal, had a long handle he could use for leverage, and weighed about twenty pounds. No one would look at him suspiciously for walking down the hall with his natural weapon. They would just think he was about to mop his room. Dorian stepped up to his adversary and smashed him over the head with the heavy steel contraption. The badly wounded inmate stumbled out into the prison's common area, his head spurting blood like a fountain. He collapsed in front of the guard's desk and medical attention came quickly, likely saving the victim's life.

"Were you trying to kill him?" I asked Dorian.

"I wasn't even thinkin' about that. Just didn't want no muthafucka takin' me for no punk bitch."

Dorian explained that if he did not do anything after Mr. Doo-rag had cut up his material and swindled him of his cigarettes, word quickly would have spread through the Lorton compound that he was an easy mark. Regardless of how much time he had to serve, Dorian said he was not going to live with that stigma, with being a target of every predator in the system. At that price, he was willing to sacrifice early parole.

Immediately following that incident, administrators transferred Dorian to a higher-security area of the prison. While there, Dorian says he participated in several of the vocational training programs available, spending time learning about drywall, painting, and other building trades. He had quit school in the tenth grade, and he was not really interested in pursuing an academic program at that stage of his confinement. Dorian did not see any benefit in going through the high school equivalency classes; they had no practical value to him. By learning the building trades, he reasoned, at least he would be able to find employment upon his release.

Despite that premise, Dorian remained committed to living his life inside the fences. In other words, although he expected to be released some day, he was not willing to challenge the lifestyles of the other prisoners around him. They ran wild in the corrupt Lorton prison system, continuing their street behavior inside the penitentiary—and so did Dorian.

Dorian explained that early in his sentence, he began working with corrupt guards. For twenty dollars he could buy an hour's worth of privacy during a visit with a girlfriend. Women he knew from the streets, or women he met through other prisoners then came to visit him. They would pass him a twenty-dollar bill that he in turn would pass to the guard. The guard then would turn his head as Dorian and his visitor disappeared into an unsupervised room for their hour of sex. For the entire time he was confined in Lorton, Dorian says he was able to buy that privacy during every visit.

Dorian did not necessarily need a female visitor. He said there was no shortage of female guards who doubled as prostitutes inside the prison. Although walls encapsulated the thousands of prisoners at Lorton, Dorian says it was a miniature city where cash payments carried the day, prevailing over most prison regulations.

I asked Dorian how he obtained the income that was necessary to participate in all the illicit activities at Lorton. He said that he earned sometimes as much as a thousand dollars each month through the prison's underground economy; just as he had on the streets, Dorian sold drugs to earn money. Because the rules were so lax, Dorian said he could smuggle marijuana, cocaine, or heroin into the prison rather easily through the visiting room. On the rare occasions when the administration tightened up on the searching of prisoners leaving the visiting room, Dorian said that friendly guards whom he had known from the housing projects where he was raised would give him advance notice. For a fee, these guards sometimes acted as mules, bringing drugs into the prison for Dorian so that he could distribute them to others.

Another popular and often-cited way of smuggling drugs into prison is to have female visitors insert the drugs into noninflated balloons. They then coat the outside of the balloon with a cooking oil that acts as a lubricant, and during a kiss in the visiting room, the balloon is transferred into the prisoner's mouth. He swallows it. Once he moves beyond the searches that separate the visiting room from the prison housing units, he either regurgitates the balloon or allows it to pass through his body and later pulls it from his stool. The high demand for drugs in prison encourages prison hustlers to do whatever is necessary to smuggle in their contraband.

THE LOVE TRIANGLE

During his third year at Lorton, Dorian says he became involved in his second violent altercation with another prisoner. Dorian explained that his problem began because of a relationship he had with a female guard. He had known her from his housing project, and she knew that Dorian was involved in the prison's drug rackets; he was a player. She asked Dorian for money, and he agreed to provide it in exchange for regular sex.

The guard's keys gave her access to offices and locked rooms where they could have privacy, so she agreed to Dorian's terms. Dorian said he had enjoyed his arrangement with this particular guard for several months, but that he was not the only prisoner enjoying her sexual favors. Another prisoner actually developed feelings for her and demanded that Dorian stop seeing her. It was a love triangle. Dorian was not one to take demands from other prisoners, so the two had words. Dorian followed up his argument by rushing into the other prisoner's cell and stabbing him twice in the chest. By then, he had shanks stashed at several locations in the prison. "I didn't want to kill him," Dorian said, "I just wanted to hurt him real bad. I didn't care 'bout him. Had to let him know he couldn't be comin' at me like that. You know how we do."

The victim of Dorian's wrath did not die, and following the prisoner code of silence, he did not reveal that it was Dorian who had stabbed him. Nor did anyone else come forward to identify Dorian as the assailant. Accordingly, authorities had no evidence with which to prosecute Dorian for the stabbing. Even if they did, however, stabbings and violence are routine and run-of-the-mill at Lorton; they are rarely prosecuted. Still, authorities were certain that Dorian was responsible, and so they arranged his transfer to a still higher security area of the prison. While he was there, Dorian continued his essentially negative adjustment to prison, participating in the distribution of drugs. Inevitably, it caught up with him.

One day he was returning to the housing units from the recreation yard. He and three friends had been smoking marijuana, and he had one gram of heroin, as well as a shank, in his pockets. As he and his friends walked through the yard into the housing units, a team of guards stopped the group and ordered a search. Dorian suspects snitches may have seen them smoking pot and turned them in. Upon being stopped, Dorian says he tried to reach into his pocket so he could grab his contraband and throw it; however, the guards saw his move and rushed him. They tackled him to the ground, confiscating the drugs and the weapon on his person.

A NEW TERM: A BADGE OF HONOR

Dorian explained that he tried denying ownership of the drugs and accused the guards of planting them on him. Prison officials did not accept his explanation. This time they had the hard evidence for prosecution. Soon, Dorian was charged in a new criminal indictment in federal court that accused him of distributing drugs inside the Lorton prison. After his conviction, a federal judge sentenced Dorian to a two-year sentence, to be served after he completed the five-to-fifteen-year sentence he was serving in Lorton for robbery. This prosecution earned Dorian a badge of honor inside Lorton, providing proof that he was a solid convict.

Dorian then went to his parole hearing. By that time he was well immersed in the prison subculture and had little hope of receiving any relief from his sentence. He was then in his early twenties and had been serving his time with others in maximum security who already had been incarcerated for north of a decade. He had no expectations of serving anything less, and he was not surprised when the District of Columbia parole board recommended that Dorian serve his sentence through to expiration. This recommendation required Dorian to remain a prisoner at Lorton for nearly eleven years of his sentence. By this time he was not particularly bothered because he did not see much distinction between his life in the projects and his life in the penitentiary.

Dorian became even more isolated from thoughts about society after his fourth year in prison. Prior to his incarceration, he had lived with his mother, and he had close ties to her. She was familiar with the ways of the streets, Dorian says, and was never judgmental with regard to his legal predicament. His mother supported him and came regularly to visit him inside the prison. She told him to try and stay out of trouble inside the prison so he could come home sooner, but at the same time, she warned him about letting anyone take advantage of him. She impressed upon Dorian that it was important for him to "be his own man." After all, Dorian's mother had introduced him to the drug rackets. She sold drugs in Washington, D.C., and was not against Dorian participating in the same schemes. Dorian began smoking and selling marijuana when he was eleven; his mother was proud that he had the wherewithal to rob the drug stashes of older kids in the neighborhood. Telling Dorian that he was growing into a man and would have to deal with the consequences of his actions as they presented themselves, his mother was fully supportive of the weapons he kept and encouraged him to use them when necessary. Prison was nothing to be ashamed of for Dorian, as his own mother had served time in a woman's prison when he was five and did not come home until he was eight. Besides his mother, Dorian has many relatives who are serving time or have in the past. Confinement held no stigma for him.

A DEATH IN THE FAMILY

After his fourth year in the prison system, his mother died of AIDS. The dreaded disease struck and killed her quickly, leaving Dorian with little time to prepare himself mentally for the loss of the one person in the world whom he actually loved and respected. Even today his eyes tear when he talks about her.

Given his prison record, the administration declined Dorian's request to attend his mother's funeral. Dealing with a close family member's death from the darkness of a prison cell brought Dorian pain that far surpassed anything he had ever experienced. "When I heard my moms died, I just used to lie on my rack. But there was no relaxin'. I couldn't sleep. But I couldn't cry either. Ain't 'bout to cry in the penitentiary, know what I'm sayin'? Everyone wantin' to do what they always do. Wanted to get their smoke on or whatever. So I just had to try blockin' everything out."

Family crises happen every day in human life and are never easy to bear. Family members who live within the community, however, have the liberty to console each other and allow pains to heal. Not so for most prisoners. As a prisoner, Dorian was not recognized as being a part of the world; he was unworthy of mourning with family at his mother's funeral.

His mother's death was an awakening, or a turning point, for Dorian. When he learned that she had died, he says he tried to find some place to be alone. A prisoner is ever aware that a guard or another prisoner can break into his space and steal the time needed for thoughts and feelings. Time is never one's own inside prison walls. There is no place to weep without being spied upon by the thousands of preying eyes that hunt for weakness. Dorian had years to serve, and after his mother's death, he purged himself of all emotional ties to the world and urged his heart to petrify.

Dorian's new family became the hooligans around him. He sold drugs with them inside the prison, providing backup whenever it was necessary. Sometimes the backup was needed for violent altercations, other times it was needed for an alibi. Whatever the situation called for, Dorian was ready to provide support for his prison family.

One of his new family members was caught in a drug bust. Dorian was not present at the time of the actual seizure, but that did not stop him from providing an alibi. The guards had been inspecting the property of all the prisoners in the dorm. They picked some prisoners at random and led them into another room for a strip search. One of the people they stopped to search was a friend of Dorian's. When he was taken into the other room for the strip search, guards found a few grams of heroin hidden in balloons that had been inserted in his rectum. The prisoner was prosecuted in federal court for this offense.

During the prisoner's trial, Dorian agreed to appear as a witness on his behalf. Dorian testified that he had been present during the strip search and that no drugs were found. After being sworn in as a witness, Dorian stated that the guards did not find any drugs during the search, but had instead planted the drugs in an attempt to extort money from his friend. Largely because of Dorian's testimony, his friend's trial ended in a hung jury.

Unfortunately for Dorian, the government did not abandon the case. During the second trial, Dorian's testimony was not effective. The government called all of the guards who participated in the search to the stand. They testified that when they conducted the strip search on the defendant, they had taken him to a private room and Dorian was not present. Because they conducted the strip search in a separate room, the guards explained that it would have been impossible for Dorian to witness the search. Not only did three officers testify, they also brought written logs of the incident with them to corroborate their testimony. Believing the officers rather than the stone-faced Dorian, this time the jury convicted the defendant of the drug offense.

Soon after the trial concluded, Dorian was indicted for perjury. He was tried and convicted. The federal judge sentenced Dorian to an additional twenty-four-month sentence, to be served after his original robbery sentence and his second sentence for distributing drugs in the prison.

The additional time did not faze Dorian. He was convinced that it would not be the last time he would be charged with new criminal conduct while in custody. If his friends in the prison called on him again, he said he would be there to support them.

At that time in his life, Dorian had no allegiance to society. He may have wanted to leave prison and begin his life again, but he did not see that as a viable option. He was living as a prisoner in one of the most corrupt prison systems in the United States, surviving the only way he knew how. All he needed was access to a shank, he said, and a piece of stone where others had a heart. For Dorian, life inside the walls of Lorton penitentiary was not unlike the life he lived growing up in housing projects. Drugs, sex, and violence were ubiquitous. He did not believe that the society outside of the prison walls wanted anything to do with him. Dorian had accepted that he would live out his life in cages with other men. Whatever came his way, good or bad, was just part of the life he had grown accustomed to leading.

A NEW LIFE: A NEW BEGINNING

One of Dorian's friends in the prison had a daughter who was Dorian's age. During a visit, Dorian's friend introduced him to his daughter. She subsequently began coming back to see Dorian, and together they would buy their hour of intimacy from one of the complicitous guards. Several months later, Dorian's new friend told him she was pregnant and that he was about to be a father.

At first, the news of his friend's pregnancy upset Dorian. He was then in his mid-twenties, and he knew he had several years of prison ahead of him. Not only did he have to finish four more years at Lorton, but he also had an additional four years to serve in the federal prison system upon the completion of his Lorton sentence. Dorian also recognized that his behavior inside Lorton's walls easily could lead him to more problems with the law. Besides that, he did not want or need the emotional baggage of a child. He just did not care, did not consider himself father material.

It is not that Dorian did not want children, he says. He came from a close family with five siblings. Had he made different life choices—choices that would not have led him to prison—he says that he would have liked to live as a family man. However, that was not his situation. As a prisoner, he would not be able to provide his child with a home, nor be able to participate in educating or raising the child. He did not want to bring a child into the world if it meant the child would be leading a difficult life, one that most likely would result in the child's having to deal with law enforcement all of his or her life. Despite Dorian's misgivings, however, the mother was adamant about carrying the pregnancy to term and raising the baby herself. She and Dorian continued their relationship as friends, and as Dorian watched the pregnancy develop, he became more involved in the relationship. After he felt the baby kick, he even became enthusiastic about his imminent role as a father.

His friend gave birth to a baby girl in 1997. She named the child Sade, after the popular R&B singer. When the mother brought Sade to see Dorian for the first time, Sade was only a few days old. He says the moment he held his infant daughter in his arms, he realized that he now had a new reason to live. The heart of stone again turned to a heart of flesh and began beating for someone else.

After the child's birth, Dorian's focus changed, and he began at once to accept responsibility for his actions. He says he abandoned his role as a purveyor of contraband within the Lorton prison and disassociated himself from the violence. He was no longer willing to serve all of his life in prison. Although he felt society had rejected him before, Sade gave him a reason to try to do whatever he could to return to the outside world again. He wanted to hasten his release so he could live as more than only Sade's biological father. Dorian realized that he was missing out on life; he wanted out of the abnormal world of cages and guards and shanks and census counts.

And thus, the birth of Sade brought the birth of a new Dorian. He kept an eight-hour job in the prison in order to avoid the idleness that always led him to problems. When he was not working on his prison job detail, Dorian participated more actively in vocational programs; he began studying independently in preparation for the high school equivalency test he now wanted to pass. By then, Dorian had been out of school for over a decade, so studying did not come easily to him. Nonetheless, he persisted and began to improve his reading, comprehension, writing, and math skills. Progress was slow, but he was moving forward.

The biggest change for Dorian, and perhaps the most important, was his commitment to stay away from the drugs and the violence that had been so much a part of his life during the early years of his sentence. He changed his circle of friends. Instead of the key players in the Lorton drug rackets, Dorian began associating with tutors who worked in the education department.

The most significant evidence of Dorian's commitment to change is that since his first visit with Sade in 1997, he has maintained a clean disciplinary record. This is the same person who during the first seven years of his sentence received not only scores of disciplinary infractions but was charged and convicted in federal court on two separate occasions for new criminal conduct.

While serving the final years of his sentence at Lorton, Dorian suffered two additional family losses. His grandmother, seventy-eight years old, was found dead in a river, presumably murdered. Several months later, his younger brother was murdered. Dorian knew his brother was trafficking in drugs, and he understood from first-hand experience the possibility of violence that was part of his brother's choices. Still, the loss of these two family members, after the death of his mother, further strengthened Dorian's resolve to develop skills that would lead him away from a life on the streets. More important than his own life, Dorian says, is doing whatever he can to ensure that his daughter does not live in the hell that has been his family's life.

Dorian finished serving his robbery sentence in 2000, and federal marshals transferred him to the low-security federal prison at Fort Dix, New Jersey, to begin his additional four-year sentence. Dorian was now thirty and had already served nearly eleven years.

The Bureau of Prisons' decision that Dorian would serve the remaining commitment in a low-security prison reflects Dorian's newly documented positive adjustment to his confinement. Since Dorian's arrival at Fort Dix, he has conducted himself in a manner that he is confident will keep him free of problems during the remainder of his sentence.

PREPARING FOR RELEASE

Continuing his commitment to develop skills that will help him upon release, Dorian began participating in high school equivalency courses, and months later was awarded a GED certificate. Since then, Dorian took a placement test and was admitted into a community college program. Enrolled in his second college semester now, Dorian hopes to complete his associate's degree before his sentence expires in December of 2003.

Dorian works full-time in food services. His shift begins at 4:00 A.M. five days each week. He reports to the kitchen and remains there until the conclusion of the noon meal. While there, Dorian wipes tables, collects food trays, and performs general cleaning duties. He chose the job, he says, because it keeps him busy and from having to interact with others. All relationships in prison, Dorian explains, are potential problems. "Sometimes I try to count how many days I can pass without saying one word to anyone."

When he is not working, Dorian studies for his classes or struggles to teach himself to type. Dorian is determined not to repeat the bad decisions he made at Lorton. He recognizes that had he adjusted more positively during the first years of his sentence, he likely would have been paroled after serving just over three years. Instead, because of the decisions he made, Dorian will serve at least fourteen years.

I asked Dorian what he expects to achieve upon his release. He says he does not give the outside too much thought. It is still too far away, he says, and too many things can happen. Dorian says that he only thinks about getting outside, not what he will do when he actually gets out. However, when pressed about what type of work he wants to pursue, Dorian said he would like to work with real estate. "That sounds like good work, buyin' and sellin' houses. I'd have time to spend with my daughter. I ain't 'bout to take any kind of job, know what I'm sayin'? Got to pay me at least a hundred thousand a year. Got to get me a Lex an all that."

Like many prisoners, Dorian has expectations that upon his release, employers will overlook the many years he has been separated from society, the fact that he is a convicted felon, that he has no work experience outside of prison, and that he has a substandard educational background. Despite having served his entire adult life in prison, Dorian expects that he will not earn less than a six-figure annual income, or at least that is what he says. He is unrealistic, and he is bound to be disappointed.

His job expectations notwithstanding, Dorian says he wants the privilege of helping to raise his daughter. He wants to do what he can to educate her and to ensure that she does not suffer the same abject misery he has endured in his life thus far.

I asked Dorian what he will tell Sade about the perils of trafficking in drugs. He says he "will tell her the bad and the good about it," explaining that "it can help you get money quick and that drugs makes some people feel good." The years of his imprisonment, and even his later adjustment, apparently, have not reversed what Dorian learned from his own mother. Dorian's story is not atypical. Many prisoners who begin serving their terms in volatile institutions seek to blend in as quickly as possible and suffer the consequences for years to come.

In the next profile, Hector Colon describes how he adjusted after being sent to a maximum-security prison at nineteen, with a sentence that exceeded forty years. It begins with trouble.

BECOMING AN ADULT IN THE PENITENTIARY: HECTOR COLON

How a nineteen-year-old prison thug began his adjustment in maximum security.

Hector Colon was nineteen when he began serving his prison term. He had been convicted for participating with others in a narcotics ring that distributed heroin in New York City. With no beard growth on his face, weighing 105 pounds, and standing under five-feet-six, Hector appeared ready for junior high school. Instead, he was embarking on a journey that would lead him to Leavenworth, the ominous maximum-security federal penitentiary in Kansas. Although not yet out of his teens, Hector received a sentence of 511 months, or just under forty-three years.

For two years prior to his conviction, Hector was held without bail in the Metropolitan Correctional Center (MCC) in New York City. Had he behaved himself during that pretrial phase of his sentence, Bureau of Prisons administrators likely would have sent him to a medium-security prison. In light of Hector's difficulties in adjustment at the MCC, however, they determined that he needed the more rigid environment of a penitentiary. His diminutive stature notwithstanding, Hector stayed in trouble. He and his clique of Puerto Rican toughs terrorized others inside the MCC and the court bullpens. Particularly, Hector told me, he and his friends would target rats—those who were cooperating with the government in the prosecution of others.

Hector Colon

A PERSPECTIVE ON RATS

"Rats was the reason we all was serving time," Hector complained.

When inmates transfer between their court proceedings and the jail, they carry news with them. The most popular news to bring back is information on which inmates have "gone bad" or turned into witnesses for the prosecution. As might be expected in the backward world of prison, a so-called good guy is defiant of the criminal justice system until the end of incarceration or life itself. The prisoners with whom I serve time characterize John Gotti as a good guy; Rudolf Giuliani is a bad guy because he "has hurt so many people with his vindictive prosecutions."

Prisoners like Hector consider themselves victims, reasoning that they would not have had problems with the law if it were not for all the snitches who went bad. It is as if the bars and institutional controls somehow block their ability to see any relationship between their current status as prisoners of the criminal justice system on one hand, and their own actions on the other. Instead, they attribute all their problems to malicious prosecutors and those who helped the government build a case against them. Hector and his crew retaliated against snitches. Inflicting violence upon them may not have made a difference in the cases of Hector and his fellow thugs, but their defiance helped them pass the time.

Allegations of someone cooperating with the government were enough to warrant a beating. If someone came into the jail with a reputation of having cooperated with the government, or if someone even looked weak, as if they "might go bad," that was enough for those in Hector's group to start their campaigns of terror. If they could not acquire shivs, they manufactured weapons out of items sold through the commissary. They would take three or four combination locks, for example, insert them into a sock, and use it as a swinging club for thwacking a target's head. Or they collected heavy batteries and used them to pelt perceived informants during meal times or while watching television. Another effective weapon was collecting hot sauce and jalapeno peppers, then squirting the stinging juice into a victim's eyes to blind him.

For Hector, the persistent attacks were a combination of recreation and revenge. Ironically, they also may have been a strategic defense for him. By creating a reputation for himself as a prison terror, he simultaneously was keeping potential prisoner predators from focusing on him. Since he was young and slightly built compared to the others, concerns about being attacked were never far from his thoughts. Hector's actions resulted in literally scores of disciplinary infractions during the months he was held at the MCC. The charges were serious. Some were for fighting, some for assault, some for possession of weapons. He once was charged with attempting to manufacture a bomb; guards found that he had been hoarding sulfur collected from matches, electrical wires, and batteries. Instead of charging him in the crowded criminal courts for his actions, administrators elected to handle Hector administratively. One way to do that was by sending him to a maximum-security prison after he received his sentence.

FEAR AND THE "HOT HOUSE"

Despite his eagerness to incite trouble while at the MCC, Hector told me that he was afraid when he learned he was being sent to Leavenworth. Leavenworth, the oldest federal penitentiary in the United States, opened over 100 years ago. Peter Earley (1992) detailed the lives of several prisoners held in this notorious prison in his book *The Hot House*. Earley, a journalist by profession, received unprecedented approval from a former director of the Bureau of Prisons to enter Leavenworth unescorted. He was allowed to mix freely with prisoners and staff members in order to collect information that would help him write about the prison, providing his readers with a glimpse of life inside the impenetrable walls. Hector read Earley's book while he was at the MCC; it terrified him to learn that he would begin serving his sentence in Leavenworth with the predators Earley had so vividly described.

Hector remembers sitting on the bunk in his cell at the MCC after having received the news of his imminent transfer. "It was one thing to receive the long sentence," he says, "but that wasn't as bad as the fear I felt when they said I was going to Leavenworth. I read about the violence inside that place, the rapes. Being small, I was worried." Hundreds of the prisoners at Leavenworth are serving life sentences and expect to die within its walls. For some, a physically small prisoner like Hector undoubtedly would prove a tempting target for exploitation. He expected others would force him to fight for survival every day. While looking outside through the narrow window in his cell, dreading his imminent fate, Hector told me that he remembers a tear falling down his cheek. The way he described his experience to me, it was like he had been in Hades reading about the fire and constant torment of hell, then learned that Satan's door was the next stop.

Despite the torment he felt inside, Hector said he knew that he could not allow anyone else to know he was afraid. After having lived for two years as a thug inside the MCC, he knew that the worst thing he could do was show fear. Instead, Hector kept his tough face on and waited for the move. When it came, and he was being processed inside the high walls of Leavenworth, one of the guard's questions gave him another reality shock. "In case of death," the guard asked, "whom do you want us to notify?" That question, Hector explained, shook him to the marrow of his bones. He did not know how to take it. When the guard told him that it was just a routine question, Hector did not feel any better.

He walked up the stairs as instructed, and the officer in charge of the tier told him that he had been assigned to cell 616. It was after 5:00 P.M. when he approached the cell, and the prisoners were waiting to be released for the evening meal. Lightfoot, the prisoner in 616 was not going to chow, though. He was sitting on his bed. When Hector approached the cell and said he had been assigned there, Lightfoot did not welcome him. Instead, he used an aggressive tone to tell Hector that he would not be allowed to sleep there for more than one night.

"Yo, my man," Hector said he told Lightfoot, "I just come in with a fresh 511 months to serve. I'm tired. I just want to sleep. We can deal with all that bullshit later."

"Naw, fuck that," Lightfoot said. "We're gonna deal with it now. My cellmate is in the hole on some bullshit and he's getting out tomorrow. He's coming back here. When he does, you're out. I don't care where you go, but you ain't staying here. Dig?"

It was not the way that Hector wanted to start off his time in Leavenworth. But he knew it was a crucial test. He had not been on the tier for fifteen minutes and already he was in an altercation that he expected could determine the remainder of his time. That is part of prison, and no matter what the consequences, Hector had to stand his ground. Every altercation has an immediacy to it, and nothing can be put off. One must face the present, whatever it may bring.

Coming into any prison brings the luck of the draw. Some prisoners are fortunate and are assigned to share quarters with a reasonable individual. Some, on the other hand, have Hector's luck and face a challenge at once. If Hector submissively backed down, Lightfoot, the Native American prisoner who already had been assigned to cell 616 and marked it as his territory, might have tried to push Hector further. Guards would be locking the two in the cell in a matter of hours, and for Hector, there was no telling what the evening would bring.

Although Lightfoot towered over him and outweighed him by at least a hundred pounds, Hector said he looked Lightfoot sternly in the eye and told him, "I'm where they sent me. We'll deal with tomorrow when tomorrow comes. You don't like that, then do what you gotta do."

PREPARING FOR WAR

Seeing that Hector was not about to retreat, Lightfoot mumbled something and went off to chow. Hector knew the altercation was not over. When Lightfoot left, Hector walked over to see Guerro, a prisoner whom he had met at the MCC but now was assigned to the same tier at Leavenworth. Hector told him he needed a blade like the ones they used at the MCC, the small disposable razors issued for shaving. Hector was an expert at removing the blades and melting them into a toothbrush for use as a slicing weapon. If Lightfoot approached him in the cell, Hector could keep him away by slicing the blade across his face. Many people in prison walk around with badly healed welts across their cheeks and necks from such razor slices.

"Man you ain't been here but an hour," Guerro said. "What you need a blade for?"

Hector explained the problem with his cellmate. "'Bout to be some shit in the cell."

Instead of giving him the tiny razor blade that Hector requested, Guerro shoved aside a steam pipe that ran through his room. Behind it was his hiding place for a weapon. Guerro pulled out a sword that Hector estimates was twenty inches in length. "In here," Guerro told Hector, "these are the blades people fight with." Guerro also told Hector to watch himself, as Lightfoot was serving a term for murder and was known to have a mean streak.

The shank was actually a sharpened piece of pointed steel. One end was heavily taped, with a looped rope around the end for effective gripping. Hector said he had never seen such a weapon but knew it would be effective in stopping an attack from Lightfoot in the event that his aggression escalated after the guard locked them in the cell later that night. Hector hid the shank down the leg of his pants and returned to his cell. Skipping dinner, he made his bed and crawled on top to read the packets of information he received during the admissions procedure. He kept the shank within easy reach by his side and intended to sleep with it.

As the prisoners began returning to the tier after the evening meal, Hector heard a loud commotion outside his room. He walked outside the door and saw that it was Lightfoot arguing with the officer in charge, telling him that he had to move Hector out of the cell because his roommate would be returning tomorrow. The officer was not budging. When Lightfoot raised the tone of his voice, the guard told him to cuff up. Lightfoot was taken to segregation, and he must have been transferred out of Leavenworth because Hector never saw him again.

Hector says a guardian angel must have been watching over him. If Lightfoot had returned to the cell, he was convinced one of them was going to be carried out by the medics. Instead, Hector had the cell to himself for the next few days. While he was alone, he had time to think about what could have happened. He felt as if he was in danger, as if death—his or someone else's—was as close as his next meal. He later learned that Lightfoot already was serving a life term, which was not unusual behind the Leavenworth walls. Hector knew that he, too, might never get out of prison. During those first nights in the cell, he convinced himself that although he might die in prison, he knew there would be no fair fights—only survivors. He began to prepare himself mentally to do whatever was necessary to survive.

When he finally did receive a roommate, it was Jack, an older, born-again Christian, whom Hector welcomed as someone who would not bring problems to the cell. Hector offered Jack the lower bunk, which many considered a privilege. Although the lower bunk made it easier to relax, as climbing in and out of the upper bunk was a hassle, Hector was thinking in terms of survival. In case of attack, he thought it would be easier to defend himself from an elevated position. During those first weeks at Leavenworth, all of Hector's moves were calculated in terms of how they would effect his survival. It was as if he was at war, living in a trench, armed and expecting attack at any given moment.

In high-security prisons, a prisoner's race, ethnicity, and geographic region of origin frequently play a role in his adjustment. That is especially true when the prisoner initially walks into the facility and is not well acquainted with the others. No formal rules of segregation exist, but the prisoners segregate themselves voluntarily. Blacks sit in one area, whites in another, and Hispanics in another. Even the food lines through which prisoners pass to eat are black and white. At Leavenworth, the racial seating areas were further divided by the inmates according to East Coast and West Coast origins. Higher-security prisons are territorial, with each group looking after its own. In lower-security prisons, on the other hand, race and other differences play much less significant roles.

STAND UP, FIT IN

Hector was young, small, Puerto Rican, and from New York. Other Puerto Ricans with status inside Leavenworth heard about him, likely through Guerro. One leader from New York City asked Hector to present his paperwork to verify that he had never cooperated with the law. Assuming the paperwork validated that he was a good guy, meaning he had never provided any assistance to authorities, he would be accepted. Hector's paperwork showed that he was indeed stand-up, and he was then allowed to eat in the Puerto Rican section of the chow hall and was introduced to all Puerto Rican members of the Leavenworth community. "They showed me all the love in the world," Hector explained. His affiliation with the group protected him in certain ways. Indeed, if anyone from outside the group targeted Hector for harassment, it would be a breach of prison etiquette, an indication that the aggressor considered the Puerto Ricans soft, and an open sign of disrespect inviting conflict.

His Puerto Rican mentors, Hector explained, taught him how to live in Leavenworth. They taught him to be awake, dressed, with his steel-toed boots laced up before the doors were unlocked at 6:00 A.M. each morning. "I learned to live my life as if I might die on any given day," Hector observed. "Being my size, I lived every minute ready for war." He never took naps in the day time. He worked full-time in the UNICOR factory. After work he exercised. During his first years in the penitentiary Hector gained sixty pounds. In order to create a more ferocious look, and to fit in, he had ten tattoos inked on his body. After his exercise, Hector watched television until the 10:00 P.M. lockdown, at which time he slept until 5:30 A.M. each morning. This became the routine he expected to live until the year 2028, when he was scheduled for release.

Hector's counselor, who is responsible for job assignments, recommended a UNICOR factory job because it would provide him with a structured environment. Each morning Hector joined his friends for breakfast in the chow hall, and from there he went to the factory where he worked moving boxes between 7:30 A.M. and 3:30 P.M., Monday through Friday. Hector dropped out of school in the tenth grade to start selling drugs. Because he did not have a high school diploma, he was required to participate in the GED program.

At Leavenworth, the factory offers a GED program for UNICOR workers. Inmates assigned to the factory spend a portion of each day in UNICOR-sponsored classes until they pass the GED exam. Hector attended the classes reluctantly; he was completely indifferent to passing the high school equivalency exam. "I expected to be in prison until I was fifty-eight, if I ever got out," Hector said. "I didn't see how an education was going to do me any good. Those classes didn't teach what I was needin' to know 'bout livin' in prison."

Perhaps half the people who come to prison lack a high school education. Congress has passed legislation tying the possibility of receiving good time credits to an individual's obtaining a high school equivalency certificate. Prisoners like Hector must participate in the GED classes until they pass the exam. Otherwise, they lose privileges such as access to the telephone, the commissary, and visitors, or suffer whatever sanction the unit team deems appropriate, including the potential loss of good time. Still, education meant little to Hector.

Hector's comfort level rose by his fourth month in Leavenworth. It was about then that he had his first altercation. He was in the television room when he found himself in an argument with a prisoner from Chicago over a basketball game between the Knicks and the Bulls. Many prisoners escape the monotony of prison by living vicariously through a preferred team's performance; they take disparaging remarks about a sporting team as a personal insult. Hector insulted the Bulls. Raheem, an avid fan of the Bulls who towered over Hector, took the insult personally. Hector then made it personal by telling Raheem, "Quit crying like a bitch." Hector said that Raheem slammed his chair down and stormed out of the television room.

Hector assumed that Raheem was going to get a knife, so Hector says he went to his room and strapped down, meaning he got his knife ready and waited for Raheem to come for him. "I was ready for whatever," Hector said. Instead of Raheem, Outlaw-Bey came through the door. Outlaw-Bey was a New York native who also led the Moorish Science Temple community at Leavenworth. Being a fellow New Yorker, Outlaw-Bey had been looking out for Hector. Out of respect for Outlaw-Bey, Raheem went to see him before attacking Hector. Outlaw-Bey asked Raheem, as a personal favor, to let Hector's inappropriate remark slide. In return, Outlaw-Bey assured Raheem that he would control Hector.

When Outlaw-Bey came to speak with Hector, he explained that at Leavenworth a prisoner should not throw insults around lightly. Raheem had been about to respond with lethal force, and since Hector had insulted him, he would have been in the right. Hector's tough-guy image had to be discarded, Outlaw-Bey explained; in the penitentiary, he had to treat every man "with the respect a killer deserves." Following that incident, Hector moved into Outlaw-Bey's cell and began studying the Qur'an. Hoping to strengthen Hector's discipline, Outlaw-Bey persuaded him to attend the Muslim classes and participate in the Muslim community.

After his first year at Leavenworth, a new penitentiary opened in Allenwood, Pennsylvania. Because it was closer to his home in New York, Hector was transferred involuntarily. By that time he had become comfortable at Leavenworth, and he was not looking forward to starting over in a new penitentiary.

A TRANSFER AND AN APPEAL

Hector says about forty prisoners rode the bus with him from Leavenworth to Allenwood. When they arrived, they were surprised to find an empty penitentiary. Another group of prisoners had come from Lewisburg first, but not liking some of the new policies at Allenwood, the prisoners rioted in protest. They were taken to segregation, thus giving the Leavenworth prisoners free reign of the prison until the next buses brought more men from other facilities. Those prisoners did not start arriving for three months. By the time they came, Hector already had resumed his Leavenworth routine. Over the next three years, he worked, woke early, found a job, and led a rather structured existence.

Three years after Hector arrived at Allenwood, while he was in segregation, he received incredible news from his attorney. The Second Circuit Court of Appeals had reversed a part of his conviction, meaning that his forty-three-year sentence could be reduced by as much as thirty years.

Understandably, the news made Hector ecstatic. He had been in the hole for insolence. When he returned to the general population after two weeks, he was enthusiastic about telling his friends that he had won his appeal. But some of the people with whom he had grown close over the years began to shun him upon learning of his news. Those people had lost hope long ago about going home. Instead of being happy for one who was about to get out, they felt a sense of loss, like they were losing a family member or a teammate with whom they expected to grow old. Their response was to ostracize Hector, to treat him as if he did not exist.

Hector was expecting a transfer back to New York for a new sentencing hearing. Instead, after a couple months of euphoria, he received devastating news. The appellate court reversed its earlier decision, saying that reversing Hector's conviction would create a precedent that would free thousands of other felons. The U.S. Supreme Court would have to resolve the matter. The emotional roller coaster ride was too much for Hector. Upon learning that his victory had been snatched from him, he says he completely lost interest in everything and just tried to get back in the groove of prison. Upon learning that Hector would not be leaving, those prisoners who had been shunning him began to embrace him again.

After several months, the Supreme Court issued its decision, irrevocably reversing a part of Hector's conviction. A few days later, he was riding the prison bus back to New York for a new sentencing hearing. When Hector entered the courtroom, his attorney enthusiastically spoke about fighting for the maximum sentence reduction.

"No," Hector interrupted him. "I want to make a deal right now for twenty-five years."

"What do you mean twenty-five years?" his attorney asked in astonishment. "I can get your sentence down to thirteen years."

"Look," Hector pleaded, "I been in prison with guys serving 800-year sentences. I can do twenty-five years a lot easier than the forty-three-year sentence I was doing. Just make me a deal."

The attorney instructed Hector to wait patiently. But when the judge began to speak, Hector stood up in court and made the case himself. He told the judge that he wanted to make a deal that would limit him to a twenty-five year sentence. The sentencing judge seemed amused at Hector's legal naivete, and like his attorney, instructed him to wait for the proceedings to play themselves out. It was good advice, for when things were over, Hector's time was reduced by twenty-seven years, to a fifteen-year term.

After receiving his sentence, Hector returned to the penitentiary in Allenwood. His unit team, including his case manager and counselor, called him in and indicated that soon he would transfer to a medium-security facility, as the new sentence he received altered the equation that determines his security needs. Hector was sent to a federal correctional institution (FCI) in Schuylkill, Pennsylvania. "I hated the FCI," Hector said. "I was used to doing time in the penitentiary, where a whole different mentality exists."

ROUGH ADJUSTMENTS

Hector explained that he had been in the medium-level facility for only a couple of months when he had a problem. Some of his cousins were confined in the same prison, and they were playing on a flag football team together. The game got rough, he explained, and some of the prisoners from the other team began taunting his cousin. Hector had his shank nearby. When the taunting started, he said he put the shank in his waistband beneath his shirt. During an argument between his cousin and one of the other players, Hector said he intervened. He lifted up his shirt so that others could see his knife. "I just want anyone to know," Hector told the group, "that anyone who got a problem with my cousin, also got a problem with me."

Although no officers were around during the incident, within a week Hector was called by one of the prison's lieutenants. The lieutenant told Hector that he was aware of the incident with the knife and that if he created any more problems he would return to the penitentiary. Hector said that he lost his cool and cursed out the lieutenant.

Hector told me that he could not believe someone told the lieutenant about the threat he had made. "That would have never happened in the penitentiary. I told the lieutenant he could shove the bitch-ass prison up his ass, that I wanted to go back to the penitentiary where men wouldn't run to the cops to solve their problems for them." Hector's outburst resulted in his being sent to segregation. And although he eventually was transferred, he did not return to the penitentiary. Instead, he was transferred to another medium-security facility, this one on the other side of the country, near Portland, Oregon.

A NEW FOCUS: SUCCESSFUL HABITS

Hector was upset about being transferred so far away from his family in New York. When he arrived in the new prison, however, he felt some relief in being separated from the peer pressure of the other prisons. Since few New Yorkers were confined in his new prison, he was free to live a bit more independently. He committed himself to earning a GED, and during his first year there, he passed the high school equivalency exam. He also participated in several programs. He says that he kept a knife nearby, but because he was not in the middle of group-related violence, he did not feel the need to keep it with him at all times. Instead, he was able to focus on developing himself.

After completing a class in photography, Hector took a job as a photographer in the visiting room. He snapped photographs of the men together with their visitors, and during his job, he began a relationship with a woman whom he met in the visiting room. They began a romance through the mail, but prison rules prohibited the girl from coming to visit Hector. The Bureau of Prisons maintains a rule that prohibits prisoners from receiving authorization to visit with people whom they did not know prior to their incarceration. Because Hector met the woman in the visiting room when she was visiting a relative in the institution, his unit team would not add her to Hector's visiting list. The woman and Hector decided to marry in order to subvert the rule, but when Hector made his request to the unit team, they transferred him back to the East Coast, effectively terminating the relationship.

I met Hector at Fort Dix. He now keeps a low profile and does not mix too freely with others in the population. "There are too many rats on this compound," Hector explained. "I don't want to talk with anyone who won't show me their paperwork, and nobody is bringing out their paperwork here. So I ain't lookin' to make no friends."

Hector says that he has no need to carry a knife at Fort Dix, and he even has learned to relax. Now he sleeps on a lower bunk and even takes naps during the day. Instead of serving another three decades, he is scheduled to be released in two years. And now that he approaches the end of his sentence, he says that he is more likely to participate in educational programs.

Hector began serving his term when he was a teenager; he will finish as a thirty-three-year-old man. It frightens him somewhat, as he knows that opportunities will be limited. He hopes to work with troubled youth in some capacity upon his release and says that he will look for opportunities during these last two years to develop his communication skills so that he can describe the dangers of living a life of crime. Despite the way he has adjusted to prison, Hector says he intends to break all connections with the criminal world upon his release. He wants to live the remainder of his life outside.

During my interview with Hector, we discussed the polar opposite values that exist in prison and the outside world. Whereas he has spent more than a decade consumed with rumors about whether others had cooperated with law enforcement, he now recognizes that in the legitimate society that he wants to enter, he needs to concentrate on other matters. Now he is working to develop his vocabulary and his diction. He has established goals to achieve before his release and is studying a book by Stephen R. Covey (1990). During Hector's remaining months, he hopes to develop the seven habits of successful people that Covey describes.

Andrew Frison, the next prisoner serving an elephant-time sentence, was not so recalcitrant during his term. Rather than mocking those who worked to prepare themselves for release, readers will learn why Andrew took affirmative steps to develop new skills.

AN EDUCATIONAL TRANSFER TO ACQUIRE COMPUTER SKILLS: ANDREW FRISON

A long-term prisoner describes passing through a prison riot while working toward an associate's degree.

Earlier this week I walked into one of the leisure rooms (a common area where prisoners may gather to watch television) here at Fort Dix, and I saw a familiar face. Andrew Frison, a young African American prisoner from New Jersey was sitting at a table talking with friends. Seeing Andrew there in the room surprised me because he had been transferred from Fort Dix over a year ago. Usually, when someone transfers from one prison to another, he does not return.

I asked Andrew where he had gone. "I was in Big Spring, Texas," he said, "on an educational transfer." This was interesting news to me, as I am in my sixteenth year of confinement, and I had not heard of anyone going through this educational transfer program. I asked Andrew to describe his experience.

Andrew initiated the transfer request in February of 1999. At that time, he already had lived over eight years in prison, the last two at Fort Dix. He began serving his sixteen-year term at the high-security penitentiary in Atlanta, then was transferred to a medium-security facility in Pennsylvania when his security level dropped. From Pennsylvania, he was sent to a prison in Talladega, Alabama, and then to Beckley, West Virginia, before his security level dropped once more, this time to low, and he was brought here to Fort Dix, where I met him in 1997.

Andrew Frison

Obviously, the federal prison system holds people from all across the country. Andrew began serving his term in 1991, and although he was raised in New Jersey, and that is where his family continues to reside, he served time in four different prisons, each in a different state, before he was able to succeed in transferring to a prison in his home state. He is fortunate. Although the Bureau of Prisons maintains a written policy indicating that it strives to place prisoners as close to home as possible, the system is crowded, and sometimes prisoners serve their sentences thousands of miles from home. I began serving my own term in 1987. Although sixteen years have passed since then, I have always been over two thousand miles away from my family in Seattle.

I asked Andrew whether he had been active in educational programs at the other facilities. He told me that he had taken a few college courses since his term began, but he was not designated at any single facility for a long enough time to earn a degree. "Besides," Andrew said, "during the beginning of my term I was doing everything I could to learn and understand law. I really wanted to find some relief from my sentence."

Perhaps a universal goal of all prisoners when they initially begin serving their time is finding a way out. Many turn to the law library. The Supreme Court has interpreted the U.S. Constitution to require that all prisoners have access to the courts. Accordingly, either law libraries or some type of legal aid program is available in every prison. Prisoners frequently turn to jailhouse lawyers for assistance. Those with a bit more ambition sometimes search for loopholes in their case that may provide them with relief.

Postconviction relief, however, comes extremely rarely, especially in the federal courts. By the time a person comes to prison, he already has an extensive legal history behind him, all of which is well documented. In the majority of cases, prisoners agree to plead guilty in exchange for less exposure to a possible lengthy prison term. Those who elect to proceed through trial, however, have mountains of legal transcripts through which they can sift for an error. Whether defendants proceeded through trial or pled guilty, once they are inside the prison system, many begin looking for relief, totally oblivious to the fact that for every one person who obtains relief, the convictions and sentences of more than nine remain intact.

It is hard to litigate from behind prison walls. Although law libraries are available, they are not nearly as well equipped as the law libraries that professional law firms accumulate. Prisoners have no access to computer databases, and even copy machines and typewriters are scarce. More important than the lack of access to legal resources is the lack of experience most prisoners have in the legal field. Most prisoners have not finished high school.

As a whole, prisoners are poorly educated. However, this does not stop hundreds of them in each institution from spending long portions of their day in the law library. They comb through complicated legal texts searching for something that may bring them relief. Despite the David-versus-Goliath odds, occasionally word eddies quickly throughout the prison that a prisoner has obtained relief from his sentence.

In a prison holding 2,000 people, my experience suggests that each month scores of prisoners will file petitions requesting relief from their sentences. During any given year, however, fewer than a handful of these inmates succeed in self-litigating a reduction in time. In a community that starves for mental stimulation, those odds still are enough to encourage newly committed prisoners to dedicate their first years to time spent in the law library, like Andrew did.

In addition to working through legal texts and studying in a mishmash of college programs, Andrew said that he also participated in some of the vocational programs that were available. He earned certificates of competency in welding and computer software application programs such as WordPerfect and Lotus 1-2-3.

FEDERAL PRISON INDUSTRIES (UNICOR)

When Andrew arrived at Fort Dix, he wanted to extend his knowledge of computer applications. To that end, he sought a job in UNICOR, a wholly owned government factory that provides employment for federal prisoners. The UNICOR factory at Fort Dix features a computer department where inmates can apply to work. Andrew sought and obtained work as a data-entry clerk, hoping that regular exposure to computers would help prepare him further for the future.

Andrew spent the first several months of his employment at UNICOR entering data into spreadsheets, word processing, and database management programs. His supervisor, though, recognized his competency and eagerness to learn; he offered Andrew a coveted position in the factory's drafting department. Andrew readily accepted this opportunity.

The drafting department at UNICOR gave Andrew the privilege to work with some of the most sophisticated drawing programs on the market. He learned AutoCad R14 and AutoCad 2000, Microstation, Visio, and Auto-Tol. Mastering these programs required years of study, and Andrew welcomed the challenge. He ordered books that further explained the intricacies of the computer-assisted drawing programs and studied them when he was not working. He hoped that he could develop enough knowledge to eventually find employment in the drafting profession. "Studying helps me forget that so much of my life is being wasted here in prison," Andrew said. "I look for any opportunity to advance my skills while I'm here. Not because I think it will help me go home any sooner, but rather because I want to ensure I'm able to find satisfying employment upon my release. I'm committed to living as a free man when I get out in 2005. There will be no more crime for me."

Andrew told me that he learned as much as his superiors at UNICOR would allow him to learn after about twenty months on the job. He was implying that his superiors limited his ability to master the programs. "In UNICOR, we're allowed access to the computers and the software programs," Andrew said. "But we're given very specific assignments. We are not authorized to delve further into the programs and are prohibited from accessing the most sophisticated features. No inmate," he continued, "is allowed to participate in computer programming." I asked him why. "The Bureau of Prisons does not want an inmate to get so far ahead that staff members cannot supervise his work," Andrew explained.

Although Andrew appreciated the opportunities he was given to learn about drafting, he was still thirsty to learn more about computers. He began making inquiries about other options through which he might learn more. He spoke with Jan Tenor, a well-respected teacher at Fort Dix. She recommended a booklet that described educational programs at other federal prisons.

The Bureau of Prisons publishes this booklet describing the various federal prisons across the United States. Unfortunately, little information is available about each prison, and it is quickly dated. Although a prisoner may use the book to find some basic information about a prison's security level, its geographical location, and some of the basic programs available, it is a poor basis for decision making. To be sure, one cannot expect an accurate picture of a new place or program from such a booklet. Most information published by the Bureau of Prisons has a propaganda-like feel to it.

For a prisoner to obtain an accurate description of any prison, he or she must talk with prisoners who are or were recently confined there. Even then, widely varying accounts are heard. One person may consider a facility to be a good assignment, while another may have horrid experiences there. My own experience suggests those who are able to find a satisfying job and living quarters adjust much easier. That way, they can more easily avoid the complications that exist in every prison, complications such as gang problems and abusive staff, for example.

PURSUIT OF AN EDUCATIONAL TRANSFER

Despite the particular booklet's inadequacy, Andrew did read about an educational program available at the federal correctional institution at Big Spring, Texas, which seemed perfect for him. It allowed inmates to earn associate's degrees in various computer application programs. He was not too optimistic about ever getting there, though, because the prison at Big Spring is in a different region of the United States. His experience in the Bureau of Prisons system suggested that transfers to other regions were rare. Nevertheless, he expressed his interest in the program to Jan Tenor, and to his surprise, he found a supporter. Tenor said she would do what she could to help.

Two days after speaking with Tenor, Andrew learned that she had written an internal memorandum to Andrew's case manager. In the federal prison system, every inmate has a case manager, and one of the responsibilities assigned to this position has to do with inmate transfers. Tenor's memorandum recommended that Andrew be considered for an educational transfer to Big Spring, Texas. Tenor argued that Andrew had proven himself to be not just a responsible prisoner, but also a disciplined student who was focused on developing skills that would help him succeed vocationally upon his release from confinement.

Andrew's case manager, Russell Boatwright, received Tenor's recommendation and asked Andrew to confirm that he wanted to transfer to Texas. Andrew explained how he wanted to develop more skills to help him upon release, and that the possibility of earning an associate's degree appealed to him. To his credit, Boatwright agreed to submit Andrew's case to the regional office. I have known few case managers who willingly put forth this effort. With Tenor and Boatwright supporting the request, the region soon granted Andrew a transfer. A few weeks later he was told to report with his property to Release and Discharge, where he would be packed out and prepared for transfer.

Andrew was fortunate to have found two supportive staff members who were actively willing to process his request for transfer. Without their intervention, it is unlikely that he would have been able to participate in the computer training program at Big Spring. Without an impressive record of adjustment and the political skills to ingratiate oneself with staff members who have decision-making or influential powers, a prisoner will not succeed in arranging transfers to particular prisons, and especially not for program participation.

Transfers cost the Bureau of Prisons money, and administrators constantly are looking for ways to cut unnecessary spending. Making arrangements for a prisoner to transfer to a desirable prison might be considered in many administrative circles as an unnecessary expense. In most instances, prisoners are transferred for institutional need. A prisoner may request a particular prison for whatever reason, but without the support that Andrew received, such requests rarely are granted.

Andrew's transfer was not easy. After he was packed out, he waited for the move. Then, one morning in late May, at 4:00 A.M., guards woke him and told him to report to Release and Discharge. At 4:15 A.M. he was locked in a barren cell. Andrew waited there for about two hours. He then was marched to a bus with about twenty-five other prisoners for the five-hour journey to the prison at Lewisburg, Pennsylvania. This was the first leg of his long journey to educate himself further.

Andrew was confined to the holdover section of the penitentiary at Lewisburg for the next week or so. Then there was a repeat of the chaining process that he went through before he left Fort Dix. Any time a prisoner who lacks community custody status is transferred outside, guards wrap a heavy chain around the prisoner's waist to hold the prisoner's handcuffed wrists in place. They also fasten the prisoner's ankles in manacles to restrict the inmate's ability to move. Guards take these extra precautions to compensate for the loss of fences and walls that confine the men while they are in prison. Traveling while in custody is both emotionally stressful and physically uncomfortable.

THE AIRLIFT

The bus took him on a four-hour trip to Harrisburg, Pennsylvania. He departed the bus and hobbled up a ramp to board an airplane filled with prisoners, all of whom were similarly chained, heading to various destinations across the United States. The plane left Harrisburg, touching down and dropping prisoners off in West Virginia and Atlanta before it arrived at the major prisoner transfer center in Oklahoma City, where Andrew was escorted off the plane and led to a new prison cell. He was required to share it with the other prisoner who already had been assigned there. A guard locked the door behind him.

All prisoners must get used to changing roommates without notice. After a prisoner is situated in a particular prison for a while, he may succeed in maneuvering into a cell with someone truly compatible. But even then, something can happen that will bring an abrupt change in living conditions. The roommate may be taken to segregation, and in these days of crowded prisons, within hours of one prisoner departing, a new prisoner may be installed in the cell. Typically it makes no difference to the staff member who makes cell assignments whether the prisoners sharing a cell are compatible. One may listen to loud music while the other likes to read; one may be aggressive and hyperactive while the other is passive. Problems also arise over smoking preferences.

Although federal prisoners may purchase cigarettes in the commissary, many state prisons prohibit inmate smoking. At Fort Dix, smoking is not authorized inside any buildings, but these rules are frequently overlooked by inmates and staff. Tension builds and tempers frequently erupt when nonsmokers are exposed to second-hand smoke or are left to clean up cigarette butts and ashes. Whatever the differences, prisoners must find ways of adjusting to their assigned quarters.

Andrew stayed in his cell at Oklahoma City for five weeks as he waited for bus transportation to Big Spring, Texas. This was a grueling wait, Andrew explained, because there was no recreational facility, and there was a constant shuffling of inmates, all of whom had different security levels. Further, he did not have his property with him. That meant no phone books or address books, so communicating with those in his support group outside of prison was difficult. He did not receive mail, did not have a radio or access to commissary to assuage the monotony of his status. "It was a lot like living in a bus station," he explained.

Finally, in his fifth week there, a guard woke Andrew at 2:00 A.M. He was told to prepare for transfer. For security reasons, guards do not tell prisoners in advance of their transfer schedules. Every minute is spent in anxiety, waiting for the move. After he was chained up again and loaded onto the bus, Andrew tried to sleep as the bus drove for six hours to the Lubbock County Jail, where he was transferred into a large cell with forty other prisoners. The prisoners were just hanging around, most sleeping on the floor. Andrew waited there for twelve hours; then, finally, the bus was loaded up again for the final leg of his journey. He arrived at his new prison six hours later.

It was June 17, 1999, when Andrew finally made it to Big Spring. The journey from Fort Dix had been difficult and very trying on his mind. He was happy to have the transfer behind him, eager to begin working in the new program. But before he could start working toward his goal, an obstacle presented itself, and it left Andrew wondering whether he had made the right decision in leaving behind the relatively peaceful environment at Fort Dix.

SECOND THOUGHTS IN A DISTURBANCE

A couple of days after Andrew arrived at Big Spring, while he still was settling himself in, a full-blown riot broke out. Although he could not verify it, rumor had it that at least one of the people involved was killed. He said the melee began in the earliest hours of the morning.

Andrew explained that the prison at Big Spring is actually an old hotel that sits on a no-longer-functioning military base. When the base closed down, the building was converted into a prison. The remodeled structure features twin six-man rooms connected together by a common bathroom that the twelve men assigned to the two rooms share. Andrew said he was fortunate to have been assigned to a room where he, at least initially, got along with the other prisoners. Others were not so lucky.

Andrew was asleep on June 20, 1999, three days after he arrived at Big Spring. Loud screams woke him at 1:30 A.M. He said he looked outside his window and saw what he estimated to be a hundred prisoners battling with each other. As a low-security prison, Big Spring was surrounded by a double-wide fence topped off with razor wire, but the enclosed buildings did not have locks on the doors. Although rules prohibited it, prisoners could walk outside at anytime to congregate in the courtyard between the buildings. On that evening, Andrew explained that he seemed to be observing a gang war.

Prisoners had pipes, broom handles, steel pieces they had fashioned into swords, mop ringers, and chairs. The fighters were using anything they could get their hands on as a weapon. Andrew's roommates told him that several Big Spring gangs were constantly battling with each other. This confrontation, they admitted, looked worse than most. He said the fight was between the Border Brothers and a group challenging them for control of the unit's drug and gambling rackets.

The battle lasted for more than an hour, Andrew said, before he heard shots being fired from the upper compound gates into the lower compound housing units. That is when the prisoners started to separate. One of the gun shots fired by Bureau of Prisons guards ricocheted off the wall and into a housing unit. The bullet hit an uninvolved prisoner in the eye. Andrew said the wounded inmate had been lying in his bed when the stray bullet hit him, causing him to lose vision in that eye permanently.

After the prisoners disbanded, the staff marched in and ordered all prisoners to lie face down on the floor with their hands behind their backs. Staff members then went behind each prisoner and fastened their wrists together with plastic straps. Andrew and the others waited in that position for twelve hours, he said, until late the following afternoon. While lying on their stomachs, with their hands tied behind their backs, the prisoners felt helpless and vulnerable, not knowing whether there would be some type of retaliation from the guards for the disturbance. Andrew said he was wondering what kind of hell he had entered as a result of the transfer.

He had been leading a relatively stable life at Fort Dix, confined, but preparing himself for a better future. Now, after only a few days at his new prison, he felt like he was in gladiator quarters, where explosive acts of violence could erupt at any moment—and Big Spring was, for the record, a low-security prison.

Once the staff members came around to cut the plastic ties that bound the prisoners' wrists, officers began holding interviews to find out what had provoked the riot. As a new prisoner, Andrew did not know anything, and he said as much when he was questioned. Rumors of inmates being killed really concerned him, although there was no way for him to verify whether deaths actually had occurred.

As a prisoner who had been focusing on developing himself while in prison, he did not want to be in an environment where he inadvertently could be pulled into prison disturbances. Andrew had been confined for about eight years already. He was well aware of the consequences of participating in group violence, and he wanted no part of it. He knew that he could control his own behavior, but he recognized that he was involuntarily linked with every other prisoner around him. His first experiences in the Big Spring prison did not engender feelings of peace or confidence in the immediate future.

Despite the initial excitement of the disturbance, the prison soon returned to normal operations. Andrew then was able to visit with Mr. Kennedy, an educational coordinator at Big Spring. Kennedy introduced Andrew to a representative of Howard College, the community college that was sponsoring the programs in which Andrew wanted to enroll. His enthusiasm was returning, but it still was tempered by the volatility of his surroundings.

After speaking with the representative of Howard College, Andrew learned that he was going to be responsible for a one thousand dollar tuition payment. It was a reasonable request, but it was information Andrew believes, and validly so, that he should have received before he applied for the transfer from Fort Dix. He wondered what would have happened had he not enjoyed the support of his mother, who agreed to help with the tuition payment so that Andrew could participate in the program.

After a few weeks, Andrew finally began his studies, and immediately he was thrilled to be receiving the instruction. He worked with sophisticated software programs and even learned some things about hardware as well. Besides studying the course materials from a theoretical perspective, Andrew also obtained practical experience by participating in an apprenticeship program in the prison's engineering department. He used the skills he was developing to draw blue prints that would be used to convert different sections of the prison.

Today, Andrew is proud to have earned his associate's degree in computer-aided drafting. He explained that as a result of his education, he can work in any type of business that involves drafting, including architectural firms, interior design firms, and all types of manufacturers who need these skills. All in all, Andrew says he is glad to have had the opportunity to complete the program at Big Spring, Texas. The transfer out there and back was difficult, and he had his share of problems, but on balance, the good far outweighed the bad.

The problem, Andrew recognizes, is that he will remain in prison until 2005 unless something happens to shorten his sentence. During that time, technology will advance while the skills he has worked so hard to develop may become obsolete. He hopes to find work in UNICOR again at Fort Dix, work that will allow him to use his newly expanded skills, but he is doubtful about that. Still, Andrew may find opportunities to develop other skills, or perhaps, he will find a program being offered at yet another prison. Maybe he will be fortunate in being selected to participate in that one, too. He remains optimistic.

Byron Perymoore Nelson, our last elephant-time prisoner, was a former enforcer for drug dealers. Upon his confinement, however, his religious faith inspired him to change his ways.

FINDING JESUS IN PRISON: BYRON PERYMOORE NELSON

One former violent drug offender describes how Christianity contributed to his prison adjustment.

Byron Perymoore Nelson was born on the island of Jamaica. When he was ten, he moved with his mother and brother to New York, where he continued his primary and secondary schooling. Byron was a gifted student and athlete. He had such an outstanding record that after earning his high school diploma, Rice University offered him a full track scholarship. After high school, however, Byron already had moved out of the family home and had been lured into the world of drug trafficking. More schooling did not appeal to him.

With a physically imposing presence, Byron initially was hired by another drug dealer to serve as a bodyguard. Together they sold crack cocaine in areas rife with violence, and Byron, armed and available, stood ready to defend his turf to the death. Eventually, Byron expanded his role in the operation from enforcer to distributor.

Although he never used or handled drugs directly, Byron agreed to fund their purchase for sales at higher prices. In effect, he had become a drug dealer. When he was twenty-one, less than three years after he joined the racket, he was set up in a sting operation and charged with the manufacturing and distribution of crack cocaine. The manufacturing charge leaves one with the impression of sophistication. In reality, it refers to a primitive

Byron Perymoore Nelson

chemistry operation combining cocaine, baking soda, and heat that results in a substance commonly known as crack.

Byron was taken to a county jail after his arrest. Because he was charged in a drug case involving weapons, the magistrate judge ordered Byron held in custody without bail; defendants charged with crimes related to the distribution of large quantities of drugs rarely are granted bail. In 1991, he began his time in a two-man cell that was so narrow he could stretch his arms out and touch both walls. And in that cell, Byron picked up a Bible.

When he was a child in Jamaica, Byron's mother and grandmother forced him to go to church every Sunday. He hated it. All the praying seemed senseless to him, but it was easier to attend and fake his way through the rituals rather than endure the whipping he would suffer if he did not. After moving to New York, his mother stopped pressuring him to attend church, so he quit attending. Byron never gave God another thought until he saw that Bible in his cell.

Somehow, the Bible intrigued him. He remembered his grandmother and mother telling him when he was a child that Jesus could save him, that all the answers to his life could be found through prayer and faith. Alone, and in an unfamiliar situation with nothing else to read and nothing else to distract him, Byron picked up the Bible. He began reading it with one intention in mind: to see if the Bible could free him from the wrath of the criminal justice system. He was not necessarily interested in spiritual support or religious redemption.

Historians tell us that when the first penitentiaries were opened in the United States, Bibles were the only reading material available for prisoners. Prisons were supposed to be places of penitence, hence the name penitentiaries. In time, however, reform took lower priority than confinement. Furthermore, the lengths of time prisoners began to serve increased dramatically. Early in the twentieth century, three years in prison would have been considered an exceptionally long term. Today, however, those with ten years to serve are considered short-term prisoners and maybe eligible for camp placement.

Textbooks often define four goals of imprisonment. One is incapacitation, that is, removing the offender from society. Deterrence is a second goal, meaning that the threat of a lengthy prison term should deter the convicted criminal as well as others from committing crimes. Retribution, a third goal, brings society's revenge on the offender. The fourth stated goal is rehabilitation. In the federal prison system, no objective instrument exists to measure whether one is rehabilitated.

Byron hoped that through the Bible he would find an answer for his question of what rehabilitation meant. At that early stage of his confinement, he did not know that rehabilitation—whatever it means—is hardly synonymous with release. The way he interpreted his predicament, by studying the Bible he would prove to himself that either religion was simply a placebo for the weak-minded, or it was in fact a tool he could use to free himself from confinement. Thus, when he initially opened that Bible in 1991, he did so with skepticism and the expectation that nothing would come from the excursion.

THE INTIMIDATOR

With a body builder's physique, Byron stands well over six feet tall and weighs approximately two hundred pounds. He is a dark-skinned black man. With his shiny bald head, goatee, and serious demeanor, Byron looks more like an executioner, an intimidating gang leader, or a prison ruffian than a humble seeker of spiritual guidance. It was on his fourth day of confinement that he opened the Bible, however, and although ten years have passed since that memorable day, he has never parted with his Bible since.

He began reading from Genesis. The jailer brought breakfast to his cell just after 5:00 A.M. each morning. After eating, Byron would begin reading, hardly leaving his cell to do anything else. He found the stories inspirational, an appealing escape from the monotony of his confinement. In time, he connected with a few other inmates in the jail who had formed a Bible study group.

Besides freeing him from prison, Byron initially hoped that studying the Bible would help him learn self-control. During those first days of confinement, when he saw all the noise and chaos around him, he knew that he would need something to help him control his aggression. Solving problems with violence or threats of violence was the way Byron had lived on the street. Considering himself an expert in hand-to-hand combat, Byron said that before his imprisonment he always carried a hunting-type knife concealed on his person. He would not hesitate to "get rid of a person" who presented a problem, a threat to himself or his operation. In jail, however, he wanted to control himself, to avoid altercations if possible because he said it was obvious to him that he could not escape the hundreds of eyes that seem to watch every prisoner.

Instead of joining other prisoners to play table games, watch music videos, or engage in staples of prison life such as extortion rackets or gambling, Byron either stayed to himself reading the Bible all day or joining three to four others for informal study groups where they would discuss the books, chapters, and versus they had read in order to derive further meanings from their readings.

After a month in the county jail, Byron said he not only was passing at least ten hours each day absorbed in reading his Bible, but he also had begun to spend a few hours in prayer. He continued to push God "to prove his existence" by freeing Byron from jail. It was a personal experiment, he explained. Byron expected that his efforts would be rewarded with divine intervention. If not, he would conclude that there was no sense in continuing.

Several months later, Byron proceeded through trial. He was convicted on all charges against him, and at his sentencing, the judge imposed a term of 204 months. Hearing the time pronounced in months rather than years took some of the initial sting out of the sentence. "When I heard the judge say 204 months, I didn't know what he was talking about. It didn't really bother me that much. After we left the courtroom and I was on my way back to the jail, I realized that was seventeen years. That hit me pretty hard."

KEEPING THE FAITH—LONG TERM

When Byron was transferred from the county jail to a medium-security prison in Schulykill, Pennsylvania, he had seven months of confinement and Bible study behind him. His experiment continued, as he still had hopes that religion would set him free—literally. After settling into the prison, the first thing he did was to walk to the chapel. He sat through the Christian services, then stuck around to mingle with some of the other prisoners. The prison held approximately twelve hundred men, but fewer than a hundred attended the Christian services. A smaller percentage of the population attended services for the Islamic and Jewish faiths.

All federal prisons have at least one chaplain who is responsible for coordinating religious services for the various inmate faiths. The chaplain contracts with members of the clergy from neighboring communities to lead services if someone is not on staff at the prison to meet the needs of a particular faith. Generally, the Christian, Jewish, and Islamic faiths are well represented in the inmate population, and chaplains are available regularly. Clerics from Native American, Rastafarian, and other beliefs visit the institution on a monthly or quarterly basis. All religious faiths share the nondenominational chapel building.

Byron freely acknowledges now that when he began studying the Bible, he saw religion as a crutch. He was alone in jail, facing a lengthy sentence, and he was looking for something to free him, something that he could grasp that would enable him to escape the certainty of a long, walk through the caverns of the criminal justice system. Many prisoners turn to religion when the gates close behind them. Some are afraid of the pressures that come with confinement and seek protection through joining a fellowship with others. Byron met with several participants of the Islamic community who said they joined the group because its membership offered them a kind of protection from the extortionists inside the fences. Others look to religious activities as a substitute for the personal bonds they lost with others as a result of their confinement.

During Byron's first days at Schulykill, he met Joseph, a Bible-study leader. They were assigned to the same housing unit. They shared stories about each other's past and what it was that had led them each to God and were committed to studying together every day. Their pursuit of spiritual awareness somehow assuaged the pains of their confinement, even if it had not yet resulted in Byron's release from prison.

Throughout his first year in confinement, Byron insists that he never wavered from his many hours of daily prayer and Bible study. Nevertheless, he says that he did not feel inside like he was being completely honest. Several females worked inside the prison, either as officers or as members of the administrative staff. On occasion word reached the population about some of those female staff members developing romantic relationships with prisoners; like many prisoners, Byron kept hope alive. Rules exist to prohibit such conduct, of course, but human nature is not always responsive to and respectful of prison rules.

With thoughts about the possibility of opening a romantic relationship with one of these women, Byron explained to me that he postured himself in ways that might make him more appealing (or intriguing) in his effort to capture a female's attention and, hopefully, affection. The first thing he would do, he says, would be to hide his Bible. As the female passed by— unmoved by his tacit invitation for flirting—he says he experienced a sense of guilt for having abandoned his faith, even if only temporarily.

Besides the airs he put on, Byron also was troubled by thoughts that never seemed to leave his mind from the time of his arrest. While on the streets, Byron had ambitions of opening strip clubs as a career move. He knew a number of women who danced in such clubs. They had explained the business to him and promised to help him by bringing him a stable of nude dancers if he would open a club. He had aspirations of engaging in this business at his earliest opportunity. After he began pursuing the word of God, however, Byron says he sometimes felt troubled that a conflict might exist between his spiritual quest and his career aspirations. He explained his internal dilemma to the others in his Bible study.

FINDING PEACE

Joseph, the person whom he respected the most, convinced Byron that he would have to purify his thoughts. Lust, Joseph explained, was a carnal sin. With such thoughts expressed, Byron said he came to realize that he was like a wolf in sheep's clothing, meaning that externally he appeared good and godlike, but on the inside he was corrupted with wicked thoughts—a ravenous and sensual wolf. It was then, in the early months of 1992, a year after his quest for God began, that Byron made a personal commitment to give himself completely to Christ. The experiment was over, as he accepted and embraced Jesus Christ as his personal lord and savior.

At that point, Byron says he began changing his thinking patterns. Instead of turning to God to help him find release from prison, he began reading the Bible with hopes of cleansing his thought processes and his soul. He began to interpret the Bible literally, following the Old Testament Israelites whom he understood to require seekers of God to divide their days into quarter parts of confessing sins in prayer, worshiping, and reading the word of God; the fourth quarter, apparently, was allowed for rest. It was then that Byron also began the habit of fasting at least one day each week, and sometimes denying himself food for as long as ten consecutive days. These were personal exercises he chose to help him control his will. By abstaining from food, Byron believed that he simultaneously strengthened his spirit, which brought him closer to God.

After that first year, Byron's thoughts about leaving prison vanished. It no longer mattered where he was. All that mattered was his devotion to God. He lived like a monk, constantly in prayer. Whereas he used to carry a knife at all times, now he never was found without a small pocket Bible on his person. He did not read novels, did not waste time on television. Such activities held no interest for Byron. To him, every hour brought him another opportunity to serve God, and he did not want to waste time on superfluous activities.

CHARLATANS

Byron's perspective contrasts sharply from others I have known over the years who fancy themselves devout Christians. In particular, I remember one adjustment group for long-term prisoners sponsored by Dr. Martin, a prison psychologist. I had participated in Dr. Martin's weekly group meetings with perhaps a dozen other prisoners for over a year. Time after time I listened to the other eleven men whine about the ten- or fifteen-year sentences they were serving, complaining how they did not deserve such severe sentences, how the government was corrupt for keeping them in for so long, or how if it was not for a snitch they would not have been caught.

Dr. Martin presented an exercise to the group one day, asking us each to identify our three highest values, what we valued more than anything else in the world. Each of the eleven other group participants said that God was more important to their lives than anything else. But unlike Byron, who had come to accept his prison term as God's will, these others were remarkably consistent in their weekly expressions of grief over the predicament of their incarceration. I rarely have encountered someone who has come to know that peace so clearly apparent in Byron.

The only nonreligious institutional programs in which Byron participated were those that he felt could help him serve God better. He enrolled in the college programs not to earn a degree or certificate, for he says he had no use for a certificate avowing that he had completed a secular program. Rather, he says he participated to make himself a more learned man in order to spread the word of God more effectively.

NEW ASPIRATIONS

Byron lifted his aspirations from owning strip clubs to becoming an evangelist for Christ upon his release. Such a career move would not be without precedent. Many people serving time in prison have become impassioned with religious beliefs during their incarceration. Malcolm X, whom I took to describe himself in his autobiography as a misogynist and violent street thug prior to his arrest, devoted himself to what he believed to be Islamic teachings during his incarceration. He later left prison to become a world leader for those of his belief. Charles Colson, a former member of President Nixon's inner circle and a Watergate defendant, devoted himself to Christ during his imprisonment. Upon his release, he built a prison ministry with the sole purpose of leading others to Christ. In a *New Yorker* interview, Reverend Jesse Jackson was quoted as observing "Every preacher is a sinner preaching salvation. . . . A saint is a sinner who got back up again"; Byron hopes to emulate these and other models of redemption.

Not all prisoners, however, find it so easy to accept and live among prisoners like Byron who have found God and Jesus: do-gooders, usually Christians, but also others who converted to and dedicated themselves to various religions. Although they are rarely targeted for abuse by predators inside the fences, prisoners who appear to be overly religious may be referred to derisively as "Bible thumpers" and even ostracized by others in the prison. Religious groups are an annex community inside the fences, part of the prisoner population but not freely mixing with it. Their members stand out, with their neatly pressed clothes and humble demeanor, always greeting those within their flock with affectionate embraces and handshakes. The religious communities resemble an island of peace in an ocean of hostility.

Some guards, too, may be reluctant to accept a prisoner's commitment to God. Byron has described instances where officers have openly accused him and his Christian brothers of feigning their allegiance to Christ as a prison ploy, charging that they will abandon their faith and revert to crime soon after prison gates open. This is a commonly held position of many American citizens as well. Byron accepts such jibes, humbly recognizing that years of interaction with recalcitrant prisoners has rendered many guards callous and incapable of believing in a human being's ability to change. The skeptics are understandable. It is more of a challenge to meet the hostilities of guards who seek to provoke Byron into misbehavior in order to prove that his Christianity is only a ploy. Nonetheless, it is only a small faction of the guards who appear to resent the religious prisoners. Generally, this would be the same faction that resents prisoners who participate in educational programs, or anything they deem as the system's coddling of prisoners. Most guards are either indifferent to, or even supportive of, those participating in religious programs, as prisoners with deep religious convictions represent one group that could be predicted to be the least likely to engage in prison disturbances.

AN UNLIKELY FELLOWSHIP

Byron described one guard with whom he developed an intense personal relationship. Such relationships are discouraged by prison rules, as administrators are convinced they present a threat to security. A guard who is too chummy with a prisoner may look the other way and purposely not see a disciplinary infraction. Worse yet, a guard may agree to bring in contraband for prisoners with whom he has a close relationship.

Despite the discouragement, after long-time observation, one officer recognized Byron as a devout Christian. The officer, too, attended church regularly and practiced his faith. "The officer came by my room and acted like he was going to do a shakedown. He moved a locker in front of the door to block anyone else from coming in. But instead of searching, he just wanted to spend time praying with me. The officer was going through a personal crisis. We prayed together; he even broke into tears. We felt

God's presence, though. When we were praying, he wasn't a guard and I wasn't a prisoner. We were just two of God's children. It was a beautiful moment." The two committed to fasting together as a devotional bond.

Readers should not be surprised that a guard would expose himself to Byron in such a personal way. Guards have extensive opportunities to examine not only an inmate's central files that describe his background and his behavior in prison, but also the thoughts he expresses to others in the community. Prisoners have no rights to privacy. All mail is potentially censored before leaving an institution, and telephone calls are recorded. When guards are assigned to posts where they have free time on their hands, for example driving around the prison's perimeter, they frequently listen to tape recordings of an individual's telephone conversations. Before the guard exposed his thoughts to Byron, he likely had more information about Byron and the completeness of his conversion to Christ than a psychoanalyst has about a patient for whom he is prescribing treatment.

Through religion, Byron found complete peace behind the fences. Although he was serving a seventeen-year sentence, he says he never felt depressed or that he was missing something in life. Rather, his Bible studies, prayer, and fellowship with other prisoners gave him a feeling that he was exactly where he was supposed to be. He says prison was where God wanted him.

RACE AND SPIRITUALITY

Other inmates, however, have not always been so happy with Byron's prominent position in the Christian community. His uncle in Jamaica is well known as a leader of the voodoo religion. Other Jamaicans who meet Byron in prison tell him that he ought to abandon the so-called white man's religion and return to his uncle's voodoo, which they believe is real. Many Muslim prisoners, too, tell Byron that "the blond-hair, blue-eyed Jesus is for the white man," that he should be practicing "the black man's religion of Islam."

Byron has been undeterred, unwavering in his faith. Religion not only has been the instrument of his adjustment to prison, he insists that it has changed his life forever. Whereas other prisoners frequently are lost in worry about one thing or another, Byron says his faith in God has brought him an ever-present peace. He never worries, he explains, because no matter what happens, he knows that he is living God's will.

In 1995 Byron's security level dropped, and he was transferred to Fort Dix. Although his level of freedom increased in the low-security prison, his adjustment pattern did not change. Immediately upon settling in, he introduced himself to the other practicing Christians there, joined a Bible study group, and looked for collateral programs to help him spread the word of God. He found several sponsored by Fort Dix's Psychology Department.

Every federal prison employs a staff psychologist who is available for prisoners having difficulty coping with their confinement. The psychologist also may initiate programs in which well-adjusted prisoners participate to share their experiences with others. These sessions are a kind of group therapy for prisoners, with discussions and exercises designed to help those who struggle with individual problems. Dr. Martin's long-term prisoners group I described above is an example of one such group.

Byron enrolled in the Alternative to Violence and the Anger Management programs. He considered himself well qualified to contribute to both. Although he led a life of violence prior to his incarceration, as a result of his adjustment to imprisonment, Byron had passed several years without a single altercation or disciplinary infraction. He later became a facilitator for the seminar groups, designing skits and leading others through discussions to expose group participants to the ramifications of violence and anger. He also shows the participants methods he and others use to cope with the temptations to violence in prison.

Attending Christian religious services is most important within Byron's communal priorities. Beyond that, his favorite program focuses on helping troubled adolescents from neighboring communities. Under the sponsorship of the Psychology Department, children between the ages of thirteen and eighteen come into the prison on field trips as part of Fort Dix's Youth Awareness Program. The prisoners provide the students with a description of their background and the poor decisions they made that led them to prison. The children, many of whom are considered at-risk because of previous altercations with the law, are free to question the inmate participants about life in prison. Byron's involvement gives him a sense of community; he feels he is making a worthwhile contribution that may persuade some of the adolescents he encounters to remain in school and lead law-abiding, crime-free lives.

In 1996 Byron was well into his fifth year of imprisonment and fully committed to serving his time in prayer. An interesting development occurred, however, as the U.S. Supreme Court clarified an interpretation of law, enabling Byron to submit a legal motion that may have provided relief. He had neither the legal training nor the funds to hire a lawyer to advise him, so he simply wrote a letter to the judge explaining why he believed the newly interpreted law applied to him. The letter he wrote resulted in a five-year reduction of Byron's sentence. Instead of waiting for release to come in 2007, he learned that prison gates would open for him in 2002. Byron had not been expecting this change in the law. When it came and he learned that his sentence had been reduced, he gracefully accepted it as God's will.

TOWERING-TIME PRISONERS

Finally we come to five prisoners with towering-time sentences, each of whom faces at least two decades of incarceration. For them, prison is their community. It becomes their home, and they adjust accordingly. With sentences that reach so far into the future, by the time they have adjusted, towering-time prisoners largely have abandoned thoughts about the communities from which they came. They pay less attention to participating in the broader society outside of prison fences than a teenager does to thoughts of retirement.

In many ways, it is the towering-time prisoners who shape the culture inside the fences. They provide advice to less-experienced prisoners on how to cope with problems and frustrations inside the fences. Others seek them out for consultation in overcoming dilemmas, either with fellow prisoners or with problems of a more institutional nature.

The towering-time prisoners bring a stabilizing presence because the community really belongs to them. Others may spend a few years, but the towering-time prisoners stay. Like leaders in any society, they have an interest in maintaining the status quo. Before Raheem attacked Hector Colon over the dispute in the television room, for example, he first sought counsel from Outlaw-Bey, a towering-time prisoner whose calming presence cooled a cauldron of intense emotions. Less-experienced prisoners cannot provide this Solomonic guidance.

Towering-time prisoners frequently provide advice that runs opposite to that which one would receive outside. Individual distinctions that bring respect and leadership outside do not count for much inside. Those serving towering sentences support their own particular—and generally criminal—code of values. Seeking to fit in or belong, less experienced prisoners emulate the behavior of these long-term prisoners, thereby perpetuating the culture of failure. This section begins with the profile of one prisoner who has served over a quarter century behind bars during his long criminal career.

CAREER CRIMINALS VERSUS FIRST TIMERS

The criminal justice system was far more tolerant when Jerry Cohen began serving time in the 1960s. Whereas today, repeat criminals face no-parole sentences and three-strikes-you're-out laws, Jerry describes how he used to serve a few years in prison, get out, commit similar crimes, then return to prison for a few more years. For him, prison was just a part of the criminal life. It was not a place where one changed one's life. The years he has served define his life. Jerry is more committed to the life inside than he is to his own family. Ironically, he describes how he has been abandoned by two wives, as well as two of his three children, during the time he has served. Many of the criminal alliances he has made over the years, however, have remained constant. He steadfastly clings to the criminal way of life.

This was also the case for convicted organized crime boss John Gotti, who succumbed to cancer in a prison hospital in the tenth year of his life term at age sixty-one. Gotti was said to have continued to operate his crime family from behind bars through his son, John Jr., until the younger man's own conviction and sentencing.

Like many long-term prisoners, Jerry has made no plans for changing his life in the future. Approaching sixty years of age, he does not pretend to want a job. After his release, Jerry expects to return to the same way of living he has known all his life. Unfortunately, such behavior has the tendency to return him to communities behind prison fences. They are communities where towering-time prisoners like Jerry live as dignitaries.

Other than during the first decade of his life, Jerry has yet to live outside of prison for ten consecutive years. And, despite spending so much of his life behind bars, he told me that looking back on it all he has not a single regret. Is that bravado, or sour grapes?

Unlike Jerry, this is Seth's first commitment. Seth represents the new generation of long-term prisoner. Whereas books describe prison societies of the past as being composed of burglars, armed robbers, and murderers, over fifty percent of the people receiving long-term sentences today are drug offenders; many have no prior criminal histories.

Most sentencing schemes today not only require long terms for drug offenses, but also eliminate an individual's sense of efficacy. Parole boards no longer exist for federal prisoners, and an individual has no means by which he can alter his fate. Upon sentencing, the criminal justice system has spoken with a finality that never existed before. Even access to courts has been curtailed. Prisoners like Seth come to prison without hope and with no incentive to change. When immersed in the prison community, they frequently adjust to it by trying to belong. By garnering reputations for violence, some prisoners lessen the chances of becoming prey themselves. They try to look fierce. Hector had multiple demonic tattoos inked on his body; Seth grew a goatee and refused to smile.

Seth had aspirations of becoming a prison revolutionary, a writer. He wanted to influence the world outside of prison, to let others know that sentencing laws were "locking young white men in prison for decades." Seth is adamant that he is a victim of reverse discrimination. Indeed, despite his conviction, he does not consider himself a criminal at all.

Like Jerry, Melvin has served several terms prior to the twenty-year term he only recently has begun. He has suffered from problems related to drug abuse since he was in his early twenties. Never able to conquer his substance abuse issues, he has returned to crime each time he has been released from prison. It seems the decisions he makes keep leading him back to confinement. Despite acting of his own volition, like Seth and other prisoners, Melvin always has considered himself a victim.

It is difficult to imagine a prisoner who works harder than the Professor, Roderick Campbell. With advanced degrees from an Ivy league school, Roderick uses his skills to help others. A jailhouse lawyer with no interest in the underground economy—a singular, and perhaps unique exception to the rule—the Professor is an aberration.

John, on the other hand, used his skills to open his own version of a store in the cellblock and used the profits of his labors to launch a career as a bookie. Originally, locked up with both his father and brother, he has passed through various stages as his confinement has progressed. Unlike most prisoners, John is not bitter about his incarceration, although he is often lonely and anxious. He now takes precautions not to behave in any way that would threaten what few privileges he has.

THE PRISONER IN THE MIRROR

As I move into the sixteenth year of my sentence, I have just over a decade remaining to serve. Whereas I began the term with pimples on my face, I now have streaks of gray in my hair. Prison has become a way of life for me. I have passed nearly all of my adult years in the community of the confined. Living shoulder to shoulder with thousands of men who embrace criminal values, I constantly studied the outside society I longed to join by reading extensively (*The New Yorker* was of particular help) in order to avoid the danger of becoming one with the prison. Whereas others advised me to live inside the fences, a day never passed when I did not work to prepare for my release. I often felt as if I were living in a cave sunk into the pit of the earth; every day presented me with an opportunity to build another step on the ladder to the top of the pit.

Time now passes differently. I divide the years into two parts rather than twelve months; in winter I feel close to summer, and in the heat of summer I feel the holidays rapidly approaching. Since the beginning of my term I have kept a journal that records my daily activities like a long-distance runner records laps around a track. Every step brings me closer to the end of the marathon, a time when prison gates will open and life as I want to experience it will resume.

My hope is that soon, my long-time record will persuade administrators to transfer me to a minimum-security prison camp. Such a facility will remove me from almost all of the volatility that exists in closed and oppressive communities. Behind fences, as John explains in his profile, I live in a society where the susceptibility for riots, food or work strikes, and other mass disturbances, as you will see, is ever present.

A HOODLUM FOR LIFE:
JERRY COHEN

Despite having spent approximately twenty-five years of his
life in prison, this career criminal expresses no remorse or in-
clination to change.

In 2003 Jerry Cohen will be released from prison. It will not be the first
time. When release comes, Jerry will be sixty-two years old, an age when
most Americans are retiring, or at least close to it. Not in Jerry's case. In
all of his life, Jerry doubts whether he has contributed more than a few
hundred dollars to the nation's social security system. Indeed, since he
was twenty-five, Jerry has never held a job. Prior to that, the mishmash
of jobs he did hold all were of the unskilled labor variety. Jerry may be
the type of offender lawmakers have in mind when they use the term
"career criminal."

Jerry can remember only two legitimate jobs he has held in his lifetime.
One was working on a construction job for a few weeks before growing
bored with the routine and quitting, and he remembers sweeping floors in
a brewery for a while. Unhappy with the hours, and not having them
changed after having worked in the brewery for thirty days, Jerry told his
superior to "shove the job up his ass." For Jerry, staying on the job for a
few months would have been considered long-term employment.

Jerry is a hoodlum. Even now that he is over sixty, he proudly describes
himself as a hoodlum. "I've been a hoodlum all my life and I ain't chang-
in' what I am for nobody," Jerry says. Besides being a self-described

Jerry Cohen

criminal, Jerry also is the epitome of a stand-up convict, one who would find himself at home, respected, and among friends in any American penitentiary.

In 1960, when Jerry was eighteen, he received his first prison term. He was sentenced to "five years indefinite" for a burglary conviction. The sentence structure indicated that a parole board had the power to release Jerry at any time, but in no case could he be held longer than five years on that conviction. He served twelve months before the parole board deemed him fit for release.

At eighteen, most young adults are graduating from high school and either pursuing a vocation or continuing on to college for further study. Jerry had dropped out of high school years before. "I was the only Jew in an Italian neighborhood from Jersey," he explains. "I did what everyone else was doing. School wasn't it. I hung out."

HANGIN' OUT WITH THE "GOOD GUYS"

His definition of "hanging out" meant waking up after noon, dressing sharp, then standing around street corners talking with "the fellas," who also were hoodlums. Not one of Jerry's friends ever considered working or building a career. By choice, they all were into running scams or burglary. They thought nothing of putting a crew together and breaking into stores to steal televisions, appliances, or anything they could get their hands on. There was no moral debate over right or wrong. Instead, they simply considered themselves a group of "good guys," the definition being that they were "stand-up."

When he was taken to the reformatory to serve his first sentence, Jerry told me he was together with several friends from the neighborhood. They passed their time playing cards, playing handball, and gambling. No one paid a thought to participating in programs of any kind. Jerry says he never concerned himself with whether courses were available to help him develop skills while he was in prison. All he thought about was getting out and returning to the only life he knew. Prison was an accepted part of life for him, and he had no apprehension about returning.

Within a week of his release, Jerry was back into his usual routine. He and his partners were scouting businesses in New Jersey they could burglarize, "doing whatever we could to earn a few dollars." They were criminals, and all that really mattered to them was that everyone in the crew acted like a man. That meant that under no conditions would anyone ever consider helping law enforcement.

In 1963 Jerry had another opportunity to demonstrate that he was a man. He was charged, tried, and convicted for burglary, his second time. On this term, he received a sentence of between three and four years. He went back into the state prison system of New Jersey. No big deal. He passed eighteen months before a parole board decided to release him.

After that 1965 release, Jerry enjoyed about a year without having any problems with the law. That is not to say he was obeying it. Nothing besides burglary held much interest for him, and, as after his first release from prison, within a week, he was "takin' down scores." Jerry was arrested and charged in 1966, but some legal maneuvering kept him out of prison on that conviction until 1968, when he returned to the state prison system in New Jersey to begin serving a twenty-two-month stretch on a two- to four-year term for burglary. He was released in 1970.

In 1972 Jerry began his fourth term, serving nineteen additional months before the parole board released him from a two- to three-year term that he was serving. Within two weeks after his release, he was indicted again on still another burglary charge. After being convicted, the judge sentenced him to a four- to five-year term, of which he served thirty-seven months. Jerry was released from that term in 1978.

Jerry was in his late thirties and already had served five separate prison terms. Although he had little formal education, he was a glib talker and mixed easily with the criminal crowd. He had woven a wide network of criminal associates during his many terms in prison, and after his release in 1978, Danny, a young friend, called him with a proposition.

NEW SCAMS IN AN OLD GAME

Danny was a kid whom Jerry had looked out for during his last prison stretch. Soon after Jerry was released, Danny told him that he had a friend who could provide him with a thousand pounds of marijuana. Although Jerry had never been around large-scale drug dealing, he knew so many criminals that he did not foresee a problem in selling it. Besides, Jerry said, in the back of his mind he was planning on robbing Danny's friend of the marijuana.

Jerry said that Danny presented him with a bag containing about three hundred pills. These were in addition to the marijuana. They were a type of amphetamine, but not being a drug user himself, Jerry had no idea what they were. Danny asked Jerry whether he thought he could sell them.

"How many you got?" Jerry asked his entrepreneurial young friend.

"We've got three million pills."

"What do you want for them?" Jerry asked, knowing he did not have a penny to his name.

"I've got to pay ten cents a pill. Get whatever you can and we'll split the difference." Danny said. "Take these as a sample."

Jerry told me that he had no idea what he was doing. He divided the sample into three packages and gave them to three separate young associates. He asked his friends to put the pills on the street and get back to him within a day with a price on what the market would bring. After consulting, they settled on a price of twenty-five cents a pill. Within one month Jerry said his three friends had sold all three million pills, leaving Jerry with $258,000 after he had paid off Danny and his friends; he did not think it necessary to split his proceeds evenly with Danny. The way Jerry saw it, he had intended to rob the drugs, so Danny ought to consider himself fortunate to have earned the six figures he made on the transaction.

Prior to that drug deal, Jerry never held more than ten thousand dollars in his hands at one time. Suddenly, fewer than two months after being released from his fifth prison term, he was flush with cash. His days of burglary were behind him. Jerry took his money and made a new start for himself in Florida. He connected with other friends of his from New Jersey and began his lucrative, full-time career as a drug dealer. He operated without problems until 1985. During his seven-year run, Jerry estimates that his drug sales netted him well over five million dollars. But, because he was a heavy gambler, as well as a connoisseur of gourmet restaurants and wines, Jerry says that today, after having served seventeen years in prison, he is without a penny to show from his so-called glory days. "I ate out five nights a week," he reminisces, "and I never spent less than a g-note on dinner. Besides that, a bad string at the race track might eat up another fifty thousand dollars. It was nothing for me to go through a million dollars a year just living."

MAFIA CONNECTIONS

In 1985 Jerry was charged with leading an organization responsible for distributing cocaine and marijuana worth tens of millions of dollars. After a lengthy trial, Jerry and his associates were convicted on the charges of operating a continuing criminal enterprise. Jerry and his partner each received thirty-year sentences. Jerry was forty-four years old.

The government also alleged that Jerry was an intimate member of the Lucchese crime family, one of New York City's five Mafia families. "The stupid bastards," Jerry explains. "They should've known that as a Jew I could have never been made." Official members of the Mafia, or so-called made members, he explained, had to be of Italian descent.

Despite Jerry's lack of ethnic credentials for becoming an official member, or "made man," in the Mafia, less than a month after his drug-dealing conviction in Florida, he was on trial again in New Jersey. This legal event, the government's largest Mafia trial in history, is described in the book *The Boys From New Jersey* (Rudolph, 1992). As prosecutors had hopes of tearing apart the very fabric of the Mafia, all defendants were facing life in prison. After a trial that exceeded twenty months, the jury acquitted each supposed Lucchese member, including Jerry Cohen. The other defendants went home after the trial. Jerry and his partner, Jackie DeNoscio, however, resumed serving their thirty-year prison terms.

I met Jerry at Fort Dix in 1999. At fifty-eight, he was then in his fourteenth year of imprisonment. He had three more years ahead of him before he was scheduled for release. That was assuming he did not lose any of the good time that he had accumulated over the years. Either way, the three years remaining was not much in terms of prison time. After already having served so much of his life in confinement, Jerry was a veteran prisoner. In fact, he was more than that. Because of his charismatic personality, his reputation as a stand-up convict, and his aura of living with close ties to the highest echelons of the Mafia—the men whom tabloids frequently write about—Jerry lives at the top of prison society.

Slender and just over six feet tall, Jerry is a handsome man. With a full head of dusty-gold hair and an olive complexion, he looks like the picture a casting director would select when choosing an actor to play a prison patrician, or the institution's equivalent of an aristocrat. What draws others to Jerry—staff and inmates alike—is his straight-forward manner. With him, there is no pretense relative to who or what he is, about what his capabilities are outside, or that he ever will be anything else.

Jerry's behavior contrasts with that of other offenders who have served north of fifteen years. They frequently invent Walter Mitty personas and escapades, telling of adventures through which they have triumphed or describe nonexistent relationships with successful criminals and business people or entertainers. Perhaps because of insecurities that torment them over having led failed lives, or at least lives that must be colossal disappointments on some level, many long-time prisoners tend to fabricate stories that could not possibly have any validity. One prisoner I know, who has been incarcerated for thirty consecutive years, tells a story each day about the close relationships he has with celebrity gangsters who were no more than toddlers when he began serving his term in 1972. Just last week during dinner, he said that he was incarcerated with some of the people made famous in the movie *Papillion*. This prisoner likes to describe himself as one of the first gangsters who moved equally well between the celebrities of his day and organized crime, and frequently brags about his jet-set life prior to incarceration.

Rather than focus on the dismal prospects of the present, or the perhaps more perplexing possibility of returning to a world from which they have been separated for multiple decades, long-term prisoners frequently find comfort either in impressing others with the glorious lives they led prior to confinement, or if their lives were not so glamorous, painting an image of themselves as sophisticated jewel thieves, bank robbers, or drug lords. They fancy themselves as men of integrity for the sole reason that they have served their time without ever having "given up" any of their criminal associates. For many, prison is a place where grown men live in fantasies. For me, after spending years around pretenders, a straight-shooting convict like Jerry is a relief.

Unless one makes a conscious effort to filter out the communal manure, decades upon decades of living inside fences seem to eliminate a prisoner's ability to use logic. Long-term prisoners are quick to latch onto and run with any rumor, to cheer in a movie anytime a law enforcement officer gets shot, or to express joy whenever the system suffers a blow. They are grown men who act like gangs of petulant schoolboys, expressing how all judges, prosecutors, and law enforcement officers should be shot for all the "good people whose lives they ruined." Prison is an upside-down world where criminals are the heroes, and those who enforce the laws are the villains. While life becomes a theatrical farce, the opinions expressed are as real as a shot in the head. Inside the fences, it is common to see grown men greet each other with simulated gun shots, or to hear conversations throughout the day that glorify murder.

Another friend introduced me to Jerry in the dining room, and since then, I have come to know him well. Like many prisoners, Jerry has no hope or expectations of making any personal changes in his life. The difference is that he does not pretend for anyone. He passes each day in the same manner today as he did when he began serving this term in 1985, which is the same manner in which he passed every one of his previous terms.

AN EXPENSIVE ROUTINE

Jerry regularly sleeps until eleven. He always appears clean shaven and sharply dressed in trousers that someone else washes and irons for him. Jerry walks to the dining room to join two or three close friends for the noon meal, where inmate kitchen workers scramble to ensure that everyone at his table has enough to eat.

After lunch Jerry returns to his room, where he either reads tabloid newspapers or passes the day playing gin and smoking cigarettes with some of the others who regularly come by his room to make social calls. On a regular basis, well-connected prisoners from other institutions who transfer to Fort Dix seek Jerry out to pass along greetings and respects from gangsters who are incarcerated elsewhere. Knowing a prisoner like Jerry can make life easier for a newcomer.

In the evening Jerry usually will eat in the housing unit. Others will have managed to smuggle tomatoes, onions, and other vegetables from the kitchen. Jerry employs a cook in the unit who chops up the vegetables and prepares meals for him and his friends so they can avoid the hassles of both the dining room and the lines associated with the use of the microwave ovens. With the meal prepared, Jerry and his friends eat together among themselves in one of the unit's rooms. After dinner he may play a few more hours of gin, then take a stroll around the prison's compound with his two closest friends.

Jerry's charm serves him well behind the fences. It has helped him secure a do-nothing job as a midnight orderly, which leaves him without responsibility. He spends his evenings either talking with friends, playing more cards, or watching television until the early hours of the morning. For Jerry, the most important aspect of his time is structuring a schedule that allows him to pass it as easily as possible.

Serving a sentence the way that Jerry does is expensive. He estimates that, on average, he has spent between five and six hundred dollars each month since he began serving his term in 1985. The money has gone to purchase items in the commissary, to pay for food smuggled out of the kitchen, and to pay for all the services—such as cooking, cleaning, and laundry—that he purchases from others. Jerry has no money of his own, but people whom he has met in prison over the years have been faithful in their friendship, with several regularly chipping in by depositing between one and three hundred dollars each month in his debit account in the commissary. As a popular prisoner, Jerry has enjoyed this remarkably high level of financial support throughout his sentence. Even in prison, he is a high roller.

Jerry does not write to anyone outside of prison, and other than his mother, his sister, and one of his daughters, he has no network of support outside that is not in some way related to the criminal world. His mother, he says, has stood by his side since his first prison term in 1963, and wherever he has been held, he always has been able to count on her coming to visit him on a regular basis. She now is over eighty, and she continues to join his sister in serving his time with him, visiting Jerry at least once each month.

AN UNCHANGING OUTLOOK

Jerry says he finds it easier to live inside these fences by not soliciting or working to maintain relationships outside of prison. He uses the phone regularly, but since federal prisoners now are limited to fewer than ten minutes of telephone access per day, Jerry uses it mainly to speak with his eldest daughter. He has two other children, but he has strained relations with them as a consequence of his having been incarcerated for virtually their entire lives.

Jerry does not lie to his family members. When they ask him what he plans to do upon his release, he tells them he does not know. The one thing he does know is that he refuses to work or to change from the type of person he always has been. A return to prison does not frighten him as much as a low-paying job, which he says he would never accept. "What kind of job could I get that would pay me forty to fifty thousand dollars a week?" Jerry asks. "That's what I need to make to support my lifestyle." He is a man who knows quite specifically what he wants.

When I reminded Jerry that he has been sharing a closet-sized prison cell with other men for more than twenty-five years of his life, he said that does not faze him. "I hope I don't have to die in prison, but I'd prefer to come back than to live from hand to mouth." Many long-time prisoners, I think, are of the same mind. Inside, they have respect and are considered men of integrity; outside, they perceive few chances to succeed.

Jerry is a gifted and talented communicator. Part raconteur, part street tough, he has a gripping story for every occasion, and within minutes he has other people laughing and smitten with his wit. Jerry Cohen seems to be perpetually on stage, much the way a famous actor might be. He has style, timing, a perfect sense of his audience—whether it is composed of hardcore felons or the staff members who make their living guarding them. Jerry Cohen puts everyone around him at ease. He is the center of attention, and others around him make noticeable efforts to obtain his favor. He could easily adapt those talents to initiate a career in sales of some sort, but he has no interest. "What could I make as a salesman?" he asks. "Four, five, ten thousand a month? How am I going to live with that on the street? By the time taxes are taken out I'd be left with about half of whatever I earned. That just won't cut it for me. I've got to find something better."

When I reminded Jerry that millions of people support families on far less than the numbers that he is talking, he dismisses them as people who don't know how to live. And he is adamant about not falling into that "working-man's trap," which to him, is a worse prison than the ones he has known for his entire life.

Many of the prisoners around me speak in the same hardcore terms as Jerry. But few are really believable. Jerry differs from most in that despite the many years he has served in custody, he readily acknowledges that he has no fear of returning to prison. Although he is courteous to everyone, he shows no deference to staff members or to anyone else. In all of the time that he has served in prison, he has not joined a single prison program. He has not enrolled in one educational course, not participated in a single activity sponsored by religious services or the psychology department. In fact, he is openly contemptuous of those who try to present themselves in one way to other prisoners while simultaneously sucking up to staff members. In fact, he is not averse to exposing someone for living like a counterfeit hoodlum.

Among all the programs sponsored by the federal prison system, there is only one through which inmates may enroll to reduce their terms in confinement. Congress has given the Bureau of Prisons authority to reduce by up to eighteen months the sentences of inmates who successfully complete a five-hundred-hour drug education program offered by the psychology department. The course takes about nine months to complete. Inmates who enroll must participate in group sessions by revealing their personal experiences with drug use. They also must sit through classes detailing the harmful effects of drugs and write an essay in which they renounce the criminal lifestyles they once led.

Jerry scoffs at inmates who portray themselves as hoodlums, gangsters, tough guys, thugs, or whatever the current vernacular may be, then enroll in such programs. What really irks him is when these people say they enroll only "to get over on the government" or to get out of jail sooner. He equates them to crybabies. "They knew what they were doing when they came to prison," he says. "They should be men about it and do their time like a man. Bending over to participate in these kiss-ass programs with all the other snivelers in prison is belittling. If they wanted to get out of prison so bad, they never should have come in the first place. Prison is a place for men."

HALF A LIFE AND NO REGRETS

Unlike others, Jerry does not talk one way around his fellow prisoners and another around staff members. He is as loyal to his values as he is to his criminal associates. Ironically, staff members respect him for the commitment he makes to his way of life. Whereas guards and lieutenants frequently wear stern faces and openly harass prisoners for the smallest of trivialities, many treat Jerry like he is a celebrity. One case manager whom others have nicknamed Mussolini because of his shiny bald pate and seemingly fascist ways actually has befriended Jerry. Indeed, when Jerry was scheduled to appear before the parole board for the possibility of advancing his release date, Mussolini asked Jerry whether he had a staff member to represent him before the parole board. When Jerry answered that he did not, Mussolini volunteered to go say a few good words on his behalf.

From a convict's point of view, Jerry is a stand-up guy. He is deserving of respect because of his allegiance to the criminal code. But why would Mussolini, a staffer who recommends segregation and loss of good time to less noteworthy prisoners if they are caught with minor contraband, agree to recommend early release for a career criminal who has never even gone through the motions of attempting to go straight? Like others in the prison, perhaps Mussolini is a theater-goer, caught up in the charisma of Jerry Cohen. Another guard regularly overlooks Jerry's violation of petty prison rules. Instead of being harassed, Jerry leads the life of a dignitary inside the fences. Staff members, perhaps, recognize him romantically as one of the last of the old-time convicts.

Jerry expects to be released from prison in 2003. Temporarily, until he is able to pull himself together, he expects to live with his sister, his mother, or his daughter. He will be sixty-two, with no assets, not even clothes. Essentially, he begins his life anew, with no experience other than having led a bungled life as a burglar and drug dealer. He has served nearly half his life in prison.

Despite the limited prospects that such a background brings, Jerry says he does not regret a single day he has served in confinement. In fact, he says that even if he were to begin serving his term again, he would not pass his time any differently. He has passed his time easily. "It's been a piece of cake." For him, that is considered a successful adjustment to prison.

If Jerry's figures of his commissary expenditures are accurate, over the course of the seventeen years he has served on this sentence, he has spent over a hundred thousand dollars. Had he managed to save half that sum, it might have made a significant difference in his ability to situate himself in the community upon his release. But Jerry says he has never thought about the obstacles he would face upon release. It was too far away for him to contemplate, so he passed his time thinking about how to get through the day. He has served his sentence one day at a time, expecting that when he left prison he would revert to the same behavior he has known all his life. With those aspirations, he saw no reason to frustrate himself by trying to learn a new skill. Jerry had no hope of rehabilitation; he was not interested in living any other life than that of a hoodlum. Crime is all he has known since childhood, and despite having served over twenty-five years in prison, he continues to see no reason to change things now. "I started off this bid with three kids, a wife, and a dog named JoJo Cohen," Jerry reminisces. "Now, two of my kids don't talk to me. Like the first, my second wife left me. And the dog died last June. I don't even know which I miss the most, the wife, the kids, or the dog."

Jerry will return to what he has known, in some way, shape, or manner.

Despite also serving a lengthy sentence, Seth Ferranti, the next towering-time prisoner, lacks the stature of a long-time convict like Jerry. Seth describes the pressure of just coming into the system, and the steps he took to fit in.

SEEKING FREEDOM THROUGH RECOGNITION AND ACCEPTANCE BY OTHERS: SETH FERRANTI

A prison radical who calls himself the Poetic Terrorist talks about his efforts to connect.

Seth Ferranti has been confined since October 1, 1993. Despite no history of violence in his criminal record, he is serving in excess of twenty-five years. For the past year, Seth has been confined with me here at Fort Dix. We live on the same floor in one of the housing units. Despite our proximity, we hardly acknowledged each other until recently. That is the nature of prison living. Hundreds of prisoners live together on the same floor of a building. We share the same bathroom, and we look and move like zombies, instinctively turning sideways to avoid making contact as we squeeze past each other in the narrow hallways. But we rarely express a greeting or even acknowledge the sullen, tough-looking faces of others.

I approached Seth because I heard that he is serving a lengthy sentence. Rumors and gossip about others spread inside these fences like a gasoline fire. Not too many people in this facility are, like me, serving sentences that exceed multiple decades.

Seth was in one of our floor's community bathrooms when I introduced myself to him. The bathroom is large, with seven toilets lined up in a row against one wall, and seven white sinks mounted directly in front against the opposite wall. The walls are bare, with only square pieces of stainless steel riveted at head level above the sinks. That dull, scratched up metal comes as close as a prisoner gets to a mirror. It is like looking for one's

Seth Ferranti

reflection on the bottom of a kitchen skillet. The room is lit with bright fluorescent lights, and a lingering smell of dried urine and nicotine permeates the air.

In the world outside of fences, bathrooms may seem an odd place to initiate an acquaintance. Each prison, on the other hand, is an isolated and abnormal community, one where nominally curious behavior not only is accepted, but often becomes the norm. The presence of guards and the physical layouts of prisons quickly shatter all notions of privacy. Every location is public, open for all eyes to see.

Fortunately, some of the bathrooms have windows that open, including the one where I met Seth. We leaned out one of those open windows so we could talk without interference or interruption from others. At 10:00 P.M. on a Saturday night, when the prison yard was closed and we were confined to our housing unit—along with the more than three hundred other exiles— that community bathroom gave us our best opportunity for a private conversation.

THE "KINGPIN" FALLS

Seth, I learned, had been convicted of operating a continuing criminal enterprise, a nonviolent but serious drug offense that prosecutors generally refer to as the "kingpin" charge. It implies that he was a leader or an organizer of others who conspired to distribute illicit drugs. Seth comes from the suburban area of Fairfax, Virginia. When he was initially arrested he had just turned twenty; he never had problems with the criminal justice system prior to his current convictions.

After Seth's arrest, however, he was released on bond because he had agreed to plead guilty. Instead of sticking around for sentencing, Seth explained that he faked his own suicide while he was out on bail and then fled to California. He began a nomadic life, meandering without much purpose, buying and selling marijuana in college towns across the United States to support himself. About two years later, Seth was arrested again, and since that arrest, he has been in federal custody.

Seth led a delusional existence following his initial arrest. He convinced himself that because he was from a middle-class family, because he had no history of violence, and because he was young, that the prosecutors would treat his crime somewhat less severely. Seth believed that as a white teenager, a long prison term would not be appropriate for his conviction. Instead, he anticipated some sort of slap-on-the-wrist punishment. He had visions of drug rehabilitation centers and work camps. Certainly, he thought, those would prove adequate responses for his offenses. "I didn't really do anything that bad anyway," he still asserts. Consistent with that perspective, he continued selling drugs after his initial arrest.

Seth was twenty-two when he boarded a bus headed to a medium-security prison in Manchester, Kentucky. His ankles were fastened with chains. The guards put handcuffs on his wrists, then enclosed those manacles in a black metal box for additional security; a chain around his waist kept his wrists securely in front of him. The prison experience not only was new for him, he also was being sent several hundred miles away from his home in Virginia.

On the drive there, Seth sat beside a convict who introduced himself as Dagger. Dagger, an "old head" who told Seth that he was forty-two and had been incarcerated for over half his life already, including the past twelve consecutive years, said he would show Seth around the prison, introduce him to the so-called right crowd.

Seth stands just over six feet tall and is of average build. With chalk-white skin and eyes of a Hitler blue, however, he felt out of place soon after getting onto the bus. About fifty other prisoners being transported with him, he says; all were in chains. Fewer than five had complexions "lighter than a brown paper bag," he said. Dagger was one of them, and Seth felt a little easier after making a white friend on the bus. He had heard rumors about prisons being divided along racial lines and was preoccupied with this thought from the start. That bus ride gave him some initial fears about just how outnumbered he was going to be as a white man, which is how Seth likes to identify himself.

PUTTING ON THE TOUGH FACE

Being new to the prison environment, and one of the youngest men inside the fences, Seth said that he felt somewhat threatened. He hardly knew himself, much less the other felons with whom he was about to share space. To Seth, they all looked mean, with their overgrown physiques, demonic tattoos, welts and scars from knife wounds that did not heal quite right on their keloid skin.

In order to fit in, Seth put a constant scowl on his face, as if he were a prizefighter staring down an opponent before a boxing match. From that moment forward, he refused to shave his face clean. "I'm not going naked," he would say. Seth grew a devil beard and prohibited himself from smiling. Even with this new, fierce look, Seth felt the need for an ally to help him adjust. He was glad to have met Dagger, whose experience and contacts would make him an excellent prison mentor.

Once Seth and the others were processed, Seth was sent to a common sleeping area where he would remain until a two-man cell became available for him. While he was settling in, Dagger came by and said he was ready to introduce Seth around to the "good guys in the joint." Before he did, though, he said he had to make sure Seth was "okay."

"What do you mean, am I okay?" Seth was confused, not quite knowing what Dagger was asking him.

"I mean you ain't no rat are you? You didn't give no one up on your case, right?"

Seth was new to prison parlance. Not coming from a background that really conditioned him for living in a community of captives, he did not know that anyone who cooperated with law enforcement in any way was anathema and a frequent target for abuse by the other convicts who considered themselves as hard as the walls around them. Seth answered that he was not a rat, that he was serving a twenty-five year sentence.

"Look man, I can dig what you're sayin'," Dagger said, "but I'm puttin' my reputation on the line by goin' out for you. I gotta see your paperwork to make sure."

"What are you talking about, my paperwork?" Seth wanted to know.

"I need to see your PSI, know what I mean?"

Dagger was referring to the presentence investigation report prepared by officers of the court for the sentencing judge. The PSI would detail Seth's background and confirm whether he ever had provided assistance to law enforcement in the past.

In the eyes of the government and many law-abiding citizens, cooperating with law enforcement and accepting responsibility represents a step toward redemption and an attempt by offenders to reconcile with their communities. In prison, however, becoming known as a so-called good guy requires just the opposite behavior of what the average American would expect. The more recalcitrant one's reputation in prison, the more respect the convict is going to receive inside the fences. Seth's twenty-five year sentence was a valid credential in prison, equivalent to a Harvard degree for a recent graduate about to enter the job market.

Seth's paperwork verified that he was okay. As long as he did not cooperate, everything else, according to what Dagger was teaching Seth, would be fine. When Dagger read in Seth's PSI that he had eluded law enforcement for two years by writing a suicide note indicating he was jumping off a cliff into a roaring river, Dagger told Seth that it was good to see another so-called solid white man. He then took Seth around to meet his crew of stand-up cons.

ASSOCIATING WITH TROUBLE

The people to whom Dagger introduced Seth were all affiliated with one white supremacy gang or another. All were serving long sentences. As Hector Colon explained, in higher-security men's prisons, many of the men associate by race, ethnicity, or geographical background. At the prison where Seth was held, there were clusters of prisoners who wanted to be known as affiliates of the Aryan Brotherhood, the Dirty White Boys, the Road Runners, or some other exclusionary group. Seth says he was glad Dagger introduced him to those guys when he began his sentence. They gave him a feeling of belonging, and he was eager to prove himself worthy of their acquaintance.

During the first years of his sentence he consorted with this crowd. Dagger and his friends spent their time extorting weaker prisoners, smuggling drugs and selling them in the prison, and forcing prisoners whom they suspected of being snitches to check in to protective custody. This meant the suspected informers would have the choice of either facing constant abuse, including theft and assault, or asking guards to lock them in a cell without access to the prison's recreation or educational programs.

Seth reminisced about one of the first power moves in which he participated with Dagger and his friends. "It was some rat motherfucker that needed to be taken off the count." His friends came by Seth's cell in the early evening. They told him to put his boots on as it was time to "put in some work." Seth did not know where he was going, so Dagger explained. He said the group knew this "bitchassmotherfucker was a rat." That, apparently, was all Seth needed to know. Dagger went on to explain exactly what needed to be done.

Two of Dagger's group were going to stand outside of the target's cell as lookouts who could warn the gang if a guard came by. The prisoner they sought was lying on his bottom bunk. Dagger explained that Seth would be the point man, the first one in the cell. Three others would follow in behind him. Dagger also instructed Seth to brace his left arm on the bed post for leverage and then stand over the target. When he was in position, Seth was expected to tell the guy what was happening. While Seth was talking, the other guys would take everything out of his locker. Seth told the guy not to move if he did not want a "beatdown."

The guy had the audacity to lift his head off the pillow. So Seth, bracing himself on the bed with his left hand, as Dagger had instructed, smashed his right fist down into the guy's mouth. After the solid punch, the guy stayed still and quiet like a wounded bird, sinking back into his institutional-issue pillow.

After they loaded all of the victim's commissary out of his locker, Dagger turned to the guy and said, "We know you're a ratmotherfucker. Check into PC tonight. If you stay on the compound, I'm coming back for more of your shit next week. If you mention any of this to anyone, I'm gonna leave you where I found you with your guts falling out."

Seth had been initiated, and having thrown his first punch for the cause, he felt worthy of his new friends. Seth says his friends gave him a feeling of power. After his experiences of going through the criminal justice system, he says he needed that. Dagger and the others with whom Seth spent his time expressed constant hatred for snitches, the government, and anyone who was not what they considered Aryan. Seth said that he hated the government, too, blamed it for all his problems. But he sometimes had rifts with his social circle, because he says he did not hate others simply because of their skin color.

Over a thousand other prisoners were confined with Seth behind the prison's fences, and when he was walking with his pack, a black might pass him and say "Yo, what's up?" or acknowledge him in some way. Dagger and his other friends, all of whom were adorned with swastika tattoos and the word "WHITE" on the back of their left arm and "PRIDE" on the back of their right, would admonish Seth.

"What you talkin' to that ignoran' nigger for?" They would ask in broken syntax.

Seth would defend his action. "Chill out man. I play sports with the guy. He's okay."

"He's okay? What are you, some kind a niggerlover?" His friends would ask. "I don't give a shit what you play with them motherfuckers. Don't bring 'em 'round us." Tolerance had not found its way inside the fences.

His initial adjustment meant continuous problems for Seth. He served eight months of his first two years in segregation. The guards had labeled him and the group with which he was fraternizing as troublemakers. Because of the reputation his clique and his actions brought him, Seth was being summoned for questioning with guards at least once each week for one reason or another. They singled him out of groups to search him, and they went through his belongings looking for contraband five to six times each week. If a problem occurred in the prison—for example, someone turning up bloody from a stabbing or a beating—Seth frequently was locked in segregation for investigation. His time was not easy, but he had his prison respect. That had been important to him.

A NEW START

After Seth's second year, a new prison opened in Beckley, West Virginia. Although Beckley remained a long way from his parents' home, he suspected a transfer out of Kentucky would help his adjustment. Seth needed a fresh start. As long as he remained behind the fences with Dagger and his racist comrades, Seth knew he never would shake his dubious reputation as a prison troublemaker. He was granted a transfer to Beckley, and on the way to his new assignment, he committed himself to serving his time without being influenced by others.

When he arrived at Beckley, Seth was twenty-four. He then realized that he had wasted the first two years of his sentence by latching on to a group of prison thugs. They brought him nothing but senseless problems. The length of time he had to serve finally began to resonate with him, and he figured out that he needed more than the white-pride trip.

Seth decided to enroll in school. He was not necessarily interested in school for the purpose of preparing himself for employment upon release. Release, he knew, was too far into the future. He needed something more immediate, something to create a life for himself inside the fences. Every time a guard ordered him to stand for a census count or strip naked for a body search, Seth's hatred for the government and all its emissaries increased. By attending school, he would work to develop his communication skills. Seth thought of himself as a prisoner of war, the drug war. In his war, the pen was mightier than the sword. By educating himself, Seth hoped to become a voice from the inside, one that would work as a relentless weapon to tear apart the establishment that was holding him down.

Seth's parents paid for him to enroll in a correspondence program at Pennsylvania State University. His first two years at Beckley, Seth isolated himself in his studies. After the school awarded him an associate's degree, he began a sustained effort to invite the media into his life. He created press packets designed to bring attention to his cause of increasing public awareness to the injustices he saw in long-term incarceration for nonviolent drug offenders. Seth's packets included newspaper clippings that described his case, verse and prose he wrote to draw attention to his feelings of being a victim, and anything else he thought would help lure the media to his cause. He printed hundreds of these packages and mailed them to celebrity fan club addresses, television networks, and magazine and newspaper editors to court publicity. It was his way of trying to reach out, to connect with a world from which he felt estranged. Fighting against the system through disturbances inside the prison had been a waste of time, but Seth expected that his education would help him become an effective combatant against the prison system and the laws securing him.

Many prisoners, like Seth, try to politicize their predicament. Even his initial teaming up with Dagger and his crew was a political decision of sorts. By trying to educate himself and reaching outside, Seth had simply moved to a larger arena.

Other prisoners, too, frequently seek to join or make contact with a cause that is larger than themselves. By virtue of their status, autonomy has been ripped from their lives. Prisoners live under close scrutiny with hundreds of rules and the threat of aggravating and immediate punishments hanging over their heads. For most prisoners, being in possession of an onion, or having a second blanket in winter months, for example, may result in the sanction of a six month loss of telephone and visiting privileges. If the person has status inside the fences, on the other hand, he might not suffer the same scrutiny.

Politically minded prisoners seek a kind of liberation they expect will come with a wider identity. As a prisoner, Seth knows his opinions have no merit inside. Were he to succeed in persuading media representatives to carry his story or use him as a spokesman, Seth was and is convinced he will have created a position of influence for himself inside the walls. That influence may take some of the sting away from the confinement that constantly slaps him in the face.

WRITING TO BE HEARD

Those who lack the wherewithal—some might say the effrontery—to reach out to the media or people of influence may seek similar power within the prison itself. They try to position themselves as leaders of prisoner organizations (such as religious or educational groups) or groups that work in some way with the community. They finagle their way into jobs that may give them influence with administrators. Some become informants to staff members, exchanging tips on who is doing what in exchange for better living quarters or an extra box of corn flakes in the morning. Still others, like Dagger, form gangs of intimidation.

After several months of waiting for his shotgun approach to attract media attention—without receiving a single response—Seth decided to become a sharp shooter. He thought the readers of *Rolling Stone* magazine represented the audience he was trying to reach, so he wrote a letter of inquiry to the editor, asking for an opportunity to write an article that would detail his so-called suburban drug lifestyle and the twenty-five year sentence he is serving as a result of it. He had never written anything more complicated than a college term paper before, but that did not intimidate Seth. He was filled with a perhaps illogical but passionate hatred for a system that he was convinced had wrongfully incarcerated him, and he wanted to express that animosity to the world.

Seth could not believe that American citizens actually knew that people like him—young white people—were serving lengthy sentences for what he thought were trivial offenses. Seth was, and remains convinced, that he is a victim. He views his arrest and imprisonment as a means to appease civil rights leaders who complained about minority offenders receiving disproportionately longer sentences than whites. As a prison revolutionary, Seth fancied himself leading the fight for the reform of all drug laws.

Seth waited again for several weeks after sending the initial query, with no response. So he sent a second letter. Less than a month later, Seth received good news from an editor indicating the magazine would work with him. The editor suggested that Seth prepare a draft of the article he wanted to publish, then submit it for review. Seth set to work at once, trying to condense all that he wanted to express into a thousand-word article. Before he finished his draft, however, Seth learned that the editor with whom he was working had left the magazine and the project was on hold. Seth would have to wait for the new editor to contact him.

After a few months of silence, Seth received a letter telling him that the new editor was not interested in Seth writing an editorial or biased story, but instead would send a professional writer to interview him for an article. Seth really had been hoping to launch his writing career, a career that he envisioned would become a torrent of invective-laden articles condemning the prison system and the draconian drug laws of the federal government. Realizing that *Rolling Stone* would not publish his own work, Seth hoped the awaited journalist would come to see his situation as dire and bring it to the attention of the thousands who read the magazine. Although he would not receive a byline, the popular periodical would expose Seth to what he hoped would become his constituency.

John Colapinto, the writer sent by *Rolling Stone,* eventually came to visit Seth. The two were approximately the same age, though the decisions Colapinto made as a younger man moved his life in a strikingly different direction. As a long-term prisoner, Seth does not see the turn of events this way. It is as if the walls not only confine his body, but restrict his rational intellect as well. For him, solace comes through casting blame on others. To Seth, it has been the evil, conspiratorial hands of government that "fucked up" his life. "I got a life sentence for some bullshit mistakes I made when I was just a kid," Seth complains. "If I thought I could get away with it, I'd kill all these motherfuckers who make the laws." Seth's revolutionary voice is remarkably consistent in its lack of remorse.

During his visit, the writer recorded his conversation with Seth and took photographs. It was Seth's big day, his chance to distinguish himself and put a face with his prison number for the readers of *Rolling Stone*. The reporter asked about life in prison, wanted to know how he copes inside. Seth told the writer about his routine. He explained how he lived with a so-called real criminal, someone serving three years for a rape conviction. The cell was small, like a walk-in closet containing one metal bunk bed, a toilet-and-sink contraption, and two small storage lockers that are supposed to contain everything Seth and his cellmate own. Seth explained that he worked in the prison factory and spent the rest of his time trying to reach outside the fences.

I asked Seth whether he was angry about having to serve his time in close quarters with someone who has only a three-year sentence for rape, one of the worst convictions to have among the pecking order of criminal convictions. "People been raping people for ages. Who gives a fuck? I'm only pissed off that I got twenty-five years for selling hippie drugs to people who wanted them. And what really pisses me off is that all those hippie, free-love motherfuckers from the sixties are now the hypocrites making the laws against the same shit they were doing when they were in college."

Many prisoners, like Seth, perceive themselves as victims of a corrupt federal department of justice. They acknowledge that they were convicted. With few exceptions, however, most grumble about the length of their sentences. While they say that they made a mistake, such prisoners fail to realize and acknowledge that a mistake implies that they made an error in what they were intending to do.

Somehow, prison walls insulate Seth from admitting and facing the truth. There was no mistake. He regularly acknowledges that he knew exactly what he was doing in selling drugs, he did it to get high and make money. He fails to recognize a connection between his actions, his conviction, and his sentence. Part of his adjustment, therefore, comes in the self-therapy he administers by blaming others for the results of the choices he made. Identifying himself as a victim gives him an emotional pacifier, providing succor for the years he is losing to prison.

When *Rolling Stone* printed the article, Seth says it left out much of what he had said. The reporter focused on the shock value of a prison story describing ubiquitous violence behind the fences but did not describe Seth's efforts to educate himself, his efforts to influence public opinion, or what he perceived as the obstacles he encountered regularly in his ongoing struggle with the correctional system that holds him. The article spent too much time, Seth complained, talking about the beatings and stabbings. It did not discuss suburban white kids being sent to prison for what he called bullshit, as he had hoped it would. He frequently says that the only reason he is locked up is because the government needed to make an example of a white guy, which is what he thought was important to bring to the attention of others. He was disappointed in *Rolling Stone* for not seeing the value in this story.

Although *Rolling Stone* did not publish exactly what Seth wanted, on page 173 of its May 28, 1998, issue, a large picture of Seth's glaring face looks daggers into the eyes of readers. His quote "I Am a Prisoner of the War on Drugs" is highlighted beneath the photograph. The story did make him a celebrity inside the prison, which gave him a taste of the notoriety he craves and expects to come his way. Seth continues to believe the article can catapult him into a career as a prison radical spokesman, culminating in a feature film. He regularly makes copies of the article to include with the press packages he continues sending to media representatives. Those packages helped place some of his writings in pulp-type periodicals that cover punk rock and alternative lifestyles. Seth brands his work Poetic Terrorism, and he is the poetic terrorist.

In 2002, Seth serves his eighth year of confinement. He does not expect release to come until 2015. Like many long-term prisoners, Seth sees his incarceration as a betrayal by a duplicitous government, one where political leaders use propaganda to incarcerate the powerless in order to take attention away from themselves. This is a common theme behind prison fences.

Seth feels that society has rejected him, so he in turn has adjusted by going on the offensive, trying to create his own power base from inside the walls. As one who has been alienated from his community, Seth seeks acceptance, and eventually power. His early adjustment brought him into the clutches of prison gangs, but he later recognized that he needed to reach outside if he was going to make a difference in his life. His adjustment, like that of many prisoners with political propensities, is about connecting with other (and hopefully like-minded) people. Seth seeks his freedom through recognition and acceptance by others.

Melvin Spears, our next towering-time prisoner, also sought acceptance through others during his early prison terms. Now, he begins the initial months of his longest sentence yet, and because of a sanction he recently received, he will serve his first year with few connections to the outside world.

FACING A MORE PUNITIVE
SYSTEM:
MELVIN SPEARS

One prisoner describes how a newcomer's mistake resulted in the loss of privileges that would have allowed him to communicate with others outside.

Thanksgiving marks the beginning of the holiday season in America. Although the last six weeks of each year is a time of celebration for many people, especially families and children, behind prison fences this period of time often exacerbates stress. I met Melvin Spears just after Thanksgiving as he was beginning a twenty-year sentence for distributing 112 grams of crack cocaine. Personal complications, however, made his adjustment to incarceration more difficult than that of other newly arriving prisoners.

Melvin is assigned to a different housing unit than mine, and were it not for Paul, another long-term prisoner, our paths may have never crossed. Paul was telling me about a disciplinary sanction he had received for giving something of value to another inmate. His problem began when he lost a radio and set of headphones that he had borrowed from someone else. As a gesture of compensation and good faith, Paul asked a family member to send money into the owner's debit account at Fort Dix. A prison guard intercepted the message. As a consequence, Paul lost his visiting privileges for one year, his telephone usage for one year, and his access to the commissary for three months.

The sanction sounded harsh to me, but as one who has lived inside these fences since 1987, I knew the Bureau of Prisons system was becoming more punitive as it became more crowded. Every prisoner has the responsibility to know and abide by the rules—or suffer the consequences. Paul was not whining about his sanction. After having served nearly a decade, he acknowledged that he had been caught. He accepted responsibility and was prepared to put the matter behind him. "Besides," Paul said, "at least I knew what I was doing. A new guy went in for sanctioning after me. He got hit just as hard and didn't know anything about the rules he was breaking."

Paul was talking about Melvin. He suggested I might be able to help Melvin appeal his disciplinary sanction. I agreed to meet Melvin and listen to his story.

Melvin is an African American in his late thirties, and although he only recently began serving this twenty-year sentence, he was not a stranger to prison. Regardless of being the type of prisoner who serves a life sentence on the installment plan, he looked distraught and disoriented when I met him, like a punch-drunk prizefighter, battered and staggering in an unfamiliar world. Melvin explained the origins of his ordeal, that he had arrived at Fort Dix only two weeks before and already had lost the privilege of communicating with his family.

THE PATH TO PERDITION

All of Melvin's problems with the criminal justice system have their roots in his addiction to narcotics. He served three previous sentences, but after each release he resumed his drug use and eventually faced new criminal charges. His first conviction came in 1984 for trafficking in pills. Melvin received an indeterminate sentence of between four and twenty-three months. Prisoners who receive such a sentence, and stay out of trouble during their confinement, usually are released on parole after serving the low end of the sentence inside, then the remainder outside under the supervision of a parole officer. Melvin served four months, but he said that was the toughest time he had ever put in. It was hard on him because all he thought about was getting out so he could get high again.

His addiction to drugs pushed him to become a dealer. Having dropped out of high school, Melvin was functionally illiterate. He served four years in the military, then found a job as a cook. On the side, he sold drugs to earn enough money to support his addiction. Further, Melvin says his girlfriend was a prostitute, and they were able to use her earnings to buy more drugs. Getting high was the focus of Melvin's life. He was so wrapped up in his addiction that he made time for little else. Indeed, Melvin had two children with a second woman, yet he did not consider it his responsibility to help raise them. Instead, he left them to be cared for by their mother.

Approximately eighteen months after Melvin's release from his first term, he was convicted again for trafficking in pills. He received another indeterminate sentence of between eighteen and thirty-six months. While he was confined, Melvin participated in various drug education programs. Those classes helped him understand his drug and alcohol addictions. He says that he learned about how drugs destroy one's health, and how an addiction damages relationships with family and friends. Melvin realized that he was an addict, but the classes did not help him conquer his addiction. He was released from that second term after serving the minimum eighteen months. Melvin then took a job with a relative as a carpet layer and attempted to lead a drug-free life.

It did not last. Melvin does not even remember how he returned to street life and drugs, but three months after his release he was using drugs once more—every day. He snorted cocaine or shot it into his veins with a needle. He continued to work at his job while he hustled drugs on the side. Then he suffered a mild overdose. Because of his previous military service, Melvin was authorized for ninety days of inpatient treatment at a Veteran's Administration hospital, and after completing that program, he passed seven months in what he called "good clean time," meaning he was able to fight the urge to use drugs. But his past came back to bite him. He was indicted and convicted for drug sales he had made over a year before. For that conviction, Melvin received yet another indeterminate sentence, this time between three and seven years. He did not adjust well during this longer stretch of time.

THIRD TIME, HARD TIME

After his third conviction, Melvin was admitted into Graterford, the maximum-security prison for the Commonwealth of Pennsylvania. He was twenty-seven at the start of that term, and had he kept his record free of disciplinary infractions, Melvin likely would have been released after serving three years. The choices he made at Graterford, however, not only brought numerous disciplinary infractions, they also brought new criminal charges.

Melvin says that when he walked into Graterford he was feeling a lot of pressure. He was angry at the criminal justice system. Through it, he had been convicted for drugs that he had sold over a year earlier. It was an act, long ago forgotten, at least by him. He was convinced that he was being treated unfairly. Although he had served two previous terms, Melvin had hoped that his problems with the law were behind him—despite his continued criminal conduct. Instead, Melvin knew that he now would serve at least three years, more than he had served on his two previous sentences combined.

Prisoners frequently deceive themselves into believing that once they complete a term of confinement or a period of supervised release, the conviction disappears. It does not. Instead, individuals carry their criminal histories with them for life. Melvin's exposure to incarceration increased with every conviction, and his ignorance of the cumulative aspect of the sentencing laws did not expunge him from receiving increasingly longer sentences with each new conviction.

When Melvin carried his anger with him into Graterford, like most newly arriving prisoners, he fell in with a crowd that held similar beliefs to his own. At that time, Melvin says that he felt like a victim. "Society was fuckin' me over," he said. "It was fuckin' over the black man." He did not attribute his incarceration to selling drugs, or recognize how his previous convictions led to his receiving this longer term. He felt like society was targeting him personally and his race as a whole. Such beliefs led him into the welcoming arms of the Fruit of Islam (FOI) clique at Graterford.

The FOI is a militant faction of the Nation of Islam (The Nation), which has a substantial following in higher-security prisons. The Nation, led by Louis Farrakahn, is a quasi-Islamic religious group that develops segregationist views and seeks to empower black people. Those who follow The Nation differ from others of the Islamic faith in that the strict requirements of repeated ritualistic prayer are not of paramount importance. Indeed, The Nation strikes some observers as being more secular than religious because of its focus on black empowerment—by any means necessary—to the exclusion of other races. Although the U.S. Constitution offers certain protections of the rights of prisoners to worship, some prison authorities target The Nation as a prison gang rather than a religious organization, and members of the FOI as its militant soldiers.

"The FOI held the same beliefs as me," Melvin said, "so I started to groove with them." Participating with the group led to a loss of autonomy. Rules of the FOI, which he still observes, prohibit him from talking explicitly about his activities or responsibilities as a so-called soldier in the FOI; some crimes have no statute of limitations. Although he no longer is an active member of the group he says that others might consider his discussion of its activities as a breach of trust—an error that could lead to severe and violent repercussions. "I would just assume [sic] not say nothing further about the FOI or the Nation," he told me. "I've moved on to a more traditional branch of Islam, but I don't have nothing against The Nation or its people."

While Melvin was adjusting to his early years at Graterford, he engaged in behavior that led to his receiving disciplinary infractions for assault and for possession of weapons. The more serious problems for Melvin, however, were the new felony criminal charges he received for trafficking in narcotics inside the prison. Although The Nation strictly forbids its members from using drugs, Melvin was not averse to selling drugs to others as a vehicle for empowerment.

When Graterford's administrators charged Melvin with trafficking in drugs, they did not use the disciplinary system. Instead of charging him administratively with a disciplinary infraction, he was processed through the criminal justice system and given an additional twelve-month sentence. Although the new term was to run concurrently with the term he already was serving, it resulted in an additional felony conviction that would provide another damaging addition to his criminal history record.

Melvin told me that while he was serving time in Graterford, his aspirations were not to come out of prison and begin life as a law-abiding citizen. Instead, he wanted to create a large-scale criminal enterprise. Through the affiliations he made at Graterford, Melvin said that he had established friendships with several leading criminals who were eager to facilitate his aspirations of becoming a large-scale drug dealer.

Like Melvin, many prisoners use their time in confinement to initiate new opportunities for crime. While in the community, it is not always easy to find new criminal alliances. Finding new suppliers or buyers of drugs, for example, is not like finding business associates, for which one can check resumes, references, and credit histories. Criminal acts require some level of secrecy, as no one can be sure who is an informant or a competitor or both.

While in the broader American community, citizens lead private lives, prisoners live in fishbowls. Every inhabitant has been convicted of at least one felony. The men carry Presentence Investigation Reports and court transcripts that document their criminal histories. Further, the men spend years together and can easily spot others who are committed to the criminal way of life simply by the way they adjust. Those who stay to themselves, participate in educational programs, and work carefully to stay out of trouble, for example, may be indicating that they are attempting to avoid further problems with the law. Such behavior contrasts with those who live in open defiance of the system, and those who look for opportunities to continue their criminal behavior inside. Accordingly, many men use their prison terms as a period for criminal networking, making alliances to help them initiate or expand criminal networks both inside prison and in preparation for life outside prison once more.

Melvin's numerous criminal convictions may have made him look like a loser to law-abiding citizens. To committed criminals, however, his papers showed that he was a stand-up convict. He was "pinched" numerous times, but he never cooperated with law enforcement in order to lessen his own exposure to conviction. In other words, whereas others might consider Melvin's criminal history a liability, in prison, his record was not frowned upon. Instead, it indicated that he could be trusted. The new acquaintances he made at Graterford were willing to help him further his criminal aspirations.

After Melvin was charged in the criminal courts for trafficking in drugs during his confinement, administrators sent him to isolation for several months. While there he found a new mentor, he says, and he had a change of heart.

He spent time in a cell next to Kareem, a prisoner on death row. With nothing but time on their hands and steel bars separating them, Kareem and Melvin spent hundreds of hours talking. They could not mix with the general population, and they had no opportunity to leave their cells for recreation. Kareem had been sitting on death row for years already, and he had used the time to reflect on the bad decisions he made that led to his fate. Instead of spewing more of the hatred that Melvin had been living with during his years at Graterford, Kareem told Melvin how he regretted the choices he had made that had led him to death row.

Kareem tried to use their time together to persuade Melvin that his allegiance to the FOI was a mistake. Instead of looking for ways to enhance his criminal status, Kareem suggested that Melvin ought to control his life, abide by the law, start a family, and leave his problems with the criminal justice system as much in his past as possible. By continuing in his current pattern of behavior and plans for the future, Kareem insisted, it was only a matter of time before Melvin would join him on death row, counting the days to execution.

Melvin said those conversations with Kareem helped open his eyes to the perils awaiting him if he continued a life of crime. Following his release from isolation, administrators transferred him to another prison. When he moved, he did not affiliate with the FOI or with other groups. Instead, he says that he stayed to himself, spent time in prayer as Kareem had suggested, and abandoned thoughts of returning to drug sales. Melvin had about another year to serve until his release. He realized that because of his adjustment, he ended up serving six years of a seven-year sentence. If he had avoided problems, he could have been released after having served only three. Melvin said he finished that term with the intentions of leading a straight life.

THE RISKS AND REALITIES OF ANOTHER CHANCE

In 1997 he was released from prison to serve the final year of his sentence as a parolee at the Veterans Administration hospital's drug rehabilitation program in Lebanon, Pennsylvania. He joined the program with the intention of changing. For the first sixty days of his release, he was an inpatient at the hospital. He spent ten hours of each day in narcotics counseling programs where he discussed his addictions with a therapist and other addicts. The classes gave him a feeling of belonging, he said, because the participants all understood each other as they struggled to conquer the same life-destroying habits.

After two months, Melvin graduated to a vocational program that helped him develop skills he would need to find employment. During the ninety-day program, Melvin trained as a clerk, learned how to file and perform light typing duties. The program provided shelter and food; it also paid its participants six hundred dollars per month but required them to save eighty percent of their earnings in order to help them settle upon their release.

While in the program, Melvin developed a relationship with another recovering addict, and together they had a child. After being released, in 1997, he found a job as a baker. The job did not pay well, but he had a new woman in his life and together they were able to make ends meet. She supported his efforts to lead a crime-free existence, and in addition to working, Melvin says he joined a Narcotics Anonymous (NA) group and attended regular meetings. Melvin says he needed the support those meetings provided. Had it not been for the meetings, he says, he would have fallen into the company of other drug users, and their regular talk about finding or using narcotics would have been too tempting for him to resist. The NA meetings provided him with a constant reassurance of how drug use ruins lives. The meetings gave him a connection, he says, and for the first time, helped him feel good about himself and the life he was leading.

Melvin told me he led a clean life for about one year before frustration set in. During that time he did not use drugs; he maintained a job; and he was involved in a steady relationship with a supportive, hard-working woman. At thirty-five, he had no intention of returning to drug use, but he was disappointed in his economic situation. He worked hard as a baker, but his bills were so high that he could not improve his living situation. Melvin said he owned a beat-up car, but no property. With a job that paid only mediocre wages, he could not foresee any changes on the horizon. After using his weekly income to pay all his bills, he was left with fourteen dollars and no money in the bank. A flat tire would have sunk him, he says.

Melvin's temptation came in the form of an acquaintance who caught him in a weak moment. "I'll give you a hundred dollars if you give me a ride to Philly," his friend told him. Melvin said it was a Friday night. He had just paid all of his bills and was left with his fourteen-dollar surplus. He knew the drive was to facilitate a drug transaction, and he acknowledges that such activities were against his NA beliefs. "But I needed the money," he said, and agreed to provide the transportation.

While driving his friend to Philadelphia, Melvin considered the hundred dollars he was being paid. The guy was transporting a small quantity of heroin, and Melvin began to ponder the possibility of using his pay the following week to purchase heroin from one of his old contacts to sell at a higher price in Philadelphia. He followed through with his plan, and thus resumed his cycle of destruction.

Over the next year Melvin became more deeply involved in the distribution of drugs, taking advantage of connections he had made through his years in the criminal rackets. Eventually he quit his job as a baker because it conflicted with his hustling, but he continued to participate in the NA meetings. His drug operation grew, while his home life became less important to him. Instead of returning home each evening after work, Melvin brought other women into his life and used them to help him further his drug sales. After a period of time, despite his continuing participation in NA meetings, Melvin returned to drug use himself.

Melvin's downward spiral had immediate consequences. He was robbed and shot in the leg. Doctors were successful in saving his leg from being amputated from the gunshot wound, but he had to spend a year in convalescence. While recuperating, Melvin continued his drug sales and even began supplementing his medication with heroin and cocaine to alleviate the pain from his leg wound.

Melvin told me that by the time he turned thirty-eight, he had grown tired of the way he had been living on the street, and he made further efforts to abandon his drug sales. A former customer pulled him back in, however, with pleas for Melvin to connect him with a supplier. That transaction led to Melvin's arrest on his current charge. The arrest came in December 2000, ending his escapades as a drug dealer. This time he was arrested by the Drug Enforcement Administration, which was his first experience with federal law.

THE SNOWBALLING SENTENCE

Upon his arrest, Melvin says that he felt some relief. He knew that his life had gone astray, that he had allowed himself to sink into a hellish vortex that had but one of two possible endings: death or prison. He felt good about returning to prison again, expecting that this time he would be able to pull his life together. When he heard that his charges carried a sentence of between ten years and life, however, he says he was a bit shaken. Still, Melvin says he was glad to have a new start. He expected to serve a ten-year term, during which time he finally would end his dependence on drugs and emerge a new man.

When the magistrate judge refused to grant Melvin bail, which would have meant his release until the conclusion of his judicial proceedings, Melvin began to comprehend how his long history of criminal convictions now was working inexorably against him. He waited in the crowded, dilapidated county jail, where his attorney prepared him for what was to come. Ten years was the minimum amount of time he would receive, the attorney explained. It was more likely that Melvin would receive between twelve and fourteen years. Melvin told me that he understood he had erred, but that he could not conceive of receiving such a long sentence. Nevertheless, he pled guilty because he says he had no defense. Prosecutors had audio and video tape recordings of his participation in a drug transaction.

After entering his guilty plea, a representative of the court came to interview Melvin in order to complete the presentence investigation. That meeting gave Melvin an introduction to the sentencing guidelines, which provide a grid that places an offender's current criminal offense on a vertical scale, and his or her criminal history on a horizontal scale. The matrix where the vertical and horizontal scores intersect provides a sentencing range from which the judge can select a sentence. Melvin was astonished to learn that his numerous past convictions resulted in his receiving the highest criminal-history scoring, making it possible for the judge to issue a sentence as long as twenty years for the same conduct for which others might receive ten years. "I don't understand how the crimes I already paid for can come back, making me serve time for them all over again," Melvin says, even today, in frustration.

When the judge imposed a twenty-year sentence, Melvin says that his knees buckled and he felt crippled. He could not believe that he would receive so much time for his actions. With no parole available in the federal system, and good time being limited to a maximum of fifty-four days per year, Melvin recognized that unless something changed, he would remain in prison until nearly 2018. Even to a man who has not spent more than three consecutive years outside fences since he was twenty-four, the time seemed unfathomable.

Melvin complains that his aggravations were compounded further when he returned to the jail. One man in his unit pled guilty to raping his nephew and received a four-year sentence. Another man, convicted of murder, received a sentence of ten years. Despite the frequency with which he had been processed through the criminal justice system, Melvin says that at this point he felt hopeless, like his life had been taken from him. When guards learned that Melvin had been sentenced to twenty years, they removed him from the housing unit where he had been assigned and placed him in isolation. He waited there, incommunicado with the outside world, for two months until federal marshals came to transport him to prison.

After being chained and loaded onto the marshals' bus, he was driven to the penitentiary at Lewisburg for the first leg of his journey. While there he was isolated from the prisoners in the general population and did not have access to a telephone. In late November, Melvin and approximately twenty others boarded the Bureau of Prisons bus heading for Fort Dix. Melvin finally expected that he would begin to unwind. He had been held in various isolation wards for nearly two months and looked forward to communicating with his family. Unfortunately, his frustrations had not yet ended. While the other men were being processed into Fort Dix, a guard came to Melvin and ordered him to cuff up.

"What did I do?" he asked in frustration.

"You'll find out soon enough."

The guard led him to the hole. No explanation was forthcoming. Melvin waited there for six days before Counselor Steel came to see him. Steel told Melvin that he had been placed in segregation because his paperwork had not followed him to the prison. Since then, his paperwork had arrived and his unit team was releasing Melvin into the general population.

THE PHONE CALL FIASCO

"Counselor Steel," Melvin said he asked, "I haven't been able to talk with my family for two months. Can I make a phone call?"

The federal prison system initiated the inmate telephone system in the early 1990s, and in April of 2001, the system was modified to provide administrators with more control. The system issues each inmate a personal identification number (PIN) that connects the inmate with up to thirty numbers that he or she has requested through the unit team, and—unless otherwise restricted—each inmate may make up to 300 minutes of phone calls per month. Each individual call terminates automatically after fifteen minutes. Inmates are not authorized to use the phone for business purposes, nor may they use the phone for three-way calls. Every inmate call is recorded for monitoring by staff members.

Unfamiliar with federal (as opposed to state) prison rules and regulations, Melvin did not have any of this information when his unit team released him from segregation. And when he asked Counselor Steel for permission to make a phone call, the counselor only told Melvin to submit to him a list of numbers he wanted included on his list. Melvin said that because he did not have his property, he could provide only the two numbers he knew by memory—his mother's number and his girlfriend's number. "No problem," Steel told him. "Give me those numbers and I'll arrange for you to get a PIN number. When you receive your property, you may add more numbers to your list."

The following day the counselor provided Melvin with his PIN and told him the two numbers he had requested were approved. Melvin called his mother. While talking with her, he asked her to make a three-way call to his sister so he could let her know where he was. He had not been warned that three-way calls were a violation of the rules.

Later that evening Melvin heard his name paged over the loudspeaker. He was instructed to report to the lieutenant's office. When he arrived, the lieutenant read him his Miranda rights, providing formal notification that he was being charged with wrongdoing. To Melvin, who did not know what was going on, it felt like he was being arrested again. After indicating that he understood his rights, the lieutenant asked Melvin whether he had made a three-way call.

"Yes," Melvin answered. "I just got here. I called my mom and she put me through to my sister because I didn't have my sister's number on my phone list."

"Well you can't do that here," the lieutenant responded.

"I didn't know that. No one told me anything about not being able to make three-way calls."

The lieutenant wrote down Melvin's response on the disciplinary infraction form and told him he would have to explain it to his unit team. The following day Melvin told Counselor Steel what happened. The counselor told him not to worry about it. He would attach a note to the disciplinary infraction indicating that Melvin had not yet gone through the admissions and orientation seminar in which inmates are informed of all the rules they are required to follow. Melvin felt some relief when Counselor Steel told him that he would intervene with the disciplinary hearing officer on Melvin's behalf.

The following week Melvin went through the admissions and orientation procedure and was transferred to his permanent housing unit and a new unit team. Upon his arrival he explained to Bolcavage, his new counselor, the problem he had the previous week. Counselor Bolcavage told Melvin that he, too, would attach a note indicating that Melvin had made the three-way call prior to being informed of the rules.

After another week, Disciplinary Hearing Officer Morton called Melvin in for his hearing. Morton read the charges to Melvin and asked him whether he had made the three-way call. When Melvin told him that he did but did not know the rules, Morton was unmoved. "One year loss of phone privileges. Six months loss of visiting privileges. Three months loss of commissary privileges. Loss of twenty-seven days good time. And I am suspending thirty days of segregation as long as you have no further disciplinary infractions for six months."

Melvin was astonished. The entire hearing lasted no more than three minutes. Once he acknowledged that he had made the call, the disciplinary hearing officer pronounced sentence and did not permit Melvin to utter another word. He had been sanctioned and that was the end of it. Justice inside a federal prison often is rough justice of the sort the legendary (and arbitrary) Judge Bean used in Wild West days.

Melvin's first day in federal prison resulted in the loss of half the good time that was possible for that year, as well as the end of communication with his family. When he approached members of his unit team to seek an explanation, they sympathized with him but offered him little hope other than suggesting he file an administrative appeal. I have agreed to help Melvin with his appeal, but I am not optimistic that a reversal can be obtained.

As Melvin remains functionally illiterate, unable to write letters, he perceives the sanction he received as too harsh—especially in light of the fact that he had never been notified of the rules. He hopes some relief will come through the administrative remedy process, but the appellate process takes about six months of bureaucratic time. In the meantime, Melvin walks through his first Christmas season in federal prison, staring down the long end of a twenty-year sentence. His bitterness has caused him to abandon the plans he had made to contribute to drug programming while at Fort Dix. "I have a lot of experience with rehab programs, and I understand all the ways that drugs hurt a man. I could have helped. But I ain't tryin' to do nothing now. These people done took everything in the world that's important to me. So why should I do anything to help? I'm tired of bein' taken for a sucker. They playin' with the wrong man." Melvin seethes as he contemplates the future. He blames this disciplinary action for his alienation from family and friends, not his own life choices that seem to keep bringing him back to prison.

After three convictions, Melvin is serving his first lengthy sentence. His anger and hopelessness have bonded him to others who are equally frustrated and disruptive. He passes his time watching rap and hip-hop videos, with no motivation to participate in education or counseling programs. Melvin is being warehoused.

Our next long-term prisoner, Roderick Campbell, refuses to even think about his release into society. In his late fifties, he does not expect to leave prison until he is nearly seventy. His only concern is fighting the system, and he uses his knowledge of the law as his weapon.

THE PROFESSOR:
RODERICK CAMPBELL

A jailhouse lawyer concerned with ethics is a rare breed.

My own experience suggests that few prisoners passed much time in libraries prior to their incarceration. I was twenty-three when I began serving my own sentence. Between the time I graduated from high school and walked through prison gates, I estimate that the number of books I had read as a young adult could be counted on one hand. My reading habits, I would guess, were not too different from the people with whom I have been living since 1987. Like many other prisoners, however, my reading practices changed once I was forced to dwell inside these fences.

Administrators erect high walls, and they cover them with coils upon coils of razor wire in order to keep offenders from physically escaping. In prison libraries, however, the men can find thousands of opportunities for mental escape. In this respect, prison libraries are like chapels—two places most prisoners avoided prior to incarceration, but gravitate toward at some point during their imprisonment. Chapels and libraries are especially popular during the beginning stages of confinement.

The prison libraries I have known are not quite like the libraries I remember before my incarceration. Without comfortable seating, for example, they do not make good places to sit and read. And, like everywhere else behind the fences, the noise is disturbing. At Fort Dix, prisoners are not even allowed to browse through the selections. Rather, they look through photocopied pages of the book covers and make selections from them. They are allowed to check books out to read in their cells, and many prisoners lose themselves in the selections of mysteries, westerns, and romance novels.

More ambitious prisoners eventually leave behind the tawdry novels for more complicated reading. Some discover there is gold to be found in the intimidating law libraries positioned adjacent to the rows upon rows of Stephen King, Louie L'Amour, Jackie Collins, and Danielle Steele. As the center or origin of intense pseudointellectual activity, every prison has its ground zero in the prison law library.

THE JAILHOUSE LAW INDUSTRY

In the 1960s and 1970s, when a much more liberal group of jurists presided over our nation's judicial system, the Supreme Court decided several cases empowering prisoners with legal rights. One of the more important cases, *Bounds v. Smith* (1977), held that states must take steps to ensure that prisoners have a "reasonably adequate opportunity to present claimed violations of fundamental constitutional rights to the courts." The *Bounds* decision, and others preceding it, including *Johnson v. Avery* (1969) and *Wolff v. McDonnell* (1974), encouraged a cottage industry of so-called jailhouse law that thrives in every prison community. Although a later court led by the much more conservative Justices Rhenquist, Scalia, and Thomas limited the interpretation of *Bounds* in *Lewis v. Casey* (1996) and other decisions, opportunities continue to exist for inmates to practice jailhouse law, thereby commandeering the most lucrative of all prison hustles.

The Supreme Court decisions of the civil rights era resulted in all federal prisons, and many state prisons, developing and maintaining rather sophisticated law libraries. These libraries contain thousands of volumes of the familiar, professional-looking hardcover books that intimidate so many who are not from the legal profession. Each book contains over two thousand pages, on paper as thin as that in a Bible, containing dense text replete with legal citations. These tomes describe decisions that jurists have handed down over the years, and skilled jailhouse lawyers make it their business to absorb this information. They master the language and use it to initiate actions in state and federal courts, on behalf of themselves but especially on behalf of other prisoners.

Prisoners are interested in filing suits for a variety of reasons, the most important of which is either reversing their convictions or reducing their terms of confinement. At some point during their sentences, virtually all prisoners file petitions for habeas corpus or some other type of motion seeking relief. In habeas corpus petitions, prisoners frequently allege that their constitutional rights were violated at trial, and as a result, their convictions should not stand.

Others file civil rights suits for damages or some other type of intervention. In these suits, the prisoners generally allege that they have been mistreated by prison officials. Or they may cite constitutional grounds for challenging the conditions of their confinement.

Prisoners also may seek access to the courts in order to resolve regular domestic issues. Like any other citizen, a prisoner confronts complications in his or her personal life, for instance, divorce proceedings, custody disputes, or personal-injury problems, and must seek redress through the judicial system. Besides these legitimate reasons for pursuing judicial relief, many also engage in the filing of what courts consider frivolous litigation. Such filing can lift some of the boredom that comes with confinement, or better yet, it can provide prisoners with an opportunity to harass prison officials legitimately.

Perhaps fewer than half of all prison inmates have graduated from high school. Courts frequently publish opinions holding that the vast majority of prisoners lack the capacity to frame or present issues competently. Indeed, one Oklahoma court held that seventy percent of the inmates at one prison lacked the intelligence to do legal research, while an Illinois court said that fully ninety percent of the inmates at another prison were incapable of doing their own legal research or writing. Recognizing this dearth of competition, many glib prisoners aspire to become jailhouse lawyers; they pass their time reading case law and legal briefs, which gives them an aura of authority when it comes to discussions of law. Those who succeed in cultivating reputations of being knowledgeable in the law frequently capitalize on these reputations by acting as liaisons between the unsophisticated and the courts.

THE EXPENSE OF EXPERIENCE

Unlike attorneys who practice in the community, jailhouse lawyers rarely have much more formal schooling or educational credentials than their clients. On the other hand, instead of passing their time by reading pulp fiction, watching cartoons, or playing cards, jailhouse lawyers spend hours reading—though not necessarily comprehending—hundreds of legal opinions and legal briefs. Their experience actually does provide them with a rudimentary understanding of how the legal system operates, and many prisoners turn to them for help in seeking judicial relief.

Like professional services outside, jailhouse law rarely comes inexpensively, the lack of the practitioners' credentials notwithstanding. The system of supply and demand prevails. Since so few prisoners have the competence or confidence to express themselves in writing, they are confronted with the uncomfortable option of paying thousands of dollars to professional advocates outside, or paying hundreds of dollars to jailhouse lawyers inside to help them litigate their claims. Since most prisoners are without means to hire outside counsel, they rely on the spurious expertise available inside.

I have had some experience working with jailhouse lawyers. As a long-term prisoner, I worried about how I would support myself after my release. When I had approximately fifteen years ahead of me to serve, I enrolled in a correspondence law school. I had no aspirations to pass a state bar exam or become a practicing lawyer. Rather, I wanted to learn about the law to become an effective litigator inside the fences. By earning a law degree, I reasoned, I would be able to combine my knowledge of law together with my extensive experience of living as a prisoner, and for a fee, help others seeking to obtain remedy in court. The money I earned, I reasoned, would help me establish myself upon my release from prison.

While attending first-year law through correspondence, I also apprenticed with Paul, a jailhouse lawyer with a thriving practice inside the fences. On this occasion of incarceration, Paul was serving a five-year sentence for having written a letter threatening the life of the President. Ironically, Paul wrote the letter from a psychiatric ward, where he was serving time in a state prison for a separate conviction. At some point during one of his many previous terms of confinement, Paul had earned his GED, but he had no further formal education. However, that was irrelevant to his practice inside the fences.

Over the years, Paul had read through thousands of legal pleadings. He understood the format of legal proceedings and had convinced others, as well as himself, that he was an expert in all matters pertaining to postconviction litigation. When Paul learned that I was in law school, he approached me with a proposition. If I would help him with the typing and writing of his briefs, he would pay me a percentage of what he would receive in return for his work; if Paul's client agreed to pay him five hundred dollars for a motion, he would send two hundred dollars of that fee to an address I provided for savings. During the year that I worked with Paul, I not only was paid several thousand dollars, I also came to realize that the version of jailhouse law that he and most of his associates practiced was nothing more than a con game, taking advantage of the unwitting prisoners whom they served.

Jailhouse lawyers frequently collect professional briefs written by attorneys, then manipulate and rewrite the arguments to suit the needs of their clients. It made no difference that other judges had already ruled against their legal arguments. They continued to plagiarize, with a twist or two. What mattered to most jailhouse lawyers was that their revamped arguments impressed others around them and enhanced their reputations as articulate advocates. The people they represented had so much experience in losing, that jailhouse lawyers could explain away an additional loss in the courts as simply another example of what they called the "corrupt" legal system.

Several people approached Paul each month with requests for his services. Depending on their ability to pay, he would quote a fee, usually ranging between one and five hundred dollars; not knowing any better, some people paid Paul as much as two thousand dollars to present their requests for judicial relief.

After a year, I became discouraged with the practice of jailhouse law and began to pursue other activities. Paul continued with his work until his release date; he once gloated to me that he had managed to save thirty thousand dollars during his years of working as a jailhouse litigator. Despite his never having won relief for a single client in the years that I knew him, Paul was adamant that he provided a worthwhile service in the work he prepared. I called it "therapeutic litigation" because all he really provided was therapy.

Most jailhouse lawyers whom I have met during my years of confinement have had about the same level of competence as Paul. They could indeed present professional looking motions and were skilled in the art of persuading the desperate prisoners around them that they were entitled to legal relief, but they were far less successful in persuading the courts. Most were outright charlatans, slightly more sophisticated con artists. Roderick Campbell, on the other hand, is a jailhouse lawyer of a different mold.

THE PROFESSOR

Unlike most prisoners, who were foreign to libraries prior to their incarceration and could not even spell the word "research," Roderick Campbell held a Ph.D. in organic chemistry from Brown University. He was a scientist. Prior to his confinement, he was a professional chemist working as the technical director for a company making laser and infrared dies for military and commercial applications.

Roderick was forty-seven years old when he began serving this twenty-four year term in 1993, and if nothing changes, he will be in his late sixties upon release. He was convicted of manufacturing a substance known as P2P, which he distinguishes from the narcotic commonly known as PCP. He had served a six-year sentence previously for engaging in the distribution of PCP, and he readily accepts responsibility for that conviction, acknowledging that a lapse in judgment led him into a criminal conspiracy.

The conviction for which he currently is serving time, on the other hand, he insists came as a result of his being targeted for harassment by federal agents. P2P, Roderick explains, is not a drug itself. Rather, it is a chemical used in the manufacture of amphetamines—or drugs known by the street names "crystal meth," "ice," or "rock."

Looking at Roderick, one would have a hard time believing that he is serving a towering sentence for a conviction related to violations of narcotics laws. That he had served a previous sentence as well seems inconceivable. Now in his mid-fifties, Rod stands tall at well over six feet. A tuft of snow-white hair, always in disarray, covers his head. He wears a set of Coke-bottle-thick spectacles. Whereas most prisoners wear sweat pants and t-shirts whenever permissible, Roderick constantly is outfitted in the crumpled, prison-issue khaki uniform, complete with a pocket protector in his breast pocket bulging with pens and folded papers.

It is a rare occasion when Roderick is not overloaded. He is a one-man law firm, never without six to ten inches of files under his arm that bulge with legal pleadings. Wherever he walks, prisoners accost him with questions about their legal standing, what they can do to obtain relief, or how their cases are progressing. Unlike most jailhouse lawyers, Roderick takes time to talk with them all and never concerns himself with whether he will be compensated.

I met Roderick one evening about a year ago, soon after he arrived at Fort Dix. I saw Roderick sitting in the law library with several law books opened in front of him, and no fewer than a dozen people standing around this man who bore a striking resemblance to a Hollywood caricature of the mad professor. In fact, the men around him who were competing for his attention referred to him deferentially as "Professor."

Unlike most jailhouse lawyers, there was not a trace of pomposity in Roderick. He was courteous to everyone who approached him, and he made a seemingly conscious effort to give everyone a feeling of ease; no question was too minor or unworthy of an interruption. I watched the Roderick Campbell Show for twenty minutes that first night and observed him skeptically at a distance for the next several months before speaking with him.

AN UNUSUAL SINCERITY

In time, I expected to find some sign that Roderick was like other jailhouse lawyers I had encountered. Instead, I came to develop a respect for his indifference to fees, for his willingness to give his time to anyone who asked. His generosity was authentic.

Indeed, Roderick is the opposite of stereotypical jailhouse lawyers. Not only is he completely indifferent to the money he could scam out of the desperate prisoners around him, he is obsessed with memorizing the holdings and citations of any case that might apply to prisoners. It does not matter whether one is looking for supporting information on drug-law sentencing or First Amendment issues, Roderick is as familiar with legal decisions as teenagers are with popular music.

When it comes to finding legal citations to support their positions, even the other jailhouse lawyers, whose careers certainly have been threatened by Roderick's superior skills and knowledge, turn to him regularly for guidance. Graciously, Roderick obliges them. Never patronizing in tone, Roderick easily quotes obscure cases that might help them bolster their often untenable arguments.

The Professor is convinced that he is engaged in a battle that must be fought. He does not charge people for legal work, but some prisoners insist on providing him with a gratuity for his services. Regardless of how many hours he spends on a case, however, Roderick considers one hundred dollars as a more-than-generous gratuity and does not accept more. This contrasts sharply with Paul and his ilk, who would not consider taking on a new client for less than a hundred dollars. Rather than focusing on money, Roderick says his ambition is to "elevate the quality of all legal work that comes out of prison." For this reason, he freely helps other jailhouse lawyers, not only encouraging them to plagiarize his work, but also to turn to him for editing services.

The Professor began serving his term at a medium-security prison in Schuylkill, Pennsylvania. Conscious of his age and health, Roderick says he accepted a job in the electrical maintenance department because he needed the physical movement. Because he became the prison's lead electrician, the institution paid Roderick approximately ninety-dollars per month for his full-time work. When he was not replacing electrical ballasts or making other routine repairs in those early days of imprisonment, Roderick already was consumed with his legal work.

Not only did he make himself available to prepare legal filings on behalf of others, he also taught three classes a week on conducting legal research and writing briefs. Prisoners appreciated the information Roderick taught.

Each of his classes, he said, attracted between thirty and forty participants, mostly men who were struggling to complete their own postconviction motions prior to the expiration of a procedural deadline. After April 1996, these deadlines took on a new importance.

AEDPA SPELLS NO RELIEF

Prior to April 1996, courts were more tolerant of postconviction motions. Prisoners were allowed to file such motions at any time while serving their sentence. The success rate however, was never high. Fewer than five percent of those who filed postconviction motions ever received any type of relief; those who did receive relief frequently were limited to a new court hearing with no change in their original sentence. Nevertheless, prisoners held out hope throughout their sentences that some legal window would open, that by filing a postconviction motion in court, eventually they could obtain some relief.

In April 1996, however, new legislation passed by Congress, the Anti-Terrorism and Effective Death Penalty Act (AEDPA), took effect. The AEDPA severely limited a prisoner's access to the courts. As a result of the AEDPA, except in the rarest of instances, prisoners are prohibited from filing postconviction motions if one year has passed since their convictions became final. Whereas no deadline used to exist, after April 1996, prisoners realized they had to race to file motions within the new one-year time constraint. Congress extinguished a significant source of hope for the majority of those incarcerated in federal prisons as result of the newly passed legislation.

The AEDPA may have been one of the reasons Roderick's legal research and writing classes were packed to capacity. Few of the students who participated, however, had the educational background to really grasp what he was teaching. Instead, most attended Roderick's classes to listen to him speak, to make contact, to attract his attention and concern. Then they bombarded him with personal pleas for help with their cases. Everyone understood the importance of the newly imposed AEDPA deadlines for filing postconviction motions. Whether they had viable issues for relief or not, if they did not present their motions to the court within the new one-year time frame, the courts would dismiss their pleadings as being filed "out of time," rendering moot whatever chances they thought existed. Incapable of saying no, Roderick ended up accepting the challenge of helping all who came to him.

THE LAW AS A WEAPON

Despite a long history of court rulings that hold that illiterate prisoners may turn to jailhouse lawyers for assistance in filing their pleadings, administrators recognize jailhouse lawyers as a threat to the smooth operation of their prisons. Not only do they help inmates challenge the legitimacy of their convictions, jailhouse lawyers also are instrumental in filing administrative remedy procedures against staff members, habeas corpus petitions challenging the conditions of their confinement, and civil actions against individual staff members for violating a prisoner's constitutional rights. A skillful jailhouse lawyer who is looking to exact revenge for any perceived abuse will use all tools provided by the federal rules of civil procedure that are within his power to complicate the life of a staff member.

For example, Donovan, a jailhouse lawyer whom I once knew, perceived that he was being unnecessarily harassed by a guard whom I will call Pincher. After using the administrative remedy procedures available to him, which in themselves brought Pincher the hassle of having to answer his complaints, Donovan filed a civil action against Pincher in federal court for violating his constitutional rights. Pincher, therefore, had to go through the trouble of working with an attorney to defend himself against a hotshot jailhouse lawyer.

Donovan was not particularly interested in winning a case against Pincher. His objective was to make Pincher's life miserable. Prison rules left him with few options, but the legal system offered Donovan tools to prosecute his case, one that could prove effective in frustrating Pincher's life. One of those tools Donovan could use included interrogatories, which are a series of questions Donovan could compel Pincher and others to answer; and another was the rule of discovery, which provided Donovan with the privilege of digging into Pincher's background in order to find information that might prove useful to his case. If it were not for the rules of the court, obviously Donovan would have had no opportunity to dig into the personal background of Officer Pincher.

Combining his legal expertise and the help of friends outside of prison who had access to the Internet, Donovan was able to cause severe disruption to Pincher's life. First he found Pincher's home address. Then, he used the Internet to obtain the mailing addresses of Pincher's neighbors. With that information, Donovan drafted a series of questions that he mailed to each of Pincher's neighbors with the sole purpose of embarrassing Pincher and his family. Among other things, the questionnaires explained that Officer Pincher was being charged with sexual harassment. Donovan's interrogatories asked questions to elicit any information Pincher's neighbors could provide about Pincher's immoral sexual practices, including allegations of pedophilia, beastiality, and perverse homosexual practices with multiple partners. The court eventually dismissed Donovan's case against Pincher, but not before Donovan used his skill as a jailhouse lawyer to disrupt the life of his nemesis. In the meantime, the suit bolstered his image as a jailhouse lawyer. He may have had significant amounts of time on his hands, but he was successful in using it to create a symphony of disruption.

In order to discourage the practice of jailhouse law, administrators frequently target those who might be spending too much time fighting the system. They may transfer a successful litigator from prison to prison as often as every three months, making it difficult for him to settle in, receive mail, or spend time researching law and soliciting clients. Or, they may take less drastic steps, such as assigning them to jobs that leave them with little time to access the law library.

Another more simple alternative is to charge jailhouse lawyers with violating a prison rule, exposing them to disciplinary sanctions. For example, one prison rule holds that inmates are not allowed to be in possession of another's property. Another rule prohibits one prisoner from giving anything of value to another. Still another rule prohibits prisoners from conducting a business within prison. Roderick learned firsthand about the tools administrators may use to slow down the work of successful jailhouse lawyers.

TEACHING THE LAW

While teaching his legal research and writing classes, Roderick accumulated sixty-three clients whom he was helping to prepare postconviction motions. When they asked Roderick to evaluate their legal arguments, typically he became discouraged with the pleadings they had produced. He says that he could not in good faith allow them to submit such diatribes to the court. He became convinced that he had an ethical responsibility to edit, and in many instances rewrite, entire arguments so that the individuals stood a modicum of a chance of being heard.

There is no doubt that scores of staff members knew that Roderick was the preeminent jailhouse lawyer at Schuylkill. In a population of twelve hundred prisoners, staff members have perhaps two to three hundred inmates who work as informants keeping the guards abreast of all activities inside the prison. Roderick attributes his not being targeted before to the fact that he does not charge inmates; another factor may have been that Roderick did not engage in the kind of guerrilla tactics that others such as Donovan used.

Roderick is not interested in personal wars against staff members, then or now. Rather, he strives to help others "find justice." Still, some human cog in the prison machine felt the need to demonstrate his omnipotence. While returning to his room one evening, Roderick says he saw an associate warden approach a guard and order that Roderick be "shaken down," meaning that the guard was to inspect all of the possessions on Roderick's person and in his quarters. During the shakedown, the guard found files containing legal information pertaining to sixty-three different inmates. Roderick was issued a disciplinary infraction for possession of property that did not belong to him. Despite each of the other prisoners coming forward to indicate that Roderick was helping them prepare their legal motions, Roderick was convicted of this disciplinary infraction and served sixty-three days in segregation.

While serving his punishment in the special housing unit, Roderick said the Special Investigating Services lieutenant read through all of Roderick's legal pleadings. He took it as a compliment when the lieutenant told him that the work Roderick was preparing ranked first among all that he had seen. And, since there was nothing in all of his papers that suggested a private war against the prison system, or that he was using his legal skills as a hustle to generate an income, Roderick explained that he came to a private understanding with the Special Investigating Services staff that once he was released from segregation, he would not face further harassment at Schuylkill.

NEW PLACE, SAME NEEDS

As a result of a lowering of his security level, Roderick has transferred to Fort Dix. Many of the inmates he assisted while at Schuylkill had transferred to Fort Dix before him. When Roderick walked across the compound, he felt fingers pointing at him, identifying him as an exceptional jailhouse lawyer. By the end of his first week at Fort Dix, strangers were approaching him, calling him Professor, and asking for assistance with their case. He stepped right back into his groove, and since his arrival, Roderick estimates that he has filed at least one motion each week. He has no shortage of patrons.

Roderick understands that many of the other jailhouse lawyers are involved in legal activity only for the money they can generate, and a good jailhouse lawyer easily can exceed ten thousand dollars per year in what amounts to tax-free income. He says that the services he provides do not threaten the hustles of others because of the enormous amount of work required to satisfy the legal needs of such a large population. Besides, Roderick is careful never to disparage the work of others, and he frequently helps others by sharing his own work or volunteering to help them frame strategies to attack particular legal challenges. Besides, he says, many of the people who see how busy he is choose to work with others who charge more, but who may have more time than the Professor to focus on their cases exclusively.

In any given day, Roderick estimates that he is approached at least twenty times by people with whom he has never spoken. Assuming that I was working with Roderick when one of his clients saw me interviewing him for this chapter, he secretly approached me and offered me a hundred dollars worth of commissary if I would ensure that his case received top priority. I told him that I had nothing to do with Roderick's legal work but assured him that he was in good hands as far as jailhouse lawyers in prison went. "I'm just really concerned," he moaned. "This is my only chance to see my kids again."

The prisoner was from Europe. He had been sentenced to serve fourteen years in prison for participating in a scheme to distribute heroin, and following the completion of his term, he would be deported from the United States. The man had married an American woman and they had two children together. Since his incarceration, his wife had left him, and if he were deported, he knew that he would not be allowed into the United States again. Accordingly, he expected that unless Roderick were able to help him find relief from his sentence, his family would be irretrievably lost to him. The man was desperate, and he saw Roderick as his last hope. Unfortunately, he did not appreciate the odds that were working against him.

Although seven years have passed since Roderick began his career as a jailhouse lawyer, filing over a thousand separate legal petitions, he estimates that perhaps only fifty men returned to court, and, of those fifty, perhaps ten received some type of sentence reduction. Still, he remains optimistic and motivated to continue the struggle. Roderick says that he believes that historians studying this period will conclude that American jurisprudence has become unduly controlled by American politics.

The Professor was forced to break from our interview for about an hour. Anthony, one of his clients, had been granted a telephone hearing with his judge. Although Roderick does all of the research and writing for his clients, it is the client who submits the *pro se* motion to the court in his own name. When Anthony received notice that the motion he had submitted had merit, and that the judge was scheduling a conference call between him, the prosecutor, and Anthony, he had no idea what to say. Roderick agreed to accompany Anthony, and if the judge permitted, Roderick would argue the points of the motion on Anthony's behalf.

The judge called Anthony's counselor at the appropriate time. When the counselor gave the phone to Anthony, the judge told him that the prosecuting attorney also was on the line and that he was prepared to hear an oral argument. Anthony explained his dilemma, that although he had submitted the motion, he did not know much about it because another prisoner had prepared his work for him. He asked the judge for permission to let Roderick argue on his behalf. The judge agreed to speak with Roderick.

"Are you a lawyer?" the judge asked.

"No, your honor, I am a chemist by profession. But I prepared Anthony's motion."

"So you are familiar with the case and prepared to argue it?"

"Yes," Roderick answered. "I am thoroughly familiar with the case."

"Very well," the judge said. "Although this is highly unusual, if the government has no objection, I will listen."

Roderick proceeded to make his argument. When he concluded, the government prosecutor had his say, and then Roderick made a rebuttal argument. The hearing lasted twenty-eight minutes. After the judge listened to both parties, he denied Anthony's motion. Roderick is now preparing a petition for rehearing.

John, the last person we will meet, describes how a thirty-year prison sentence was perhaps the best thing that ever happened to him.

TWENTY-SEVEN YEARS OF INTROSPECTION: JOHN VINCENT BAUMGARTEN

One drug trial resulted in a father and his two sons splitting ninety years of prison time.

On February 10, 1997, federal agents arrested John Baumgarten and his younger brother, Tony. One month later, his father, John Sr., was arrested as well. All three defendants were charged and indicted in the same federal case involving trafficking in cocaine. Each male in the Baumgarten family was facing a possible sentence of life in prison, without possibility of parole.

John was thirty-three years old at the time of his arrest. His brother Tony was thirty-two. Neither had been arrested before and neither knew what to expect from the criminal justice system. Their father, John Sr., on the other hand, had served a brief sentence several years before and was somewhat prepared for the rough storms ahead. Further insinuations that his wife, the boys' mother, might face criminal charges as well made it a tough time for the Baumgarten family.

Adjusting to confinement brings trauma to anyone. Usually, however, the person who is arrested has family support to help in some way. In the Baumgarten family, unfortunately, the stress was exacerbated because all three adult males had been taken into custody at once. Previously, they had supported the family with a hair salon they owned and operated. With their incarceration, the business had to close its doors permanently.

John Vincent Baumgarten (right), Tony (left), John, Sr. (center)

PRETRIAL SEGREGATION

The three men spent their first two years locked in segregation at a prison in Petersburg, Virginia. This, too, was unusual. In most cases, newly arrested prisoners are placed in the confined but communitylike environment of a jail or detention center; they are free to interact with others and have access to television and daily use of the telephone. Prisoners held in segregation, like the Baumgartens, on the other hand, are confined to a small cell for all but perhaps one hour per day. They do not have free access to the telephone, and they live under quite restrictive conditions, tormented by the unknown that is to come.

The father, John Sr., a strong man in his early fifties, was torn apart emotionally. Facing a life sentence was difficult enough for him, but knowing that his two sons were passing through the same gauntlet had severe physical and psychological effects on him. He was anxious and confused. He could not sleep or eat.

The case focused on the distribution of cocaine. There was no violence alleged in their offense, and drugs were not found with any of the defendants. Others who had been implicated in the distribution of drugs, however, were cooperating with law enforcement and provided evidence linking all three of the men to the conspiracy. John Sr., knew that it would be difficult to persuade a jury of the group's innocence with the testimony of the cooperating witnesses. Still, he elected to plead not guilty. Yet he urged his sons to plead guilty and cooperate with the government in order to spare themselves the ordeal of a lengthy prison sentence. "The government only wants me," he would tell them. "Let me take the weight for this, and you boys get on with your lives."

John Jr. had two young children himself, and raising them had been his pride and passion. Being away from them was Kafkaesque, a bizarre experience that made his life before confinement seem like a blur; there appeared to be no bottom to the abyss in which he and his family were sinking. While his father was pleading with him and his brother to save themselves, his mother was coming to visit him and insisting that he make no decision out of weakness, that he exercise strength and choose whatever path sat right with his conscience. She did not want him to allow worries about her or his father to influence his thinking.

To John and his younger brother, Tony, their father's decision to proceed through trial settled the matter. If he was going to take his chances before a jury, they were not going to make it harder on him to spare themselves. They were in a ship with all pumps working. If it was going to go down, they chose to sink with it.

The three Baumgarten men went to trial on their drug charges and were convicted. John Sr. received a sentence of thirty-three years; Tony received thirty years. Both sentences were longer than John Jr.'s twenty-seven year sentence. That may be because when the judge asked the others whether they had anything to say prior to sentencing, John Sr. and Tony expressed no remorse. Instead, they made lengthy and bitter complaints about the manner in which they had been prosecuted. Like many defendants, the Baumgartens felt they had been unjustly convicted.

Instead of railing against the criminal justice system before his sentencing, John was more taciturn. He did not exactly express contrition, but neither did he say anything that could be construed as recalcitrance. His lack of defiance at the sentencing hearing may have resulted in his lower sentence.

Soon after sentencing, John Jr. and Tony were separated from their father in the county jail and transported to the federal prison at Cumberland, Maryland. Their father remained behind as Bureau of Prisons administrators determined his assignment. The family members had hoped to serve their time together, but this was not a decision within their power to make.

For two years, John and Tony had lived inside the squalor of the Maryland county jail system or in segregation at Petersburg. By the time of their transfer, they were mentally fatigued and distraught about having to leave their father behind, not knowing when, if ever, they would see him again.

THE ISLAND OF CONTROL

When John Jr. and Tony finally were marched off the bus and processed into the medium-security prison, however, they were pleasantly surprised. Instead of a larger version of the rancid jail cell with hundreds of transients that they had grown accustomed to over their first two years, they found their new environment inside the Cumberland federal prison relatively calm. Of course, double-wide high fences topped with shiny concertina (razor) wire surrounded the entire prison, but compared to the enclosed concrete-and-steel tombs in which they had been held, the prison seemed open.

After being processed and assigned together to a two-man cell, John and Tony tried to settle in. During those first weeks everything seemed surreal, as the reality of their sentences had not set in. John said that when the jury returned its verdict of guilty, he actually felt some relief because he was so eager for all the pretrial and trial complications to move into his past. He says that he expected to be found guilty and was eager to put the jail disorder and frequent transfers behind him so he could prepare for the many years ahead that he was certain to serve.

At Cumberland, John was surprised how much food was available and how he and his brother were able to structure their days inside. They began exercise routines and walked around the prison's compound together while trying to get a feel for what their lives would be like over the next two-plus decades.

Within a month, their father arrived at Cumberland and was assigned a cell adjoining the one John and Tony were sharing. A few other prisoners on the compound had read about the Baumgartens, and they approached the trio to express their support.

The newspapers frequently profiled the Baumgarten case during the trial because it featured three defendants from the same family. All of the defendants received towering time, so it was clear to others in prison that the three Baumgartens were "stand-up guys," meaning that they did not cooperate with the government in the prosecution of others. The other prisoners, therefore, showed them respect, offering them toiletries, shower shoes, and anything else the Baumgartens would need as they tried to settle into prison routines. But for the most part, the three stuck together. They did not develop close relationships with anyone else in the prison, and the family bonds that John, Tony, and their father shared encouraged their insularity. After a month, John said, he began to accept that he would have to live his life behind the fences.

During that first month, John began to realize how alone his father, his brother, and he were. Their contacts with the outside world began to drop off almost at once. The only steady family contact was John's sister, Sherie. The relationship with his sister, Donna, was on again, off again. His mother abandoned all three after the sentencing. He did not even know an address for her. Prior to his incarceration, he used to wonder what it would be like to die. His incarceration gave him a taste of death. His heart still beat, and all of his biological signs indicated life. But he felt alone, as if the world had written him off as dead. Prison felt like a tomb beyond the reach of the living.

Today, John says he bears no animosity to Donna, his mother, or others who have abandoned him. If any of them ever were to choose to play a role in his life, he would welcome them. But he is adamant about not wanting to pressure them with guilt into a relationship. "If they want to get on with their lives," John observes, "I support them. If they want to come back into mine, I'll give them all the love I have. I'm a prisoner, so I'm leaving the choice up to them. I'm not trying to force myself or my predicament on anyone."

ASKING FOR HELP

Without much family support outside, however, it was difficult for John to settle into prison. He had no access to money. Although the system issues basic clothing—such as pants, shirts, and boots—it requires prisoners to purchase all recreational clothing and many toiletries from the commissary. The irony is that it offers few jobs that allow prisoners the opportunity to earn enough money to purchase these items.

John needed a pair of sneakers for exercise. He calculated that he would have to work at his job for a year before he would earn enough money to afford the sixty-five dollar sneakers sold in the commissary. He called Gayle, the mother of his son, Johnny, and asked if she could afford to help. She readily agreed, sending him one hundred dollars. When John received notice in the mail that this money had been deposited in his account, he says he broke down emotionally, finally recognizing that not only was he a long-term prisoner, but a pauper in his mid-thirties as well.

Gayle was generous in providing John with that initial money. But having to turn to her for alms made him feel less than a man. He had been supporting himself and raising his own family prior to incarceration, and he was shattered by the thought that prison would render him permanently dependent on others for support. He decided to do something about it.

John was able to secure a job in the prison's barber shop. The job itself provided John with only fifteen dollars per month in income, but it was customary at Cumberland for the other prisoners to provide a small gratuity in commissary items for the haircuts they received.

DOING THE HUSTLE

John began accumulating commissary, cans of tuna, bags of chips, candy bars. When he had enough, he augmented his income by opening his own store inside his cell. The commissary allows prisoners to purchase items only one night each week, and it also limits the amount a prisoner can spend in a given month. John's store had no such restrictions, but customers incurred a fifty percent premium for the convenience John offered. If a person took two cans of tuna from John on Monday, he had to bring back three cans of tuna, or its equivalent value, in order to remain in good standing. This prison hustle helped John land on his feet inside. It also catapulted him into yet another prison racket. When his stockpile of commissary items built up, he began offering bookmaking services for sporting events, collecting fees to receive and guarantee bets from other prisoners.

The federal prison at Cumberland holds close to fifteen hundred men. Starving for any type of mental escape, many turn to sports betting, and John made a practice of providing all types of betting services. His brother and father were opposed to John's activities. They valued the privilege of serving their sentences together and worried that John's illicit activities would bring unwanted attention from the guards. Prison authorities recognize gambling as a serious threat to the security of the institution. Tony and his father were concerned that if John received a disciplinary infraction, or if he even were suspected of running a gambling ring, administrators would give him a disciplinary transfer to another prison.

Despite their admonitions, John continued his actions until his second year, earning approximately three hundred dollars each month for his efforts. The money allowed him to eat better, to purchase athletic apparel, to use the phone, and to purchase services like laundry and cleaning from others through the thriving underground economy. Besides providing John with enough money to make his life easier in the prison, his hustles were his way of adjusting to confinement.

By now, however, the lieutenants had caught on. They began calling for John to report to them. They told him that they had been hearing gossip about his activities and that they were going to keep a close eye on him. Guards began stopping him frequently for searches. They would plow through his room looking for clues in his locker, in his bed, or anywhere they thought he might be hiding evidence that could lead to charges being lodged against him.

Finally, his family and a close friend whom he had made in the prison persuaded John that he was going about his adjustment in the wrong way. His behavior, he realized, was not too much different than how he had been behaving on the street. He also realized that only problems could come from it, not only for him, but for his family, too. After his second year, John made a commitment to changing his adjustment pattern.

CHANGING GOALS

Instead of operating his gambling enterprise, John began setting goals to achieve during confinement. Cumberland does not provide prisoners with access to weights, so John began an unconventional body-building program, collecting plastic bottles to fill with water and use as weights for resistance training. John would place the filled bottles inside his laundry bag and curl the bags to build size on his arms, or attach a bag to each end of a mop handle, which would serve as a barbell for chest and shoulder presses. John stands five-feet-six, so building physical mass was and is important to him. Already at nineteen inches, he hopes to build arms that measure twenty inches in diameter with a flexed bicep.

John's participation in the underground economy, followed by his efforts to focus on body building, substituting water bottles for weights, represent typical strategies for long-term prisoners. The time can be like a walk through the desert, long and dry and lonely, without breaks in between. Or prisoners can look for independent activities that interest them, illegitimate or legitimate. If they are fortunate they may find a long-term activity that may give them solace, providing some mental or spiritual therapy, as they watch calendar pages turn and presidential administrations change.

Besides body building, John began participating in every class available inside the prison. College courses were not offered at Cumberland, but skilled inmates taught several classes in the Continuing Education program. John studied business management, finance, and drawing. With hopes that someday relief might come to nonviolent first offenders, John was trying to accumulate certificates verifying that he has consistently participated in programs to distinguish himself positively within the prison.

During his third year at Cumberland, John's case manager told him that his security level had dropped. This meant he would have to be transferred to a low-security prison. Cumberland is designed to hold only medium- and high-security prisoners.

John would have liked to believe that this change was a result of his more positive adjustment. He knew, however, that his security level dropped only because he had not been charged with a disciplinary infraction, and because the time he already had served on his sentence brought him below the twenty-year threshold that separates low- from medium-security prisoners. Time served is the only way a prisoner can distinguish himself formally in the federal prison system.

Because of their longer sentences, John's brother and father would not transfer from Cumberland. He would be alone. This made the impending move difficult because there was no telling when, if ever, John would see them again. Many things can happen in prison—riots, disturbances, racial problems. With the longer sentences offenders were receiving, John felt the level of tension rising inside the fences. His brother would not become eligible for a transfer to low security for three more years; his father would have to serve even longer before his security level would drop. John was particularly concerned about his father.

SEPARATION ANXIETIES

Although John was confident neither his father nor brother would engage in disruptive behavior, he knew they could not oppose others if the prisoners began acting with a herd mentality. The crowding seemed to escalate the chance for a prison disturbance that would threaten the possibility of either his father or his brother joining him at the low-security prison. Besides that, his father was approaching sixty, and although he was in good physical shape, John realized that health problems could arise, and he would have no way of comforting his father.

All of these concerns, however, were beyond John's control. His security level had dropped, and it was only a matter of days before administrators would order John to pack his property for transfer. He and his family tried to make the most of their final days together.

John promised both that when he arrived at his new destination, he would continue his good behavior and not revert to running gambling pools or doing anything that could result in his having problems in prison. Likewise, his brother and father vowed to stay clear of problems to enhance their chances of uniting as a prison family again, and as soon as possible.

In the fall of 2000, John was told to report for transfer. He said his farewells, trying not to look back as he walked away, avoiding any sign of emotion; during the walk, he said it felt like he was having a heart attack. He transferred to the federal prison at Fort Dix, and when he stepped off the bus, he had two goals in mind: to associate only with those who were adjusting positively, and to learn Spanish by Christmas 2001.

Unlike Cumberland, Fort Dix allowed prisoners to work with weights. John, therefore, built his schedule around three activities. He spent his mornings lifting weights, his afternoons studying Spanish; and his evenings cutting hair in the prison's barber shop. Making a conscious effort to stay out of trouble, John associated with few other prisoners. Fort Dix gave him a fresh start, and when he gave up the hustles, he became determined to use his time wisely.

THE FORTUNE OF FAMILY

The highlight of John's life now is when Gayle, his former partner and the mother of his son, brings his children up to visit him. John and Gayle have a young son, Johnny, who now is fourteen. Gayle also brings John's daughter, Breanna, who is fifteen, on these visits.

Gayle and John had a close relationship as teenagers. She gave birth to Johnny in 1987 and urged John to lead a conventional family life. At that time, he was twenty-three and did not appreciate his freedom or the responsibilities of a family. He made decisions that he now regrets. Instead of staying home, he cavorted through Baltimore, associating with people and activities that led to the long term he currently is serving. Life has been a labyrinth for John. He took some wrong turns. Now he struggles to find the path that will lead him to where he wants to be.

Gayle and the children make the long drive from Baltimore to Fort Dix about once each month, and John's anticipation of these visits helps him maintain discipline. Administrators have it within their power to withhold visiting privileges or telephone privileges for the slightest infraction of prison rules. Knowing this provides John with a strong incentive to conform.

As a federal prisoner, John is allocated fewer than ten minutes per day for telephone access. He would like to talk with his family more frequently, but the stringent time allotments make such a wish impossible.

Young Johnny and Breanna live in different households, so John must call them separately. Fortunately, they are old enough to understand his limitations. They write frequently, three to four times each month.

The regular visits, however, are John's bridge to the world. The children and Gayle usually arrive when the visiting room opens, just after 8:00 A.M. on a weekend morning. John looks forward to spending a full seven hours together with his family. The visiting room is not particularly comfortable. Bright fluorescent lights, visible surveillance cameras, and uniformed guards stand watch as the visitors try to converse with and comfort their loved ones. The children talk about school, about their activities, about their friends and plans for the future. John uses the time to guide them in the best way he can, trying to strengthen bonds that he wants to last a lifetime, cherishing every second together.

He holds Gayle's hand during the visits, and it is difficult to suppress their long-time feelings for each other. But although John's life has stood still for years, Gayle's life has moved on. Nearly five years have passed since John was taken into custody. The time has changed him. Not only his discipline and temperament, but his values, too. During their most recent visit, Gayle broke down in tears, asking John why it took the dramatic step of imprisonment for him to mature. He did not have an answer.

REFLECTION AND ASSESSMENT

John readily admits that prison has been good for him. It has illuminated the miserable life he led prior to incarceration. "I was never happy before my imprisonment," John says. "As crazy as it sounds, this is the only time in my life that I've felt happy."

Like monks who sacrifice worldly pleasure to find peace in solitude and asceticism, John's austere life in confinement has given him an opportunity to reflect on his earlier choices, including his initial adjustment behind bars. Those five years of introspection, together with the natural process of biological maturity, have brought John a clarity of thought and helped him develop an appreciation for what is important in life. Family and relationships, he has come to learn, are the only matters of importance now. Accepting this has brought John an inner peace, giving meaning to the time he now passes.

During a recent telephone conversation, Gayle told John that she worried about the possibility of falling in love with John again. This news brought John a whirlwind of emotions. He had been alone, living among only male strangers for five years. The tenderness of a woman's love has been completely absent from his life. Initially, Gayle's revelation lifted him with feelings he never expected to surface during the twenty-plus years he had been preparing himself to serve. For several days he floated in euphoria. He knew he was more fortunate than the other men around him, most of whom had no female relationships outside. John was determined to encourage this possibility of love and win her heart again.

The one thing about communications from prison, however, is that they always are exaggerated. Prisoners live in a constant state of deprivation, having few choices, receiving few gifts. When such opportunities are presented, they sometimes feel like manna, divinely supplied nourishment for the soul. Good news is easy to latch onto, as if the more one hopes it to be true, the more likely it will be. Manna is what Gayle's statement meant for John. After a few days of contemplation, however, he began to feel selfish for even thinking about pulling her into a romantic relationship.

AN AUTOMATIC LONELINESS

There is so little change behind these fences, every aspect of life becomes as automatic as night following day, or the changing of the seasons. When John first thought about the possibility of love, it felt like a panacea, as if a new romance could remove his loneliness. But as time passed, he thought with more clarity about his life. Emptiness.

John knew that he was happy because he had finally taken control of his life. He had learned values that he expected would eventually lead to a more fulfilling life. He was not there yet, however, not ready to bring others inside the fences.

Over the years he had conditioned himself to survive by shutting off all feelings and emotions. With his own mother and sister abandoning him, it became important for John to learn to live alone, like an iceberg—solid and cold without the warmth of human contact. Loneliness became as constant as a morning beard. He has his weights, his studies, and his job, but inside, at this point, he feels close to death, and he believes that romance would drag Gayle into this morbidity.

Love, John says, means understanding one's limitations. He knows that as a prisoner he has no one to hold him when he is down, and no one is happy to see him come home after a day of work. Instead of encouraging Gayle's romantic interests, John wrote her a letter explaining that there was no happiness for her with him—only loneliness. John said that instead of working to build a romance, they should continue building a friendship that would last forever. To him, a romance is dangerous, as he recognizes the long odds against any woman withstanding the many years they would live apart.

Besides Gayle, John enjoys a correspondence with two South American women, Kathy and Magali, both of whom are family members of his Spanish tutors. With them, too, he tries to build solid friendships, but romance is not a part of his life right now. As a long-term prisoner on a quest for personal development, he has found that building strong personal friendships enriches his life. He cherishes these friendships and does not ask for more.

John has promised his two South American friends that by Christmas he will have the skill to engage in a fifteen-minute conversation with them completely in Spanish. He studies several hours each day to help him reach this goal. Once he masters Spanish, John says he will turn his attention to learning Italian.

John corresponds with his father and brother at Cumberland at least once every two weeks. Besides discussing each other's regular routines, their recent correspondence has brought a measure of hope to their lives. A jailhouse lawyer at Cumberland brought to Tony and John Sr.'s attention a much heralded and recent Supreme Court case that presents the possibility of relief to the Baumgarten trio. They all recognize that nothing is certain, but the prison litigator prepared and submitted a motion on each defendant's behalf. Now they wait for the mail each day, on an emotional roller coaster that they hope will result in some type of resentencing.

Since the legal motion was filed, John says he has had difficulty sleeping. He does not know what, if anything, will come of their request for relief. Nevertheless, he cannot stop thinking about what it would mean for his life. He says all he wants is a family, and to live as a faithful husband and a good father.

John survives through dreams of participating in the lives of his children. He wants to accompany them to school functions, to enjoy sporting events with his son, to give his daughter's hand away in marriage. Through his decisions as a younger man, he realizes he has forfeited these privileges.

John categorically and unequivocally states that he will never jeopardize his freedom or his relationships again by committing another criminal act. And, he says that he will spend every day of his remaining time preparing to lead a law-abiding life. Ironically, John acknowledges that he is not yet ready for release. He has more through which he must grow. John says that he had this discussion with Gayle and others who are close to him. He told them that if the court miraculously granted relief and resentenced him, he would ask the judge to allow him to serve two or three more years in prison. He is learning things about himself behind these fences, he says, that are helping him become a better person.

John says that after release he will welcome whatever employment opportunities come his way. Unlike other prisoners who have grandiose expectations for employment, John says he would be happy to begin flipping hamburgers at McDonald's, that he would strive to be the best hamburger cook in the organization. He just wants to begin living and resents those around him with shorter sentences who frequently whine about their time, while simultaneously avowing that they will resume their criminal behavior upon release.

AVOIDING CONFRONTATION

Prison is an abnormal place, a world where much has been taken away and one constantly is subject to the behavior of others. One cannot avoid others, all are locked behind the same fence, share the same bathrooms, eat in the same dining room. The level of tension is fierce and everpresent, and some respond to the monotony in different ways.

Every prisoner faces the prospects of theft and aggressive, arbitrary behavior on the part of other inmates. John says he overlooks everything he can, but there are some things that would be impossible to overlook without making him uncomfortably vulnerable. To help him contend with the chaos, he thinks of his visits with Gayle and the children and avoids many confrontations. Nevertheless, although John can control his own behavior, he knows that he cannot control the behavior of others.

John does not expect that he would ever be the target of direct exploitation, but he knows the temperaments of his fellow prisoners, many of whom search for excitement or acceptance by joining prison cliques or gangs that thrive on thievery and disruption. If an unknown person stole something from John's locker, like a pair of shoes or a watch, John would let it be known that he was angry. Because of his commitment to his family visits, however, he would swallow the loss rather than actively pursue the hunt for retaliation. If he learned the identity of the thief, however, he would have no choice but to respond.

The system accepts only one response: to tell a guard what happened. Although such behavior is normal outside, there could be nothing more disgraceful for a long-term prisoner. John knows that if he ever was violated in any way, and he knew the identity of his aggressor, there would be no alternative but to strike back swiftly. Such a possibility fills him with anxiety. He may be calm on the surface, but he knows that at any given moment someone else's behavior can upset and change forever the fragile peace he has built for himself behind bars.

And, it is not only the other prisoners. For the most part, John finds many guards to be indifferent. Most allow him to serve his sentence responsibly. Some, on the other hand, seem to enjoy a sadistic pleasure in agitating, perhaps bolstering, their own self esteem by provoking others. John described an encounter he had with Officer Andersen, a guard who is in training for a position as a lieutenant.

John was in a friend's room when a light fixture came crashing down onto his friend's head. The accident caused his friend a deep gash requiring several stitches. John immediately called the guard from the housing unit to come to the room so his friend could receive medical attention. After taking care of the injured prisoner, Andersen asked what had happened. John explained the entire episode. When John finished, Andersen looked at him and said, "That's the biggest crock of shit I've ever heard. I'm locking you in segregation for lying to a staff member and on suspicion of assault." Andersen told John he would change his story after a few weeks in segregation.

Eleven other men lived in the same room, and they quickly spoke up, telling Andersen the same version of events as John had provided. Only then, did Andersen agree to postpone his threat to lock John away in segregation. But the altercation, Andersen's intimidating demeanor, and his labeling of John as a liar left him seething for days. "He didn't want to hear the truth," John said. "He had me figured for a liar simply because I'm a prisoner."

About a week later, John was returning from the barber shop when he happened to run into Andersen. Andersen, pleasantly, asked John how things were going, as if their previous conflict had never taken place. John seized the opportunity to respond to the incident.

"You know Officer Andersen, the thing that really bothered me about that incident was not going to segregation. That's just part of the bid, and I can deal with that," John said. "What bothered me was your intimidating tone and accusations of my being a liar."

"That shouldn't bother you," Andersen replied. "You're a convict and I'm an officer. Nothing I say should bother you. Don't you know that all I have to do is bark a little like that about going to segregation in front of most of these inmates and they'll crawl on their bellies whining and telling me anything I want to know to avoid going to the hole?" Andersen explained that he has to try everyone, and because John wears a prisoner's clothing, he'll always be tried by guards.

Andersen's explanation gave John pause. It helped him cope by giving him a clear definition of his place behind these fences. He is not a human being. In the eyes of his captors, he is a prisoner. It is his business to adjust. Not theirs.

John is not scheduled for release until 2018. He will be fifty-four years old. Besides Gayle, his family, and his Spanish pen pals, his father's three sisters—Franey, Concetta, and Maryanne—have begun communications with John. Their presence in his life is welcomed and helpful. Despite the love he receives, John says he has learned to live with pain and constantly reminds himself that at any moment the peace he now experiences may shatter. He tries not to get used to anything, even the relationships, because those, too, can stop abruptly.

John's release date is further away than that of most prisoners at Fort Dix, yet he is never bitter and tries to make the most of every day. His adjustment is working for him.

CONCLUSION

French sociologist Emile Durkheim (1893, 1897) wrote about the need of citizens in any community to bond together. Crime, he suggested, provides them with an opportunity for bonding. To support his theory, Durkheim offered evidence from newspaper stories and headlines regularly featuring stories of crime. Such stories unite the public with specific fellow human beings to talk about, inferior and loathsome men and women whom they could hate together.

For decades, politicians have recognized this powerful function of crime. As a consequence, they curry favor with voters by expressing their own disgust and anger toward the criminal class and those who break the laws of society. Politicians encounter little opposition to their tough-on-crime platforms and their demands for more prisons and tougher sentencing laws. The result, of course, is that our nation's prison population has grown at an exponential rate. More people are incarcerated, and fewer beds are being vacated because prisoners have increasingly longer sentences to serve.

When I began serving my term, cells that were designed for single occupancy held two people. Today, a third person is assigned to those same cells. The communities inside prisons are crowded, and like citizens outside who bond by expressing their hatred for criminals, inside, the criminals bond by rejecting the society that has extinguished their hopes.

Hardly a day passes when I do not hear prisoners complain about rats (informers), corrupt prosecutors, inept law enforcement officers, the unfairness of the courts, and legitimate suckers. I have not seen one film since 1987 where the prison audience did not join in seeming unison cheering for the villains. At dinner last week, one long-term prisoner in his late thirties was describing his admiration for cat burglars; another was referring to armed robbers as being considered "good guys who had the courage to do things right." He explained to me, "Robbery is an honorable racket."

Even lilliputian prisoners with relatively short sentences to serve frequently ingratiate themselves with those serving longer terms by whining about the so-called corruption of the criminal justice system and their alleged wrongful incarceration. After sixteen years of listening to the same complaints everyday, I marvel at the remarkable consistency with which the same specious arguments permeate the four quite different prisons where I have lived. Rather than accepting responsibility for their crimes and adjusting in ways that could facilitate successful emergence from prison, many prisoners join in solidarity by rejecting the values of the broader society. As has frequently been said, prison becomes the university for criminal behavior.

As David Garland wrote in his 1993 study on social theory, prisons have become an accepted aspect of life for the Western world. Whatever the reasons for their initial design, prisons (and associated strategies of punishment) have expanded and persisted. Garland tells us that during the course of their evolution, most Americans have come to accept prisons as the only reasonable response to crime. Many citizens—perhaps a majority in most modern societies—believe we could have no society without prisons.

Western civilization has made stunning technological changes and advances over the past two hundred years, but little corresponding progress in regard to its responses to crime. Only the details have changed, such as lengths of sentences and conditions of confinement. Few people question whether there might be a more effective manner of responding to crime than long-term imprisonment. As for those charged with the responsibility of governing prisons, scant attention is paid to prisoner adjustment patterns. The vast majority of administrators expect nothing more than for an offender to serve the length of time to which he was sentenced. After living in the abnormal communities that exist behind fences year after year, however, few offenders are prepared to return to their communities as law-abiding citizens.

Vinny, one long-term prisoner who has become a friend to me over the years, is scheduled for release in one month from this writing. He has been incarcerated for thirty calendar years, since 1972. To provide some perspective, Nixon was then in his first term and wireless phones existed only in Dick Tracy cartoons. Vinny is now nearly sixty, has no home, no automobile, no clothes, no money, no work history, and no job. When he departs, he may receive up to a one hundred dollar gratuity and a bus ticket to the city he used to call home.

In prison, Vinny has lived as a well-respected convict. How will society receive him? What are his chances of success outside? The only contacts he has now are other felons whom he has known over the years. By creating policies that hindered his ability to build a network of support with law-abiding citizens, administrators ensured that after thirty years, the only people Vinny knows are other criminals. The warden did not explain why she denied Vinny halfway-house placement. After thirty years of imprisonment, I cannot think of anyone who was more in need of assistance upon release. Yet Vinny will receive none.

Western civilization has enjoyed stellar technological advances in some measure because of its response to failure. When experiments do not work, researchers do not replicate those flawed research designs. Rather, they modify them. If an airplane does not fly, engineers would not use the same design to build more planes that do not fly. Instead, engineers would find their errors, correct them, and create new designs.

Prison administrators have not followed this model of scientific success. Our prisons foster us-versus-them attitudes and values that are the antithesis of the societies to which most offenders return. Nevertheless, the United States continues to build more prisons, and administrators do not miss many opportunities to enhance their punitive nature. The overarching goals of prison administrators and research scientists must be quite different.

The prison system devours an ever-increasing portion of every taxpayer dollar. Why then are citizens seemingly so indifferent to what prisons accomplish? If the goal is simply to warehouse prisoners for lengthy periods of time, during which time most prisoners will adjust in ways that leave them even less able to function as law-abiding citizens, then the administrators who govern them succeed brilliantly. Widely disseminated research on recidivism shows that the prison system represents a catastrophic public policy failure, but perhaps prison administrators view those data differently than this writer. Wardens and their colleagues create a culture that further reduces the capacities of people convicted of violating elements of the social contract that holds society together. Is this merely an accidental strategy, or is there a method in the madness?

Why do administrators refuse to use incentives in their management equations? In what ways does society benefit by funding cultures of deprivation that spew out tens of thousands of people like Vinny who have virtually no chance of finding a legitimate place in society?

It is not hard to see how prison bureaucrats benefit from preserving, protecting, and extending the status quo. By creating artificial societies where long-term offenders adjust by conditioning themselves in ways that encourage further failures upon release, administrators ensure the proliferation of their business. In other words, poorly adjusted prisoners provide short-term and long-term job security for prison administrators and staff. Returning prisoners translate into the need for more prisons; more prisons translate into the need for more staff. The bureaucracy multiplies like dandelions in the rural areas where most new prisons are built.

Such a strategy is hardly unique to members of the criminal justice profession. One of my mentors told me that when the March of Dimes Foundation had helped wage the successful war against polio, it did not close its doors but rather switched focus to birth defects. Part of its motive may have been to help children, but considerations of self-preservation seem also to have been present. Professionals who work for institutions—unlike doctors and lawyers who practice privately—are careful to protect those institutions and their jobs therein. What would happen to prison jobs if all offenders prepared themselves to lead crime-free lives upon release? What if there was no more recidivism?

By denying prisoners the definition and example of a success model, no prisoners know what administrators expect other than for them to serve time. Policies tell prisoners what they cannot do but offer little guidance on how to rebuild their lives. In fact, prisoners have no means whatsoever to distinguish themselves formally.

Classification models do not take into account prisoner accomplishments. The prisoner who works hard throughout his term, studies diligently, acquires new skills, and demonstrates his commitment to leading a law-abiding life encounters more problems and resistance from the system than the prisoner who serves his entire term hibernating or playing poker and watching soap operas. What even-handed observer would not find this fact of life bizarre, insufferable?

By not providing prisoners with opportunities to enhance their quality of life inside, administrators ipso facto encourage prisoners to do nothing but allow time to pass. Many inmates thus adjust by joining in solidarity with others in the prison community who hate and reject society's values. One could not devise too many recipes for failure in American society that succeed as brilliantly as long-term incarceration in today's correctional institutions.

Changing this dismal equation would require administrators to replace the culture of deprivation with a meritocracy of sorts. By providing prisoners with a degree of control over their classification status, more would reject the values of the institution—of failure—and work toward developing skills that would help them succeed upon release. Since corrections administrators have no incentives to reduce recidivism rates, however, and every incentive to welcome offenders back into correctional institutions after their release, it is likely that they will continue to govern prisons with sticks rather than carrots, to create ever-widening chasms between law-abiding citizens and those serving time.

Unfortunately, my experience suggests that all except the most highly self-motivated prisoners will continue adjusting to these punitive policies in ways that increase their estrangement from society's values and their chances for failure after release. Unless taxpayers call for change, I expect the cycle of failure to continue.

REFERENCES

Bounds v. Smith 430 U.S. 817, 97 S.Ct. 1491, 52 L.Ed.2d 72 (1977).

Clemmer, D. (1940). *The prison community.* Boston: Christopher Publishing.

Covey, S. R. (1990). *The seven habits of highly effective people.* New York: Simon & Schuster.

Durkheim, E. (1893/1964). *The division of labor in society.* New York: Free Press.

Durkheim, E. (1897/1966). *Suicide: A study in sociology.* New York: Free Press.

Earley, P. (1992). *The hot house: Life inside Leavenworth Prison.* New York: Bantam.

Etzione, A. (1999). The good society. *Journal of Political Philosophy, 7,* 88–103.

Garland, D. (1993). *Punishment and modern society: A study in social theory.* Chicago: University of Chicago Press.

Irwin, J. (1970). *The felon.* Englewood Cliffs, NJ: Prentice Hall.

Irwin, J. (1980). *Prisons in turmoil.* Glenview, IL: Scott Foresman.

Johnson v. Avery 393 U.S. 483, 89 S.Ct. 747, 21 L.Ed.2d 718 (1969).

Johnson, R. (Ed.). (1982). *The pains of imprisonment.* Beverly Hills, CA: Sage.

Lewis v. Casey 116 S.Ct. 2174 (1996).

Rudolph, R. (1992). *The boys from New Jersey: How the mob beat the Feds.* New York: William Morrow.

Sykes, G. (1958). *Society of captives.* Princeton, NJ: Princeton University Press.

Wheeler, S. (1961). Socialization in correctional communities. *American Sociological Review, 26,* 697–712.

Wolff v. McDonnell, 418 U.S. 539, 94 S.Ct. 2963, 41 L.Ed.2d 935 (1974).

INDEX

About the Author

Michael Santos was imprisoned in 1987, when he was 23, for convictions related to the distribution of cocaine. Despite his having no history of violence, and this being his only term of incarceration, he was sentenced to a nonparoleable term of 45 years. Assuming he continues to receive the maximum amount of good time, Michael expects to remain incarcerated until 2013.

During his imprisonment, Michael has earned a B.A. from Mercer University and an M.A. from Hofstra University. In his first book, *About Prison,* Michael described his observations and experiences during his first decade of confinement. Through his network of support, Michael maintains a Web site at PrisonerLife.com and encourages readers to interact with him. He continues to write about the prison experience and the people it holds. Readers may contact Michael at the following addresses:

Michael O. Santos
10115 Greenwood Avenue North
PMB 184
Seattle, WA 98133
E-mail: info@MichaelSantos.net
URL: www.MichaelSantos.net

DATE DUE

SEP 10 '03			
OCT 27 03			
APR 19 04			
MAY 10 04			
2-18-05			
DEC 1 05			
5/12/09			
4-23-10			
5/26/11			
12 April 2012			
5-3-12			